Praise for Kabbala Pat

"Sandy Anastasi's knowledge and insights into the Kabbala are amazing! I have a whole new perspective about the world around me with the knowledge I gained from this class. I am truly grateful for the experience of learning about the Kabbala, I am a better person for it. I would gladly take it again as with most of the classes I have taken with Sandy, I always seems to get exactly what I need for where my life is at that moment."

— Sandy Rola, Student

"I've been a user of binaural beat meditation CDs and technologies for almost 5 years now and I'm always skeptical when I hear of new meditation techniques that are superior. However, I've grown to trust Sandy's recommendations over the years, and she kept speaking of this book with such passion and enthusiasm that I had to try it out. I'm very grateful that I did! There is something about all the archetype patterns and visualizations that somehow skirts around the skeptical ego and communicates directly with the unconscious aspects of ourselves. I was immediately hooked, and felt significant shifts on many of the paths. I highly recommend this to anyone who is interested in personal development, consciousness, and just feeling happier in their life!"

— Rick Manelius, PhD in Engineering

"Sandy's Kabbala Pathworking Class was instrumental in my being able to appreciate who I am! Her class helped me to understand the uniqueness of each of our paths! It is a very enjoyable step of continual enlightenment! "

— Eunice de Guire, Student

Books by Sandy Anastasi

The Anastasi System Psychic Development Series:

Level 1: The Fundamentals

Level 2: Energy and Auras

Level 3: Tools and Toys

Level 4: An Introduction to Channeling and Spirit Communication

Level 5: Developing the Energy and Skill in Spirit Communication

Level 6: Healing in Spirit Communication (to be released)

Astrology:

Astrology: Art and Science

Intermediate Astrology

Tarot:

Tarot Reader's Workbook: A Comprehensive Guide from Beginner to Master

Kabbala:

Kabbala Pathworking

KABBALA PATHWORKING

An Experiential Exploration of Your Higher Self & the God Consciousness Within You!

By Sandy Anastasi

Notices

Kabbala Pathworking

Copyright © 1992-2011 Sandy Anastasi

ISBN: 978-0-982-56691-6

Acknowledgements

A work of this magnitude has required the help of so many people that it is impossible to list them all here. If you have been a student of mine, a fellow Pathworker at any time during the last 25 years, I thank you for your support, your insight and your dedication. You, more than anyone, made this work not only possible, but also necessary. Thanks go to John Maerz of AIIS for his initial organization of an unwieldy pile of writings and his unique ability to arrange music to accompany the Paths. Special thanks are given to my IT manager, Rick Manelius, and my editor, who happens to be his wife, Emily, for the dedication and perseverance needed to bring this manuscript to its present state of readability and use. Thanks go to Rick for his creativity in arranging my website, www.sandyanastasi.com, so that readers may listen to the Paths there. My thanks also go to Leslie Bielen who wrote the forward for this book. Her encouragement and creative suggestions have been most helpful. I want to thank my long-ago student Joyce Reed for her wonderful artistry in designing and drawing the mandalas, and Heidi Chan, Debbie Ronning, Sharon Wojno and Paul Foglia for doing the research and formatting Paths 11, 12, 13, 14, 15, 17, 19, 20,21, and 22. Your efforts have been appreciated by hundreds of Pathworkers already. My personal assistant, Lisa Freeman, is always high on my list of people to thank, as is my husband, Ron Tourville. Your love and support make everything possible. Finally, thanks go to all of YOU who are reading this, for YOU have made it all worthwhile.

Table of Contents

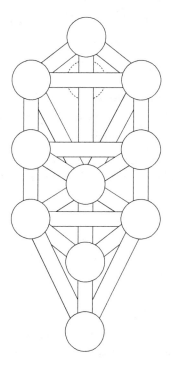

Foreword

I have known Sandy Anastasi as a teacher, mentor and friend. Her breadth and depth of knowledge is far-reaching. In this particular work she combines learning the basics of Kabbala and learning about yourself at the same time, making the process fun. This is a scholarly book, but not as an academic understanding of the Kabbala. Rather, it is about experiencing the Kabbala and how you relate to its paths. This is about becoming a scholar on who you are and why.

By reading or listening to the paths as presented in this book, you enter a world of experience that will change your life forever. It is a world known only to you. In each path you will uncover and rediscover aspects of yourself that you may sense, feel, be aware of, or for which you may not have a clue. Each one you work with will provide you an experience that opens the gateways to a better understanding of you and your world.

This book gives you one of the best gifts your soul and spirit could ever ask. In each path you will find out about parts of yourself, and each time you go through the entire book, all 32 paths, you will unearth and unravel aspects of yourself you long forgot or never knew.

I have personally experienced the contents of this book several times as a student, self-study student and facilitator, and each time my experience was different. I learned more on different levels and heard and sensed things differently each time I progressed through the paths. It takes commitment to proceed through all 32 paths, and it is worth every second! I encourage you to keep up with the practice of the paths. To not do so is like leaving yourself at a rest area while on a road trip, never getting to your destination.

To say that Sandy Anastasi has provided you with an engaging process is an understatement. She has offered you an adventure. Each path takes you places within yourself where you have not been before, but in a manner that makes you feel safe to explore and examine. Like everything else in life, you get out of it what you put into it. The joy of having this book is that you can set your own pace and determine how deeply you delve into your findings. The first time you may go easy on yourself. With later visits you may feel the need to go deeper. It is all up to you. In the end you will not be the same. The changes may be dramatic or they may be subtle. I guarantee, though, that changes have occurred. I know you will have an unforgettable experience with this book. Have a fun time!

Leslie Bielen, PhD - Retired Administer, Florida State University System

Author's Foreword

My study of the Kabbala began in an unusual way... I dreamed it. Let me start at the beginning.

I was studying astrology, numerology, crystals, color therapy, psychism, Tarot, religion, philosophy and history all at the same time. That may sound a bit odd, but I have always learned in an eclectic manner. I would take a single thought or concept, and follow it through all of these areas until I understood it from many points of view. In my studies, I was continually frustrated because I could see all of these areas I was studying had a common thread that helped me to understand the concept I was following, yet I could not tie them together directly. I fretted over this. I kept looking for the common denominator. My Guides kept directing me to study the Kabbala. I would dream that I needed to study it. I would be in a book store and have a book on Kabbala fall off the shelf and land on my foot. So, of course, I tried to study it. Unfortunately, back then the only books available were all firmly based in Jewish tradition, and in fact, most were in Hebrew. Not only was I not Jewish, but I also was not particularly religious. All the religious language got in the way of my learning, and I set those books aside and remained frustrated but still searching.

My Guides took pity on me. Before long, I found myself awake in my dreams, sitting in a large classroom filled with hundreds of other students, learning the Kabbala in scientific and mathematical terms from a nice looking middle-aged fellow in jeans and a white shirt with rolled-up sleeves. I later found out that I was studying on the astral with Kuthumi, Lord of the 2nd Ray, who had experienced several incarnations here on earth – one being St. Francis of Assisi, and another Pythagoris. Apparently, he affected those other students as deeply as he did me – in the following years, many, many excellent Western-oriented and non-religious works on the Kabbala appeared. Interestingly, they all follow the same format. He is and was a great Teacher. And it is time for the Kabbala to be accessible to everyone in our lovely world.

I have studied and taught the Kabbala for more than 25 years. Initially, my teachings were classroom lectures describing the Kabbala and its origins and meaning in great detail. Learning about the Kabbala in this manner is a typical exoteric tradition that allows the student to learn through observation and study. This is the most universally accepted method.

Then I came across *The Sword and the Serpent*, an early book by Denning and Philips that utilized pathworking to explore part of the Kabbalistic Tree of Life. Their approach showed me a new way of learning about the Tree of Life. Through pathworking, a process of guided visualization utilizing universal archetypes, I realized it was possible to *experience* the Tree of Life by actually walking the Paths via guided imagery. I had discovered an esoteric means of teaching the Kabbala. Through this arcane method, the seeker actually learns about the Kabbala experientially.

I researched and/or channeled many of the Paths in *Pathworking the Kabbala* and developed others with the aid of my students. Heidi Chan, Paul Foglia, Sharon Wojno and Debbie Ronning, pathworkers from my earliest groups, helped to develop many of the Upper Tree paths. John Maerz, my long term fellow traveler on this path toward enlightenment set the Paths to music. Joyce Reed, an extremely gifted artist and fellow pathworker created the mandalas that we use as a focus to enter each Path. I have guided pathworkers along the Tree of Life during all these years. But even after all this time, I still consider myself a mere student of this ancient Western Yoga. So, the Kabbala has been called, and so I believe it to be. It is a true path to enlightenment – one of the very few we still have in the Western world. The study of the Kabbala is a life-long commitment, and one that will lead you to whatever level of enlightenment you are capable of reaching.

I put *Pathworking the Kabbala* together during the 1980s as a teaching tool, though it wasn't until the early 1990s that a group I was teaching encouraged me to put it in book form. The effects of walking these Paths on the students I've seen come and go over the years proved to me its effectiveness. Each Path in this book deals with a different aspect of human consciousness. We work the Paths starting at the bottom of the Tree of Life and move upward. Each Path is learned and understood by absorbing the qualities of the two Sephiroh, or Spheres of Consciousness, that join to form it. The Lower Tree, the Paths from Path 32 through Path 24, help the pathworker to balance the inner and outer world. It is while walking these Paths that I see students coming to terms with and actually mastering their physical world challenges. Challenges concerning health, finance, family and social issues begin to fall into place. Often the families and friends of pathworkers begin to experience amazing changes and insights into their own lives just by being around the seeker and interacting with him or her. It is not uncommon for pathworkers to dream of elements on a path before they actually 'walk' it, or to even see those elements appearing in the physical world around them. I encourage pathworkers to keep a diary and record their dreams to enhance the experience.

Pathworking the Kabbala teaches you to navigate the astral realms both in the waking and the sleeping world. It teaches you awareness, insight and understanding. It teaches you to alter the world around you by altering yourself as you expand your own consciousness. It opens you to new worlds of possibility both inside and outside of yourself.

Pathworkers who choose to move on to complete the upper paths on the Tree of Life, paths 23 through 11 (paths 1-10 are the Sephiroh themselves and are learned along the way) will find their psyches expanding exponentially. It is on the upper paths that we uncover and learn and develop the innermost parts of ourselves. It is on these upper paths that we begin to have a better understanding of the greater universe around us, and to have insight as to where we might belong in it. We learn to tap into parts of ourselves that were previously undiscovered.

Walk these Paths in joy, and then walk them again and again and again. Each time the world that opens behind your closed eyes will be different. Each time you will grow in a new and more wonderful way.

In Light,
Sandy Anastasi

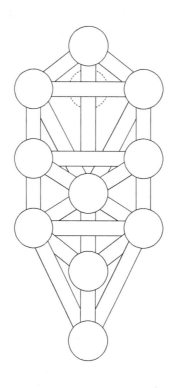

This book is dedicated to The Great World Teacher

The Lord Kuthumi

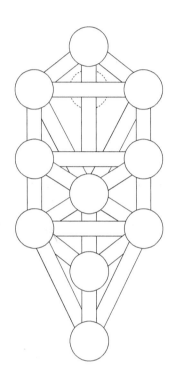

An Introduction to Kabbala & Pathworking

The figure below (Figure 1) is called the Tree of Life. As you can see, it is a schematic of 10 circles called Sephiroh, joined by 22 lines. Combined, the 10 Sephiroh and 22 joining lines are known as the "32 Paths of Wisdom." The entire Kabbalistic Philosophy is based upon this figure.

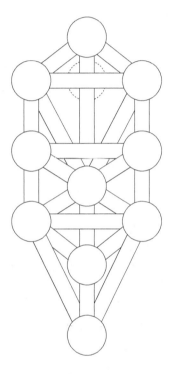

Figure 1

What Is the Kabbala?

Here is a basic history:

The earliest root of the Kabbala (note that there are many different spellings and all are correct) is found in the early days of the Jewish religious tradition. The Jews preserved the Tree of Life schematic, and the Kabbalistic system of thought derived from it. In the early days of the Jews, when they were still living as desert tribes, fathers would pass the Tree of Life down to their eldest sons by drawing a line-drawing in the desert sands. It was a secret and a totally verbal tradition.

To Kabbalists, this line drawing of 10 Sephiroh joined by 22 Paths explains the creation of the universe. It explains man's consciousness. It explains how energy becomes matter. It explains how YOU evolve out of matter to become something greater than you are.

And now, out of this very simple line drawing that began centuries and centuries ago, we have a system of thought called the Kabbala that has given rise to virtually hundreds of books.

It is a system that now permeates all of Western culture. Every single Western magical tradition and most religions, use the Kabbala as a basis for their practices and philosophies – often unknowingly!

Kabbalistic thought enters into every Western religion, not just the Judaic religion. All of the little symbols - the Star of David, the five-pointed star, the cross, the basic concepts of where the Godhead is and how it and we evolve - all of this comes from the Kabbala, from the Tree of Life.

So, if you could look at this as a root of almost everything we have in Western culture traditions and beliefs, you would be working with a workable model.

I don't believe that the Jews actually invented the Tree of Life, although most Jews certainly would claim so. In fact, in traditional Judaism, only males 40 years or older who first mastered the Torah are permitted to study the Kabbala. That should tell you something about how important the Kabbala is in Judaism! You'll note that earlier I said that the Jews "preserved" the Tree of Life. My belief is that they carried this system of thought with them out of Egypt. I believe that in the West it was the Egyptians that initiated all of these higher realms of thought, among which I would include the earliest roots of Astrology, Kabbala, and the Tarot.

One of the things that I have seen in my investigation of metaphysical philosophies - including Astrology, Numerology, I-Ching, Tarot, and many other forms of Western Occultism and some Eastern traditions, is that parts of every one of them can be traced back to the Kabbala. The Kabbala is at the root of all of them!

For example, look at the I-Ching. It is derived from 64 Hexagrams. The Kabbala has 32 paths leading down into creation and 32 going back up to the Godhead. That total is 64!

Note the number 64 is derived from the root number 8. There are eight original planets that ancient astrologers worked with long before the discovery of the three outer ones in our solar system. Each of these planets, as you will later see, has a correspondence to one of the Sephiroh and one or more of the Paths as well!

Connections to the Tarot are even more obvious. There are 22 Paths (the lines) joining the Sephiroh (the circles). Those 22 Paths correspond to the 22 Major Arcana Cards of the Tarot. The 10 Sephiroh correspond each to the four 1s, the four 2s, the four 3s, and so on, up to 10 (see Figure 9). The Sephiroh also correspond to the Court Cards of the Tarot if you remember their numerological value is 10.

So, the Kabbala fits Numerology, Tarot, I-Ching, Astrology it corresponds to everything in metaphysics and still more in our mundane world!

I have even had students who had a strong background in biology look at this diagram and say, "My God, that's a DNA molecule!"

So, the Tree of Life also corresponds to things that have to do with biology, chemistry, physics; it is not something that has to be limited to Western or Eastern occultism.

This is why some of the most brilliant people in our world spend their lifetimes studying the Kabbala! It is a truly amazing system of thought that seems to explain how everything in our world works.

I think the best definition of all is that which describes the Kabbala as the only true Western Yoga.

Here is a quick summary that will compress into this introduction a great deal of material that I usually put into a much lengthier discussion. Remember, study of the Kabbala as a system of thought could take years.

Anyone who has studied the Kabbala all of his or her life will be laughing now because the Kabbala is a system of thought that becomes a life-long system of study, if you are going to do it using your brain. But there are two ways of learning about the Kabbala; two ways of evolving utilizing the Kabbala as a road map!

The first, obviously, is to use your mind. This method involves study; you would study the correspondences, many of which you will find in the following pages. Study would include all the different meanings of each Sephiroh, or the type of consciousness that each Sephiroh represents. To study the Paths you would learn to blend the meanings of the circles, or Sephiroh joining either end of the Path.

The Kabbala can be understood, studied and practiced intellectually. In fact, most people who study the Kabbala do so through intellectual study, by reading others' thoughts and ideas on the subject and studying ideas of how the evolutionary processes described by the Kabbala happen. If you were to pursue the religious Jewish Kabbala, you would be studying the wars of the Angelic realms in God's creation of our world. The other, less commonly practiced method of studying the Kabbala is through Pathworking. Let me diverge for just a moment to explain and discuss Pathworking.

Pathworking is guided visualization, which in this case taps into archetypical images, forms, names, and words in order to produce a specific effect in the person who is guided. I can't say that the affect each path will have on a person traveling it in his (or her) mind will be the same. In fact, I expect that every traveler will have a totally different experience and response. This is because the symbols used on the Paths are largely archetypal and each person reacts to them differently depending on his personal, cultural and evolutionary background, as well as his personal need. The only thing I can be assured of is that they affect everyone on very deep levels of being, deep enough to effect changes in consciousness and subsequent changes in life patterns.

When you travel the Paths via audio device you will lie down or sit back in a comfortable position, in a dimly lit room away from phones, doorbells, cats, dogs, children, etc. All of the Paths are set to music and it is my voice that you will hear throughout all of the Paths. I wrote the Paths, though many of them use archetypal imagery found in other literature. My early Pathworking students initially developed many of the upper Paths, and I later elaborated on them until they reached their current form. All were intensely researched, but the actual writing was channeled. I believe I had a great deal of help from the Lord Kuthumi and the Brotherhood of Light in the creation of this work.

When you do the Paths on audio, whether you are in a group or by yourself, it is a good idea to surround yourself with white light. If you're by yourself, you might visualize a counter-clockwise spiral of white light moving upward inside of you, and a clockwise spiral of blue light surrounding you. The white light helps to raise your inner energy; the blue light is protective.

If you are in a group you can do the same thing, but first stand in a circle and hold hands, left hand palm up, right hand palm down. Visualize a column of white light spinning counter-clockwise in the center of your circle, and a wall of blue light spinning clockwise surrounding your circle of people.

I have participated in Pathworking groups that used the Lesser Banishing Ritual of the Pentagram to protect and call in the Archangels. You will find this a particularly rewarding way to begin your Pathworking when you are either alone or in a group. You will find a copy of the ritual at the end of the first chapter. Feel free to print it and use it!

I have found Pathworking in groups to be an especially rewarding experience.

If you are doing the Paths by reading them directly from this manual, it still helps to follow the above procedure.

The object of Pathworking is to take you through the actual experience of the Path. You are there. You live the Path. You learn the type of consciousness represented by that particular Sephiroh and the Path that you are traveling, that part of your road, by living it. You learn by experiencing it directly. Behind your closed eyes your ability to feel and visualize grows until you are watching a movie no one else can see. In this way, each of you reading this will experience every Path in a totally individual way.

I have found that studying the Kabbala intellectually at the same time that you are Pathworking the Tree of Life works beautifully. Although Pathworking speaks as much to your unconscious mind as it does to you conscious mind, giving your conscious mind the tools to understanding while feeding the unconscious mind the direct experience is a combination that can't be beat! In a sense, by intellectually understanding what each Path is aimed at achieving you create more fertile soil in which the seeds that are planted by your experience may grow. To this end, a glossary of supportive books is included following this introduction.

Even though this work is concerned with Pathworking, I consider, for the above reasons, that some working knowledge of the Tree of Life is imperative. The following pages cover what I consider to be the bare essentials of understanding that are necessary in order to make the best use of the Pathworking itself.

Please look at Figure 2.

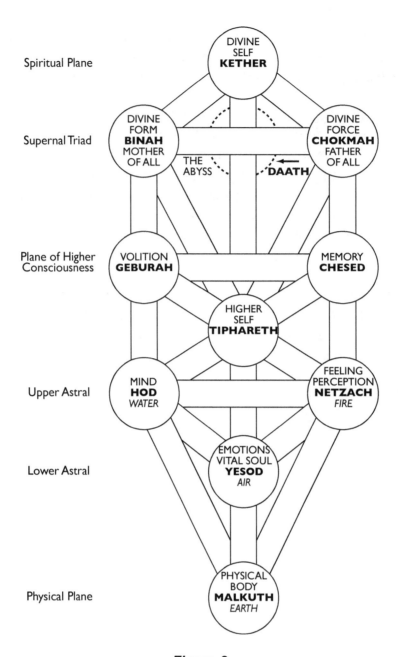

Figure 2

Above the top of the Tree, above the Sephiroh named Kether, are three "outpourings" of God-Force, which Dione Fortune, in her *Mystical Qabbalah*, (a classic work) calls the Ain Soph Aur, a name coming directly from the Hebrew Qabbalah. These outpourings are sheer energy. Those of you wanting to know more about this cosmic manifestation should read Dione Fortune's *Cosmic Doctrine*. Our Pathworking will not take us to this unmanifested level. The energy at this level is so subtle, it can almost be said to be "before the beginning."

According to Kabbalists, the actual point at which "universal consciousness" begins is the topmost Sephiroh, which is called Kether. It's very difficult to describe Kether. I feel that this is one Sephiroh that is easier to understand from Pathworking than from study. It is almost easier to understand it by metaphor, or by feeling, than by intellectual understanding. The best definition I can think of is an image of God, on the very edge of self-awareness, saying to himself, "Oh!" – It is as if the possibility of awareness, of existence itself, has only just occurred.

You might relate to this a different way. Imagine yourself in a deep sleep. Suddenly, there is a ray of light that brings you to wakefulness. You are actually awake, before you realize that you are awake. That is Kether. It is that sudden first moment of awareness. And of course, it's a lot more than that as well. It is a moment unknowingly pregnant with all possibility! For now, think of it as the point of beginning. It is, at this moment in our awareness, simply beyond our conception.

From Kether, we get an initial outflow of force, which forms the second Sephiroh, Chokmah. (This is pronounced Hokmah - however, don't worry about pronunciation, since Hebrew is a lost language; it survives in its original form only in texts, and no one truly knows the original pronunciations anymore!)

Chokmah is a massive outpouring of energy. It is sheer force. If you could imagine a star exploding, you would have a fair idea of the force involved. It is undirected and undifferentiated energy. Within you, you also have that kind of potential power, potential force. It is another aspect of your consciousness, just as Kether is. However, the Sephiroh on this topmost portion of the Tree are so far beyond our worldly experience that for the most part we are unaware of those forces within ourselves. That's something that we are going to be trying to "wake-up" as we proceed in our Pathworking.

From Chokmah, the energy flow moves down (or, as the case is in our schematic, across) to Binah. Chokmah is often seen as the Father of All because that explosion of force is considered male. But, you would have no universe; there wouldn't even be a physical reality around you, if there wasn't something to catch that explosion of energy, contain it and give it form. That something is Binah, which is often seen as the Eternal Mother. If you looked at these top three Sephiroh on the tree, what we call the *Supernal Triad* in Kabbalistic terms, you would be looking at God the Father, God the Son and The Holy Spirit; or at the Father, the Son and Mother Mary in more traditional Western religious terminology. I think it's fascinating, that when you get into world religions, almost all of them have the three aspects of God represented in some form.

In the Judaic religion, from whose mystical philosophy we get the Kabbala, there are 10 aspects of God; each one is one of the "divine" names of the Sephiroh. In the Old Testament there are 10 different names for God - each time he acted in a different manner they called him by a different name.

One of the things I have enjoyed doing with the Kabbala is drawing correspondences between the various Sephiroh and mythological figures, and the God-names from various existing religions. Where I felt they were appropriate and give insight into the nature of a Sephiroh, I have included them in the correspondences preceding each Path.

In a sense, each one of us is God on a smaller scale. The I-Ching tells us, "As above, so below." If God can be represented by 10 different names in His 10 different aspects of consciousness, then so can we!

Kabbalists say that beneath Binah and Chokmah is an invisible Sephiroh called Daath. Daath is found in what is termed *The Abyss*. The early Kabbalists claimed that you cannot access the higher consciousness represented by Kether, Chokmah and Binah unless you are dead because, according to them, you first have to cross through the unseen Sephiroh of Daath, and the Abyss, in order to make that transition. Most Western occultists do not believe that. However, to truly access these Sephiroh you must be out of the body. And that is one of the things we will learn through our Pathworking — how to get out of the body, a process known as astral or soul travel.

As we go down or up the Tree we must make the crucial "jump" across the Abyss. In our Pathworking we will work our way up the Tree toward Kether and will develop the tools necessary to make this leap across the Abyss as we progress. We'll learn what changes in ourselves have to be made, what we need to let go of, what we need to alter or revise within ourselves in order to jump that portion of the Tree and to be able to access the higher consciousness represented by the three Supernal Sephiroh, though we may never know these highest forms of consciousness completely while in physical form. This will be the closest we can come to the Godhead while in human form.

Following the life force's movement into Binah, it comes down the Tree diagonally across from Binah into the fourth Sephiroh, known as Chesed. Chesed is usually looked at as *memory* because what was so clear up in the Supernal Sephiroh diminishes and is lost on its way across the Abyss. So, what begins in Kether is powered by Chokmah and is given form by Binah, is seen as a memory of inspiration in Chesed. It cannot be exact. To understand this more clearly, think about a project you first planned in your mind. Think about how perfect you imagined it was going to look when it was done. Now, remember what it really looked like when you were done with it. Did it approach the image you originally had in your mind? In most cases, the answer will be no.

You see, as the energy moves across the Abyss, something of the clarity of the original idea is lost. Adjustments are made. So, what comes up in Chokmah is the memory of what was initiated in Kether, Chokmah, and Binah. Chesed is generally the Sephiroh with which we associate Higher Guidance and teaching. It is also a masculine force as it is on the masculine side of the Tree of Life.

As a matter of fact, if you are looking at the Tree, everything on the right side could be considered male in nature because it takes its character from Chokmah, which is the topmost Sephiroh on this side. By male, I mean generative force. And everything on the opposite side of the tree, the left side as you look at the schematic, is considered feminine, or receptive force, since the topmost Sephiroh on this side is Binah, which is feminine in nature.

But energy spins as it descends into matter, much like the double helix molecule in your DNA is seen to be a spiral when observed under a very powerful microscope. So even though Chomah is on the masculine, generative side of the Tree, it assumes a soft and gentle, almost benevolent demeanor as its primary focus is to be a receptor upon which the blueprint from the top three Sephiroh can take form. Many Cabbalists believe that Chesed is the highest level we humans can attain in our consciousness while still in our physical forms.

Chesed, though receptive to the Supernals becomes generative in a Fatherly way to Geburah, the fifth Sephiroh — hence it is often seen by World Religions as God the Father or King of the Gods.

The energy of creation moves from Chesed directly across the Tree to Geburah. This is a very important Path. It is known as the Second Major Initiation.

Let me say a few words about the Initiations on the Tree of Life. All of the Major Initiations on the Tree of Life are Paths that join the opposing sides of the Tree. There are three in all. The Third Major and most important Initiation is the first horizontal Path already discussed when tracing the descent of energy through the Supernal Triad. It joins Chokmah and Binah. The First Major Initiation is near the bottom of the Tree, on the Path connecting Hod and Netzach. Many Kabbalists look at all of the other Paths as "Minor Initiations," but all agree that the three horizontal Paths that join the two sides of the Tree of Life are the three Major Initiations.

Now let's get back to tracing the path energy takes down the Tree, as it descends into matter in what is commonly referred to as the Lightning Flash.

The next Sephiroh in the line of descent is Geburah, pronounced GeVorah by many modern Kabbalists. It is known as *volition* in the old texts. Geburah has a distinctly "martial" flavor and can be a shattering experience. This Sephiroh is interested in change. It is involved with action. It is not the totally receptive intelligence of Binah; rather, it strips and shreds and eliminates that which does not work. You see, it is refining the 'blue print' for creation supplied by Chesed. It is dynamic; even though it is a feminine Sephiroh, it has many generative characteristics we associate with maleness. and its nature is decidedly militant. In many old texts Geburah is seen as the avenging Angel or Goddess.

After the energy leaves Geburah it descends in a line leading back to the center of the Tree, to balance. It enters into the sixth Sephiroh, called Tipareth, commonly pronounced Teefareth. Those Sephiroh that lie along the middle of the Tree are neither intrinsically male nor female. They are both, depending on how the energy is used. When it is used generatively they are male; when used receptively, female.

Tipareth is the believed to be the seat of your Higher Self. An Astrologer would relate this to the Sun. Tipareth is a point of balance. All of us, when we are at this point in our development, are aiming toward finding that stillness inside when we meditate. We are aiming at turning off the mind and the senses, and finding our internal peace, stillness and joy. When we do that, we are working to embrace the energy of Tipareth.

Tipareth is not directly connected to the physical plane. In conjunction with Geburah and Chesed, it comprises the Ethical Triad. Together, these three Sephiroh make up what we call our Higher Consciousness.

And whereas very, very few of us are accessing anything that comes from the Supernal Triad at the top of the Tree of Life, most of us are accessing information from our Higher Consciousness every day, whether or not we are consciously aware of it. Our conscious awareness of what we are accessing will depend on how much attention we are paying, and how still we can make our inner voice. But all of us do access these three Sephiroh. Remember, though, they are not physical – they are internal.

The last four Sephiroh, those on the bottom of the tree, constitute the physical plane. They don't all lie on the physical plane, but they make up aspects of consciousness that deal mostly with it.

The four lower "Initiations" on the tree have to do with assimilating an understanding of each of the four lower Sephiroh.

The first of these, coming down the Tree, is on the right side of the Tree below Tipareth. It is called Netzach. Netzach represents our feelings and our desires; it represents our association with nature, with instinct and with the plant and animal kingdom. It represents our ability to just blend into pure feeling. The energy coming down the Tree crosses over or flips at this point, reflecting the spinning of the higher Sephiroh, but the affect is more dramatic. This is much like the right brain controlling the left side of the body in the human form. This placement on the Tree would appear to make Netzach masculine in nature, but the spiraling energy moving down the Tree causes Netzach to act in a feminine manner so it is usually characterized by a female form. Netzach is associated with the fire element though – a masculine element. This correlation shows the physical plane is a reflection of the higher planes. The energy, of course, becomes coarser and denser as it moves downward into creation.

The next Sephiroh, Hod, is on the base of the feminine side of the Tree. Like its counterpart Netzach, the energy is flipped here, so Hod is very masculine in its action and effects even though it is on the feminine side of the Tree. Hod represents the mind, the mental nature. It represents civilization, society and all of its constructs. It represents groups and organizations, magic, government and even monetary systems. It is usually represented by a masculine figure or a hermaphrodite. Hod is associated with the water element – a naturally feminine element, again, showing the reflection of the spiritual realms in the physical.

Netzach and Hod together comprise what is called the Upper Astral Plane. The Path that joins them is the First Major Initiation. So when you have gained the ability to control your mind and your emotions, and thereby navigate the Astral Plane, you have completed the First Major Initiation.

The next Sephiroh following the path of energy as it moves downward is in the center of the Tree again. It is called Yesod, which deals with the emotional nature and the intuition in both an emotional sense and sensitivity sense. As a matter of fact, Yesod correlates to the Lower Astral Plane. It also is the doorway into the astral, and along with Hod and Netzach together, comprises the *Astral Plane.* These three Sephiroh together are called the *Astral Triad.* Yesod is associated with the air element, a traditionally masculine element. Yesod's action is both male and female, both generative and receptive, depending upon how its energy is used. When energy is coming downward into creation, Yesod is receptive to it, but when Yesod is projecting that energy downward into the physical realm of Malkuth, it is generative. All manifested reality has its last stage of formation in Yesod before manifesting in the bottom most Sephiroh, Malkuth. And all dreams and ideas in Malkuth find their conceptual form in Yesod, so you see Yesod can be receptive to Malkuth as well! In that knowledge is the key to your being able to create the reality you wish to live in, and also the key to your conscious evolution beyond the physical plane! Yesod is an important Sephiroh to master. It is associated with Illusion – learning to navigate through the illusions we create with our minds and our emotions is a first step on the Path to Enlightenment. Hence, we find Netzach on the Middle Pillar. More about that later!

The bottom and densest Sephiroh on the Tree of Life, also on the 'Middle Pillar,' is Malkuth. Malkuth deals exclusively with the material, the physical; the purely mundane. It deals with money and finance — not the planning of it, just the interaction of spending and obtaining. It is stuff. It is the physical shell itself. It is the fight or flight reflex. In Kabbalistic texts Malkuth has sometimes been described as "the Fallen Angel." It is sometimes hypothesized that Malkuth is Daath, the invisible Sephiroh located in the Abyss, fallen to the physical plane. It is associated with the earth element, feminine in nature and therefore the most receptive place on the Tree. That is why material form happens here. This is where all of us find our physical selves right now. This is our starting point on our Path to Enlightenment as we begin our Pathworking experience.

That takes us through Figure 2. Before we move on though, look at Kether a moment more. You will see that this is where the World of Ideas emanates from. In our Pathworking, as we open more and more doors leading toward Kether, we are going to be able to gain inspiration regarding progressively higher levels of ourselves.

The other Sephiroh on the Tree of Life showing life force energy coming into creation can also be associated with other Planes of Existence when the Theosophy model is combined with an understanding of the Kabbala. For more detailed information regarding these planes than is given here, consult the works of Alice Bailey and Madame Blavatsky. Here is a brief overview:

The *Causal Plane* is the plane that extends through Daath, joining Chokmah and Binah. The Causal Plane is the root of everything that exists. When we eventually get to this level of our Pathworking, you will be getting so deeply inside of yourself that you will be able to affect the very structure of your body and your being because you will be working on the Causal Plane. You'll be able to structure your life according to your own thinking. That's what this is all about — literally *creating* your body and your world according to your own thinking!

The *Higher Mental Plane* is the next plane coming into existence. It includes Chesed and Geburah. It is the plane where your Guides and Helpers mostly reside. Those of you who are in touch with your Guides right now will find that the highest of your Guides come from this level, along with much of your inspiration.

Following the life force energy on its way down the Tree into creation we next find the *Egoic Plane.* This plane includes the Central Self, Tipareth, seat of the Higher Self. It is called the egoic plane not because everyone who opens the door into Tipareth becomes self-centered, but rather because you must have a very strong ego in order to enter that consciousness. It requires an ego strong enough to make the sacrifices of self necessary to enter that consciousness. For this reason Tipareth is also often called "the Sacrificed God." Together, the Higher Mental and Egoic Planes constitute the *Creative World of Mental Patterns*. This is where ideas take form. Those ideas are the root of all creation.

Next, as the energy moves down the planes, is the *Lower Mental Plane*, also known as the *Upper Astral Plane*. It is sometimes called the World of Forms and the Plane of Invisible Forces. The astral plane, you see, is where everything that is going to become physical takes its final form before it enters the material plane. So, as we explore this plane through our Pathworking, we are going to be able to send our thoughts more clearly, to manifest our intentions more swiftly. We are going to be able to get more deeply in touch and in control of what is going on in our lives.

The part of you that lives on the lower astral plane, which is sometimes called the seat of the Vital Soul, has a lot of energy tied up in your emotions. When you learn to work with them, learn to make them a part of yourself, but not a part that rules you and your life, instead of fighting or ignoring them, you free up enormous reserves of energy. That is what is going to happen as we pass through Yesod.

One of the problems with those who work extensively with their psychic ability, is that in developing these abilities they open the doorway into those planes just above the physical — the lower and upper astral planes. But without a "road map" it is very easy to become lost in the astral world. So, for example, someone who does psychic healing could be working with a patient with a back problem and accurately sense that the problem is rooted in anger toward a husband, but then immediately get carried off into a flight of fancy where he (or she) sees the husband beating the wife; this may not even be true, it may simply be an image floating around on the astral that the healer linked into accidentally. This is the problem of being a psychic without a road map. It's too easy to tap into whatever is floating around out there!

One of the things that will begin to happen for you early on in our Pathworking is that you will get your own road map. You're going to be able to maneuver your way around the astral plane and know what you're looking at, without getting sucked into other people's emotions, worries or fears! This is a big part of mastering the dead ends and difficulties of the astral plane.

Finally, down in the physical body itself, in Malkuth, you have Objects, and Relative Reality — relative, that is, according to whatever you *think* reality is.

Now, please look for a moment at Figure 3.

Sphere	Key or Note	Instrument	Natural Sound
1	D	Flute	Breath
2	C	Violin	Wind
3	B	Cello	Rain
4	A	Harp	Waves
5	G	Drums	Thunder
6	F	Organ	Crackling

Sphere	Key or Note	Instrument	Natural Sound
7	E	Guitar	Switching
8	D	Piano	Stream
9	C	Horn	Echo
10	B	Orchestra	Footfalls

Figure 3

As you get to know the Sephiroh, you will see that they have many correspondences. Kabbalists learning the Tree of Life through study may spend many years contemplating these correspondences to our world in an effort to gain deeper understanding. One of their most intrinsic and basic correspondences is sound.

Vibration, or sound, is the simplest and most complete definition of any of the Sephiroh, and their musical notes speak for them. Both the Sephiroh and the Paths have specific vibrations, specific musical notes and related sounds. If you have a favorite instrument, or musical key, you may get some insight into the Sephiroh and Paths you are most comfortable with from this figure. They will probably be your favorite Paths and Sephiroh as you proceed with your Pathworking.

For example, if your favorite instrument is the guitar, you will probably feel very at home in the Sphere of Netzach and enjoy all of the Paths leading into and out of that Sphere.

It is also worth noting that if you are having a challenge in your life that relates to a specific Path on the Tree of Life, you can listen to music or other sounds relative to the Sephiroh connecting either side of the troublesome Path and by doing so enhance your ability to deal positively with the situation!

Let's look at the next figure, Figure 4:

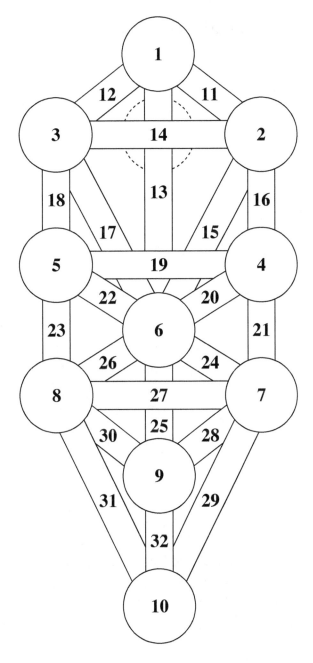

Figure 4

In Figure 4 you will see that each one of the Sephiroh also has a number, as do each of the Paths.

You can see by the way the Sephiroh are numbered that if you were to draw a line from 1 through 10 consecutively, you would end up with a diagonal crisscrossing of the Tree. Spiritual energy comes into manifestation in a downward, clock-wise flowing spiral. If you use your imagination a little, it looks rather like a snake. Figure 5 shows this downward spiral of energy, the 'Lightning Flash,' fairly well. Its snake-like flow has given it the name 'Serpent Path.'

Serpant Path and Chakras

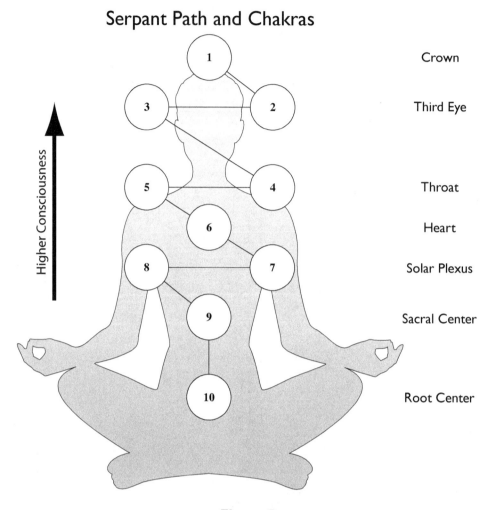

Figure 5

Kundalini, the *Serpent Power* as it is sometimes referred to in the East, refers to the life-force, or the energy lying dormant at the base of your spine. This snake-like spiral joining the Sephiroh in Figure 5 shows you the *Serpent Path* that the life-force energy takes as it is released in its counter-clockwise spiral back up the Tree of Life.

This is a good point at which to introduce a new concept to you. Not only is the Tree of Life a road map for raising consciousness through Western Yoga, it also represents your physical body.

Those who know something about the chakras, or psychic energy centers, know that these are energy vortexes through which the energy of Spirit enters to literally supply your body with the life-force that it needs to live.

There are literally thousands of these chakras, or energy entrance points, in your body, but only seven of these are considered of major consequence.

The lowest of these is called the Root Center. It is located at the base of the spine. The entrance point of the energy into this chakra is called the *perineum* — a point midway between the scrotum and the anus for a man, and at the vagina for a woman.

On the Tree of Life, the Root Center corresponds to Malkuth. So, when you explore the Malkuth level of consciousness you are exploring the consciousness of your Root Center.

When you begin to explore Yesod, you are now beginning to explore the type of consciousness associated with the Sacral Center. The Sacral Center is located about two inches below the naval, along the spine.

The Serpent Path takes you next to Hod. Hod represents one half of the Solar Plexus Center, while Netzach represents the other half. The Solar Plexus Center is located at the base of the sternum, or breast bone.

If you are questioning why the Solar Plexus Center works through two Sephiroh, while both the Root Center and the Sacral Center each only work through one, here's the answer: If you study the "biology" of the chakras, you'll find that each chakra has a corresponding "ductless" gland, a sort of physical counterpart in the body, which permits the biochemical balance within the body to be directly regulated by the energy activity (or lack of it) in the chakras.

The Root Center has only one corresponding ductless gland called the gonads. The Sacral Center has one also: the spleen.

But the Solar Plexus Center has two corresponding ductless glands; the adrenal glands correspond to Hod, whereas the supra-adrenals correspond to Netzach.

This represents the *conscious* versus *unconscious* action of the ductless glands — the conscious being part of the feminine side of the Tree at Hod, the unconscious being part of the masculine side at Netzach. Literally, the Tree becomes your body!

The next center is Tipareth, which corresponds to the Heart Center. The ductless gland associated with it is the thymus.

The next two Sephiroh, Geburah and Chesed, are again the unconscious and conscious counterparts of one of the chakras. Both of these Sephiroh correspond to the Throat Center. The biological glandular counterparts are the thyroid and the parathyroid. However, at this level, the serpent energy spins with reversed poles so that Geburah relates to the parathyroid (unconscious) and Chesed relates to the thyroid (conscious). You will note that this also coordinates with the ruling of the right brain for the left side of the body and with the left brain ruling the right side of the body.

The next two Sephiroh, Binah and Chokmah, together represent the action of the Third Eye Center (or Brow Center). They correspond to the anterior (conscious) and posterior (unconscious) pituitary glands.

Lastly, the topmost Sephiroh, Kether, corresponds to the Crown Center and the pineal gland.

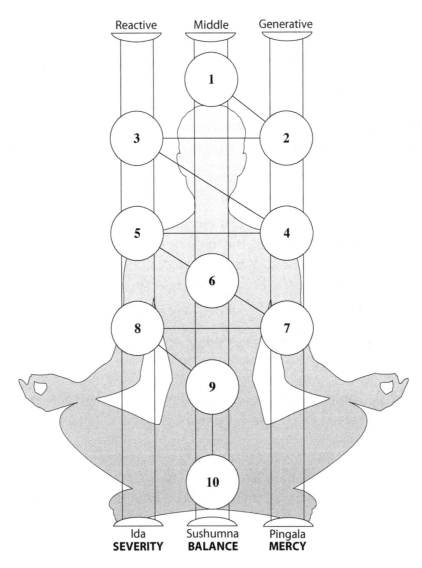

Figure 6

In Figure 6, three new factors from Eastern Tradition that relate to the Tree of Life are also shown. These are the Ida, the Pingala, and the Sushumna. Note that the Ida and the Pingala, the "side-channels" of energy in the Eastern Tradition, correspond to the female and male poles on the Tree of Life, Binah being at the head of the female side of the Tree, Chokmah being at the head of the male side. The Sushumna represents the *middle pillar*, which in us is the central pole of the body, including the spine.

Now, the reason I wanted you to see the correspondences to the body is because as we look at this *Lightning Flash*, we are also looking at the rising of the Serpent Power or Kundalini. This is the reason why the Kabbala has been termed the only true Western Yoga. Because when you talk about Yoga, you are talking about the release of the energy that is going to allow and aid the development of the higher consciousness of the entity. All Yogas stimulate the rising of the Kundalini energy and therefore the consciousness.

Just as in Kundalini Yoga, in all of us most of the energy is in the Spheres of Malkuth and Yesod. Most of it, in fact, is tied up in the Root Center. We will learn to release the energy from each of these centers. This happens automatically in Pathworking the Tree of Life as we learn what these centers are all about through inner exploration. We develop them by becoming relaxed and comfortable working with them.

This energy that is released then becomes available for our use in our own higher development. This is what the serpent path is really all about.

As the energy comes down into manifestation YOU are created! What we will be doing in Pathworking the Tree is reversing the direction of this flow. You are going to gradually learn how to take that energy out of its foundation in matter and bring it up to higher and higher levels.

Now, please notice that the Tree of Life is also divided into three columns. The columns, as I noted above, correspond in man to the Ida, the Pingala and the Sushumna. What those three columns say to the Kabbalist, (looking at the Tree as if it is your own body) is that the right side is the Pillar of Severity, the left side the Pillar of Mercy, and the middle is the Pillar of Mildness.

The Pillar of Severity, on your right-hand side, is also the feminine pillar, being on the side of the Tree with the feminine Binah at the top. It is called the Pillar of Severity because every Sephiroh and every Path that ties into this side of the Tree deals with learning in 'the school of hard knocks' — that is, learning only through direct experience. It deals with the principle of reaction. You learn through re-action, through finding yourself in situations you must work to overcome. You expand only because you must. You act against resistance. That is the feminine re-active pattern.

On the other side of the Tree, on your left hand side, every Sephiroh and Path tying into the Pillar of Mercy is characterized by volition. This side of the Tree is masculine, taking its pattern from the masculine Sephiroh, Chokmah, appearing at the top of the column. This side of the Tree is generative. On this side of the Tree, you learn because you take a chance. You learn and grow by 'acting out.' You learn because it was fun, and you tried it. It's an entirely different kind of experience than the right side of the Tree.

Now, neither side of the Tree represents balance, does it? As we evolve we drift back and forth, and back and forth, like a pendulum swinging from one side to the other. And as we reach the point where we begin to balance the energies on the Tree, we find ourselves on the Central Pillar, the Pillar of Mildness.

The fastest root to higher consciousness is to travel up that Central Pillar. People like Priests and Nuns, people who learn meditation, people who do Indian sweat lodges, become involved in the study of Shamanism, or mysticism, or metaphysical teachings that teach the value of inner harmony and balance, are all learning or working upon the Central Pillar. All of these approaches teach techniques for staying on the Central Pillar, so that the aspirant can evolve more quickly, without having to swing back and forth between one outside Pillar and the other.

In this Pathworking series we will NOT stick just to that Central Pillar. We will explore every Path leading between every two Sephiroh. We are exploring ALL of the 22 Paths that join all of the Sephiroh.

Our purpose is to learn to experience all of these types of consciousness. I also want to emphasize that the person who is swinging back and forth between the polarity of the two outer Pillars on the Tree is no worse that the person who lives his life exclusively on the Middle Pillar. Everyone is going to get to the top of the Tree. Evolution is a guaranteed process. We are all just at different stages of evolution, and we all go about it differently.

For example, there is no way we could know, but perhaps the person we see being tossed back and forth between the two outer Pillars in this life, was a Priest traveling the Middle Pillar in his last life, and in this life his evolution requires disharmony!

Who could argue with the possibility that the person in a state of balance right now has only attained that state of harmony because he has had ample prior life experience traveling the Pillars of Severity and Mercy?

My point is that there is a place for every action, for every feeling, for every emotion, for every thought.

In this series we will follow our own evolutionary process as we travel up the Tree from Malkuth. You will note a definite difference in the "flavor" of the Paths each time you switch Pillars.

Now, ultimately we want to be balanced enough that we can access the consciousness at Kether, which lies at the very top of the Middle Pillar. But we will achieve that balance and harmony in the time-honored tradition of exploration and experience, as well as meditation and inner seeking.

Let's discuss the character of each Sephiroh a little more. Please move on to Figure 7:

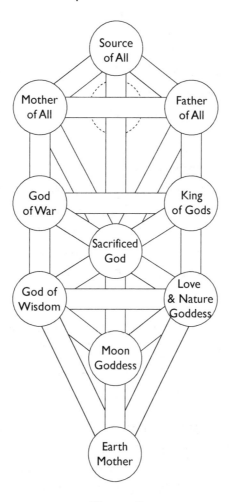

Figure 7

Figure 7 is a breakdown of the Sephiroh according to what types of Gods and Goddesses you would associate with each. I included this figure because today many people are getting involved in mythology, or paganism, or even Eastern religions with a multi-God and Goddess Pantheon. If you have insight into any of these, you will find that your understanding of the "character" and "history" of the various Gods and Goddesses will enhance your understanding of the Sephiroh they relate to.

For example, if you looked up Mars, the Roman God of War, and studied his acts and temperament, this would give you a lot of understanding about how the fifth Sephiroh, Geburah, acts.

The sacrificed God of Christianity, Jesus Christ, would be associated with the Sephiroh corresponding to all sacrificed Gods, Tipareth. This same Sephiroh would also include Buddha, Lao Tzu and Krishna.

Whatever aspect of the God-force you wish to look at, you will find it on the Tree; and by relating your understanding of it to that Sephiroh it most strongly relates to, you will gain a deeper understanding of and insight into the action of that Sephiroh.

It has been said that God is within all of us; I would expand upon that. All of the Gods, or in other words, all of the Aspects of God, are within all of us! To *know* ourselves is to know God, and to know God is to know ourselves. What an interesting enigma, certainly one worthy of life-long study.

Please take a moment to refer back to Figure 4, which was a schematic of the Sephiroh and Paths by number. You will be traveling all of the Paths in reverse order, from 32 back to 11. You will not be traveling the Paths relating directly to the Sephiroh (1-10) because you will be learning about these indirectly, through your study of the Paths tying into them. For example, once you have completed all three Paths leading out of Malkuth, Paths 32, 31, and 29, you will have achieved a very complete understanding of Malkuth.

Once you have brought the energy up into Kether, upon completion of Path 11, you will complete your Pathworking with the Lightning Flash Path, which will bring all of these levels together, giving you access to all, while completing your life's mission (whatever it may be) in Malkuth, the physical plane.

Please, if you are doing the Pathworking on your own, either from this manual or on audio, allow at least a week between Paths for your consciousness to adjust to the new energy, before you move on to the next. However, I do not recommend a wait of longer than two or three weeks between Paths. Too long a wait causes you to lose momentum.

After you have completed Pathworking the Tree of Life there is no limit to how many times you can repeat the Pathworking experience. Each time you will gain new insights and new experiences. While you are going through the Paths, if you have difficulty with one, or if you especially enjoy one, go ahead and do it several times before moving on. If you are experiencing an issue in your physical life that you feel has made you stall at one of the Paths or Sephiroh, you can help to resolve it by reading or listening to the Path again.

The Paths themselves actually represent the change of conscious between one Sephiroh and another. For example, in the 32nd Path, the first actual Path you will be traveling, you move from Malkuth to Yesod. In so doing, you will get a very good look at and insight into Malkuth, but will only just open the door into Yesod. It is your opening that door to the higher Sephiroh that allows you the extra insight into the lower one, so that you can more fully understand it.

The Paths that lead into the bottom of any Sephiroh open the door into it. The Paths that lead up from the top of each Sephiroh teach you about the Sephiroh. So, by the time we have explored all of these Paths leading into and out of any one Sephiroh, you will completely understand the type of consciousness it deals with, because you will have seen and understood it from every point of view.

Let's look at the numbers of the Paths and Sephiroh from a numerological viewpoint for a moment.

If you find your life-path number in numerology, you will be able to locate the Path and/or Sephiroh on the Tree that is your primary lesson in this life, just by looking at what Path or Sephiroh number it corresponds to.

Here's how to find your life-path number:

Simply add the month, day, and year of your birth together. The final result is your Life Path number. You will end up with a two-digit number that is the Path itself, and that can be reduced again to a single digit that is the Sephiroh that is most important to you in this life's journey. I'll use my birthday as an example:

My birthday is (month) 06 + (day 20) + (year) 1952. Add them together using simple addition. The result is 1978. Now reduce that final figure to a two-digit number by adding across: 1+9+7+8 = 25. My life path is 25. Now I can further reduce that to a single digit of 7 by adding 2+5. So, the seventh Sephiroh, Netzach, will also be very important in my life. That means I need to pay special attention to my experiences as I complete each Path that leads into or out of Netzach, in addition to the Path 25 itself!

Of course, all of the Paths are important. But those that deal with issues having to do with your life-path will be particularly important.

One more special note will help here: When you figure out your two-digit Path number, if it is greater than the number 32, you will need to count backward for your Life Path number. For example, if your double digit was 36, subtracting 32 from 36 gives you 4 – so, your actual life Path would be found by subtracting 4 from 32, because for numbers greater than 32 you are actually counting back up the Tree of Life. Your single digit Sephiroh number would remain the same.

Another thing that you will be interested to find out as we go along is that each Path corresponds to a different element: air, earth, water or fire. Depending on what element your Sun sign is in astrology, those Paths that deal with your element will also be particularly important to you. The earth signs are Taurus, Virgo, and Capricorn; the water signs are Cancer, Scorpio and Pisces; the air signs are Gemini, Libra, and Aquarius; and the fire signs are Leo, Sagittarius, and Aries. And, of course, different

Paths are assigned to different Astrological signs and planets. The Path corresponding to your Sun sign and its element will be particularly important, as well as the Path corresponding the ruling planet of your sign.

For example, someone who is an Aries will find the Path from Tipareth to Chokmah very important because it is an Aries Path. He will find all Paths leading into and out of Geburah important because Geburah is the Sephiroh corresponding to Mars, Aries ruling planet. The Path leading from Hod to Netzach, being a Path that corresponds to Mars also will be very important. I think you get the idea.

So again, even though all of the Paths are important in their totality, there are specific Paths that will be especially important to you.

See Figure 8 for detailed correspondences.

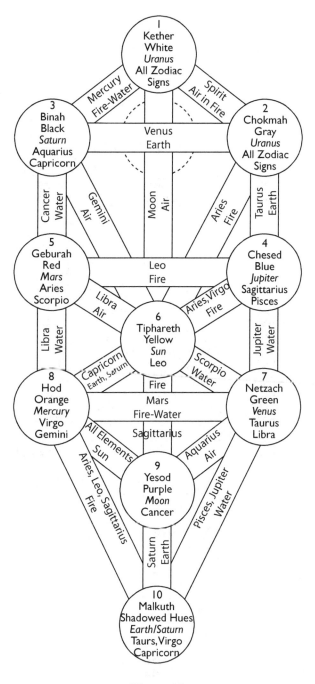

Figure 8

This figure gives you a color and a planetary representation for each Sephiroh, as well as the sign and element for each Path. The key on the bottom right of the page shows you the name of the symbol for each planet. The ruling planet(s) for each sign are also listed on the bottom of the page. This will help you to find your own most important Paths. Make a note of your Sun sign and its ruling planet and figure out your Life Path. From there it's easy! Here are the planetary correspondences to each Sun sign — Aries/Mars, Taurus/Venus, Gemini/Mercury, Cancer/Moon, Leo/Sun, Virgo/Mercury,

Libra/Venus, Scorpio/Mars and Pluto, Sagittarius/Jupiter, Capricorn/Saturn, Aquarius/Saturn and Uranus, Pisces/Jupiter and Neptune.

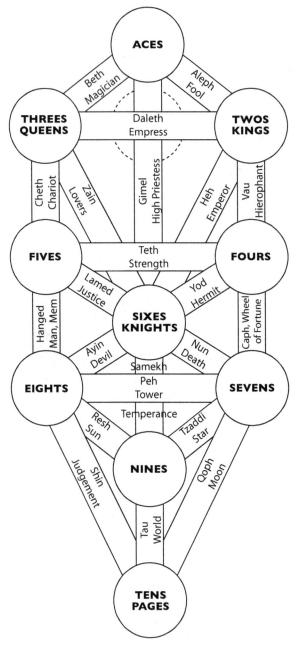

Figure 9

Figure 9 gives you the Kabbalistic correspondences of the Paths and the Sephiroh to the Tarot cards. Even if you don't read the Tarot, you might want to pick up a deck of Tarot cards to work with as you do the Paths.

Each Path, as you can see, has a very definite Marjor Arcana Tarot card that corresponds to it. I have found that if you sleep with the Tarot card that represents the

Path you are working with, it brings information and experiences from that Path into your dreams and into your life. It also teaches you the Tarot more intensely than if you studied the Tarot cards according to more usual methods. The Path IS the card.

Now, the Sephiroh, you'll notice, correspond to the Tarot Minor Arcana — that is, Kether to the 4 Aces, Chokmah to the 2s, etc., on down the Tree. The Court Cards, or people cards, also correspond to the Sephiroh, as per this figure. They are also the 10s.

Let's look at some of the more traditional Kabbalistic correspondences in Figure 10:

Sphere	Divine Name	Archangelic Name	Choir of Angels
Kether	Eheieh	Metatron	Chayoth Ha Qadesh
Chokmah	Yah	Ratziel	Ophanim
Binah	Jehovah Elohim	Tzaphqiel	Aralim
Chesed	El	Tzadqiel	Chasmalim
Geburah	Elohim Gibor	Kamael	Seraphim
Tiphareth	Jehovah Aloah Va Daath	Raphael	Melekim
Netzach	Jehovah Tzabaoth	Haniel	Elohim
Hod	Elohim Tzabaoth	Michael	Beni Elohim
Yesod	Shaddai El Chai	Gabriel	Kerubim
Malkuth	Adonai Melek	Sandalphon	Ashim

Figure 10

Figure 10 shows the Hebrew Divine Name for each Sephiroh, the Archangel of each Sphere, and the Choir of Angels for each Sphere.

The Choir of Angels that exists within each Sephiroh is very important, too, because they are actually the energy that gives that particular Sephiroh its quality. We will be working with the Choir of Angels of each Sephiroh along the way, too. You will become familiar with their energies. You are going to learn to focus on their higher power.

The Choir of Angels and the Archangel will help you to raise your consciousness as you work through each Path. Some of you will see these as outside of yourself, and some of you will see them as a part of yourself. Whichever way you choose to see and experience them is fine, since it is truly both. The inner world and the outer world are not so very different.

Figures 11A and 11B give Hebrew Divine Names for the Sephiroh and the Paths, as well as the type of 'Intelligence' traditionally associated with each. Contemplation of these will shed additional light on each Path and Sephiroh as you work through them.

Sphere #	Sphere Name	Type of Intelligence
1	Kether	Admirable or Hidden
2	Chokmah	Illuminating
3	Binah	Sanctifying
4	Chesed	Measuring, Cohesive, Receptacular
5	Geburah	Radical
6	Tiphareth	Mediating Influence
7	Netzach	Occult
8	Hod	Absolute or Perfect
9	Yesod	Pure
10	Malkuth	Resplendant

Figure 11a: Types of Intelligences (As defined in Mystical Qaballa by Dione Fortune)

Figure 11B also gives you the Hebrew letter for the Path. We will be working with the letters of each Path because that is known as the Divine Sound of the Path. You will see the Hebrew letter designed into each of the Path Mandalas, which are pictures that relate to and help to draw you into each Path you do. You will color each one before doing the Path and then gaze at it as you drift into the guided visualization for each Path.

Path #	Path Name	Type of Intelligence
11	Aleph	Scintillating
12	Beth	Transparency

Path #	Path Name	Type of Intelligence
13	Gimel	Uniting
14	Daleth	Illuminating
15	Heh	Constituting
16	Vau	Triumphal or Eternal
17	Zain	Disposing
18	Cheth	House of Activities
19	Teth	House of Spiritual Beings
20	Yod	Will
21	Caph	Conciliation
22	Lamed	Faithful
23	Mem	Stable
24	Nun	Imaginative
25	Samekh	Probation
26	Ayin	Renovating
27	Peh	Active/Exciting
28	Tzaddi	Natural
29	Qoph	Corporeal
30	Resh	Collecting
31	Shin	Perpetual
32	Tau	Administrative/Governing

Figure 11b: Types of Intelligences (As defined in Mystical Qaballa by Dione Fortune)

The last figure, Figure 12, is a reference sheet you will be using extensively. The more YOU participate in each Path, the more effective and meaningful that Path experience is to you.

Path	Color	Stone	Tarot Arcanum
32	Indigo	Onyx	The World
31	Orange-Red	Fire Opal	Judgement
30	Orange	Chrysoleth	The Sun
29	Red, Crimson	Pearl	The Moon
28	Violet	Glass	The Star
27	Red, Scarlet	Ruby	The Tower
26	Indigo	Black Diamond	The Devil
25	Blue	Jacinth	Temperance
24	Blue-Green	Snakestone	Death
23	Deep Blue	Aquamarine, Jade, Chrysolite	Hanged Man
22	Emerald Green	Emerald	Justice
21	Violet	Amethyst, Sapphire	Wheel of Fortune
20	Yellow Green	Peridot	The Hermit
19	Yellow Green	Cat's Eye, Opal, Zircon	Strength
18	Yellow, Red-Orange	Amber, Emerald, Turquoise	The Chariot
17	Orange	Tourmaline, Alexandrite	The Lovers
16	Red-Orange	Topaz	Hierophant
15	Red, Scarlet	Ruby	Emperor
14	Emerald Green	Turquoise	Empress
13	Blue	Moonstone	The High Priestess
12	Yellow	Agate	Magician
11	Pale Yellow	Chalcedony, Topaz	Fool
LF	White	Clear Quartz	

Figure 12: Path Correspondences

Each time you travel a Path you can enhance that experience by holding the stone associated with the Path in your hand. This could be either the type of stone, or a stone of the color related to the Path, also shown on this sheet. The stone held in your hand as you travel the Path will become charged with the experience of the Path, and will help you to recall and use this consciousness in the future. The charged stone may be carried with you in your day to day life to help bridge your daily life and your Pathworking. This may help to turn challenges into success stories.

You can also enhance your experience of the Path by wearing the Path color when you travel it. For example, when you do the 32nd Path you should be wearing indigo to bring this energy in the most strongly. Likewise, you may wear indigo in your daily life to bring Path 32 influence into your activities.

You also can use the Tarot card for the Path and have it with you as you travel the Path. Sleeping with it under your pillow for a few days prior to doing the Path, and a few days after, will also enhance the experience.

So, this reference sheet will help you to be more in tune with each Path as you travel it. The more of these 'extra' influences you include with your Pathworking experience, the more successful it is likely to be!

A reaction sheet also is included and should be completed immediately following each Path. It is intended to be filled out when the Path is so fresh in your mind that you can easily record physical and emotional reactions to it. Based upon this, you will be able to establish some ideas of what you feel the Path will help you to accomplish in your life and the effect it might have on you. You should do this each time you repeat a Path as well, and compare your new insights to your previous ones. That may give insights into how you have grown and into what your current life experiences are focusing on now.

The way I like to conduct a Pathworking session myself is to review my reaction to the previous Path before beginning work on the present Path. To this end, a diary sheet is included for you to fill out following each Path. It should be filled in each day during the week following your completion of the Path.

When you complete this you should be asking yourself if you had received from the Path what you had expected to. Your insights on a daily basis will help you to see how the Pathworking may have altered your normal reactions to daily experiences.

It's not unusual, as you move through the Pathworking, to begin to "live" aspects of the Path prior to actually doing the Path. It's also not surprising for people around you to start experiencing some of the things YOU are experiencing on the Paths. Pathworking has the effect of enhancing your consciousness, and through you it may touch many of those close to you!

Now, please look at the mandala supplied for the first 'mini-path' that follows this chapter. A mandala is a picture and its purpose is to relax you and move you into the correct mental state to experience the Path more readily. It is intended to "suggest" the proper mode of entrance onto the Path you are beginning. Each Path you do will have its own mandala.

The mandala you see here is intended to help you to enter our introductory mini-Path. The purpose of the mini-Path is to give you a short Path to introduce you to the skill of Pathworking.

This particular Path is short, and will serve to help you to become familiar with the four elements we will be dealing with throughout the Pathworking series, as well as to act as a clearing and grounding preparation before you begin the Kabbala Pathworking itself.

Welcome to Kabbala Pathworking. Enjoy and Grow!

Pathworking Checklist

General Instructions:

Please note that you do not need to do EVERY item listed to benefit from this work. Simply setting aside 45 (undisturbed) minutes per week to listen to each path will work wonders for you. The additional items are for those wanting to maximize their experiences. Do as many as you feel like doing with your available time/interest.

Prep Work 1-2 Days Before Completing the Path:

- Highly recommended: Print and color the path mandala.
- Highly recommended: Do anything that clears your mind, body, and emotions.
- Optional: Place the Path's corresponding Tarot Major Arcana card under your pillow.
- Optional: Place the Path's corresponding crystal under your pillow.

Setting the Stage:

- Block out 45 minutes of COMPLETELY UNDISTURBED time.
- Recommended: Anoint your Third Eye with the oil for the Path you are about to do.
- Optional: Wear an item of clothing that is the color associated with the Path.
- Optional: Hold a stone, crystal or personal jewelry item you would associate with this Path in your right hand.
- Hold your Mandala before your eyes and gaze at it.
- Turn on the recording and begin listening to the Pathworking audio as Sandy lists the correspondences on the Path.

The Path:

- Allow your mind to relax and your eyes to slowly close as you begin your journey.

Immediately After:

- Record your immediate reactions, preferably in your book.
- Note how you felt physically and emotionally both during/after completing the Path.

- Record any special parts of the Path that you reacted to strongly. List all of the things you think this Path will help you to deal with or overcome in your life.

-

The Week Following the Path

- Record any special feelings or changes you see in yourself.

- Note any significant dreams or dream symbols.

Additional copies of this checklist are available for at www.SandyAnastasi.com.

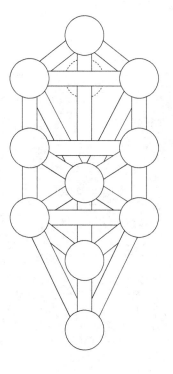

Mini Path

Take a few moments to gaze at your Mandala. Then, slowly let your eyes drift shut.

Our quest begins here.

Path

As your mind drifts, clear it of this present time and place. You open your inner eyes to a beautiful and intoxicating landscape. You walk through a green meadow; tall mountains rise in the distance. You are in awe of their majesty. Wind ruffles the tall heads of grain in a field nearby. And gurgling splashes of sound emanate from a stream.

The sun pours down over all. A welcome warmth filling your senses. You stretch up your arms, reaching toward its eternal warmth. Letting the light of the sun penetrate your body and your spirit. The sun's rays glint off the distant mountains like sparks of fireand the mountains reflect light in every color of the rainbow. Soon a gentle rain begins to fall.

At first, you revel in the cool drops. And soon you are thoroughly wet. Having nothing to lose, you enter the stream, and the rain coming down runs off of your body to merge with the waters of the stream. Somehow, in spite of the rain, the sun still shines down upon you. And soon you find yourself in the middle of a torrential sun shower.

Rain and sun beat down upon you, and all tension and worry is washed out of you and carried away by the stream in which you stand. Before long, you feel thoroughly clean in body, as well as in spirit. The rain stops and you climb from the stream to lie among the flowers lining the stream bed.

The scent of wild flowers and the call of wild birds surrounds you. Your mind begins to drift into the natural sounds and feelings all around you. You feel totally distant from the everyday life you have left behind. You begin to wonder what it would be like to carry this peace and tranquility, this feeling that all is right with the world, with you always.

You watch the flight of an eagle far above you. And for a moment, your awareness looks out through his eyes. You feel the fierce freedom of flight, the exhilaration as the strong air currents carry you up, up, high over the mountain range. You revel in your freedom. You are thrilled at being able to see everything so clearly, so completely.

Your attention snaps back into your own body. And you wonder what it would be like to have that clarity of vision, and that sense of freedom, objectivity and total oneness with the world around you, active in your own life.

A vision of the tree of life appears before you. And you see it now, like a roadmap, complete with road signs, speed limits, warnings and informational signs. The vision pulses like a beacon and you know that this roadmap will guide you along a path that will teach you, like the eagle, to fly high above those distant mountains, to reach the highest peaks of your own potential - a potential you yet barely know exists.

Excitement fills you. Your whole being vibrates with excitement and expectation.

You are ready, ready, to begin on a path toward your own higher development, a higher development and enhancement of self that will have far reaching and beneficial effects on your entire life.

Your consciousness returns once again to your physical body and you feel yourself refreshed, revitalized and ready to begin your journey.

Let your awareness return to this time, to this place. And be ready to begin the 32nd path.

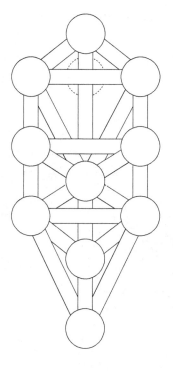

Path 32

Correspondences

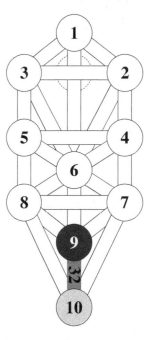

— Sphere of Malkuth —

We commence our journey in the Sphere of Malkuth, the Kingdom.
The Hebrew Divine Name is Adonai Melek.
The Archangel of the Sphere is Sandalphon.
The Choir of Angles are the Ashim, or Souls of Fire.
The Planetary correspondence is the Earth, or Saturn.
This Sephiroh is symbolized by the gateway, or cavern entrance.
Colors are all shadowed natural hues.
The element is earth.
The stone is onyx or granite.
The number is 10.
The Tarot correspondences are the four Ten's and the Princesses or Pages.
The metal is lead.
Plants are the red poppy and thrift.
The musical note is "B."
The magical image is a young woman, crowned and throned.
The spiritual experience is a vision of the Holy Guardian Angel.

— 32nd Path —

The 32nd Path is known as the Governing Intelligence, because it governs and co-ordinates the planets of our solar system and the physical plane we live on.
The Hebrew letter for the path is Tau, meaning "sign" or "cross."
The planetary influence on the path is Saturn.
The corresponding Tarot Major Arcanum card is the World.
The element on the path is earth.
The Symbols are the labyrinth, darkness, the white cypress and the fish-goat (sigil for Saturn).
The stone is onyx.
The scent is sulphur.
The color is indigo.
Living beings are creatures of nightmares, elementals and the guardians of the gates into the lower astral plane.
Mystical experiences include the passing the portals of the lower astral, rebirth and a look into the mirror of your unconscious mind.

— Sphere of Yesod —

The Sphere of Destination is Yesod, the foundation.
The Hebrew Divine name is Shaddai El Chai.
The Archangel is Gabriel.
The Order of Angels is the Kerubim, the Strong.
The corresponding planet is the Moon.
The number is 9.
The Tarot correspondences are the four Nine's.
This Sephiroh is sometimes symbolized by the garden, the sickle or scythe and the moon.
Minerals are crystal and silver.
Colors are violet and white.
The living being is the stag.
Religious and mythical figures include all varients of the Horned God.
The musical note is "C."
Plants are the mountain ash, iris and water lily.
The magical image is a strong and beautiful naked man.
Now close your eyes, and lay your mandala aside.

Invocation

"May we be encompassed by the name Adonai Malek and established in the temple of Malkuth, the Kingdom. May the portal of the 32nd path be opened to us, and may we journey thereon in the power of the name Jehovah Elohim to the gate of the Sphere of Yesod. And in the name of Shaddai El Chai, may the gate of Yesod be opened to us and may we be firmly established in the wonders of that Sphere."

Path

As you open your inner eyes you find yourself in a deep prehistoric forest.

Giant trees surround you and the sounds of great animals are all around you, as they move through the darkness of the surrounding forest.

You move carefully through the dense foliage yourself and soon come in sight of a cave leading deep into a steep hillside covered with the same giant trees.

The cave fascinates you; it seems to offer protection, warmth, and solitude.

You enter, and begin to explore.

You've entered the uppermost level of your own psyche and in your exploration of this outermost cave you find all sorts of things you've forgotten have been important to you over the years! In your exploration you come across a nearly hidden entrance way into a cave lying deeper into the hillside than the first.

Eagerly you enter.

Again, it's fascinating.

You at first think this cave is empty, until in the dust on the floor you begin to identify fossils from the distant past and you can detect, in the dim light from the doorway, cave paintings on the wall.

A deep part of your inner being calls out, "I have been here, I remember." You explore the fossils and paintings for a time and it seems that as you do, a part of your long-distance memory begins to awaken and you are able to access other places and other times. You find you are becoming fascinated with time! You bring your attention back to the present again and look about you, only to see yet a third entrance way into yet another and still deeper cave! Again, you enter eagerly.

This cave is totally dark and you can, at first, see nothing.

Silence surrounds you.

You hear only water dripping in the distant darkness and smell the humid scent of the earth.

You wait, although you don't really know what for.

Soon, a Sphere of white light approaches. As it gets closer you see that the white light comes from a glowing silver sickle carried by a being who is also glowing so brightly that you cannot see their face.

This is Sandalphon, Archangel of the Sphere of Malkuth, who will guide you on your journey inward.

The Archangel says nothing, but merely turns and moves down a passageway, which has suddenly appeared directly before you.

You quickly move to follow.

As you are lead onward you perceive that there are many protrusions coming down from the cave ceiling above and up from the floor below, as well as sticking out from the walls. There are holes and sheer drops in the floor.

You soon realize that to move ahead safely, you must remain on the path the Angel shows you.

You follow deeper and deeper into the earth and the path becomes steeper and steeper.

You realize that you are moving through a maze-like system of caves and tunnels that constantly take you further and further into the bowels of the earth.

You feel uncomfortable with the weight of tons of earth and rock that seems to push down from above, but at this point you cannot go back; you must trust your Guide and move forward.

Suddenly the brilliant light of the Angel disappears into what looks to be solid rock! You are left in utter darkness. You stumble forward in the darkness to find a narrow fissure, almost too tight to pass through; but as you squeeze through, you again see the light! Thankfully, you let it bathe over you; it seems all too meager now, with the darkness pressing in all around you.

You walk onward and the path levels out and opens into a cave.

A bit of light filters downward from a partially blocked opening far above.

In the dim light you are able to see the precious metals - veins of silver and gold and others that run through the granite walls.

Here and there are precious gems, unpolished, yet still recognizable in their natural state, studding the walls.

The cave is beautiful and you lose track of your Guide as you stop to look around.

Then you look down and see crushed bones and skulls that you have been walking on! Suddenly the cave seems oppressive and stifling. For the first time on this journey you begin to feel afraid. Where are you going? And with that thought you realize you've lost your Guide! In sudden panic you begin to search frantically for the light of your guiding Angel.

Your Guide's been waiting patiently for you at the dark opening of yet another passage leading downward.

You want to follow, and yet you feel an inner resistance. A feeling of resistance to the darkness of what lies within yourself and of what may be encountered on the lower astral plane as a result of the lack of knowledge of yourself! This feeling of resistance has a name. It is the reflection on this lower Astral Plane of your divine Guardian Angel, who at this level can only communicate to you in feelings and urges.

The feeling of resistance you feel is a built-in protection to prevent you from going unguided into the depths of yourself before you are ready for the journey.

But you are ready and your Guide awaits you. With sheer force of will you focus on first taking one step forward and then another and then another.

Soon, you are through the wall of your own resistance and you continue to follow your Guide downward.

The path twists and turns, moving clockwise in a steady spiral downward and inward.

It opens into yet another cave.

In this cave you walk among everything you have treasured in your life. You see jewelry, furnishings and riches of all sorts. Some of this is your own, some pieces you have wanted and worked hard to try to afford. You see clothing of all sorts and every type of device, toy and other material thing you have ever desired.

You realize it's all here for the taking. You begin to revel in the jewels, the gold and silver, in the sheer joy of having, having and having.

Suddenly, a strange image comes to your mind. You seem to see this treasure cave as a dragon's treasure hoard. You see treasure upon treasure piled almost to the ceiling, with the great, slumbering beast perched on top of the pile. He can't spend his hoard and he can't use it. His only joy in living is to get this treasure and then spend his life hoarding and protecting it.

The vision disappears and you are again in the treasure cave of your own desires. But somehow, the jewelry, furnishings and other objects have lost their beauty, their attraction. You are suddenly filled with sadness.

A gong sounds and the light pouring from your Archangel-guide flashes brilliantly over you. You realize that you can no longer be bound to the things of your past, that you are free of the bondage to the material things that you have acquired. Now, your inner perceptions begin to awaken as the guiding light washes through you! When the light dims, you are outside the treasure cave. No longer bound to the past or owned by your possessions you can again move forward following your Guide.

With your new found inner perception, you begin to see earth elementals of all kinds and you perceive the Choir of Angels of this Sphere, the Ashim, as the fiery points of light surrounding your Guide.

You come to a chasm whose edges are joined only by a narrow bridge. Your Guide moves smoothly across and waits for you on the other side.

You begin to cross, but suddenly, the bridge, the cliff edges and even the air around the bridge are alive with elemental beings. In their dance they try to distract you from your path.

But you look away and follow your Guide and the Ashim across the bridge.

On the other side, you continue your clockwise spiral down and as you proceed, the spirals get smaller and smaller, just as the path gets steeper and steeper.

You begin to lose sight of your Guide again, as the spiral gets tighter. You hurry to catch up.

Out of the corner of your eye you seem to see strange beasts and half seen flashes of demons, beings of the lower astral and of the Lords of Chaos. You become dizzy in your hurriedness. You look straight ahead, away from the astral forms.

Suddenly, your descent ends. Your Guide is again waiting for you, before two massive doors of bronze and tin. Carved into the center of each is the figure of a young virgin, crowned and throned.

On each side, the massive doors are guarded by tall, beautiful and naked men. As you look at them it seems that, superimposed over them both, are the images of hoofed feet and the head and horns of a goat.

These guardians look deeply into you and ask, "Who are you and why do you seek to pass through here?" You look to your Guide, but no answer, nor hint of what to say, is given to you. Yet you know that this is a test and to fail here means to return back the way you came in spite of all your gained experiences.

You tell the guardians your name, and then you say, "I seek to be reborn onto the level of the astral realms and in the Sphere of Yesod!"

The guardians stand back and the massive doors open to you! You find yourself in a large empty cavern with no openings other than the one you entered through, which now closes solidly behind you. There is no way out of here except through rebirth! Your Guide did not enter with you. You are alone in total darkness. The weight of tons of earth again presses down. You feel the cold and damp of the womb of the earth. Around you there is only stillness and silence. Even the astral forms that have hovered for so long at the edge of your vision are gone.

It feels as though an eternity passes, as you slowly allow your consciousness to drop deep into communion with the rocks and earth of the cave around you. You are the earth, you are the rocks, you are the water, and you are the darkness and the silence.

You feel energy within you lying dormant yet growing and expanding.

Suddenly, your body begins to fill with warmth and energy as light fills you and you begin, like the walls around you, to glow with an inner radiance equal to that of your Guide.

The light energy within you continues to build and build as a counter-clockwise spiral of energy within you begins and moves faster and faster; suddenly you are lifted up, up, and up, as if you are being sucked up and out of this womb of the earth to be born on a green and glorious hilltop high above! You are under the stars and the moon. Their combined light bathes you and fills you with ecstacy. Soft strains of music drift across the hilltop to you. You go to investigate.

Your guiding Archangel Sandalphon stands waiting for you next to a deep, dark well. The music emanates from it.

The Archangel motions for you to look into the well and as you do, you see that the still waters of its surface act as a mirror.

At first, as you look, all you see is your own reflection. But as you look deeper, other faces flash by, that you recognize as past versions of yourself. You look into the face of antiquity, into your own roots and the very roots of your race. Finally, at the very bottom, you see the Saurian symbol of the fish-goat, symbol of Capricorn. You realize that your journey into matter has ended and that your conscious evolutionary journey begins here.

Your Angelic guide speaks to you now, for the first and last time. "Remember, on the journey you now begin, the only obstacles come from within!"

Sandalphon begins to shimmer and soon, in the Archangel's place, you see a great stag.

He turns and leads you onward toward the Sphere of the Moon, Yesod.

As you move forward you feel a fierce resistance in the air around you.

It's as if a stiff wind was blowing you steadily backward. You push, and push and suddenly the resistance is gone.

You stand now in a beautiful, lush garden surrounding a 9-sided temple with a silver door. Ash trees surround the entrance. You move inside.

You can feel this is a place of power. The very air vibrates.

The walls inside the temple are carved in relief and on them you see stags, centaurs, dogs and wolves. You see the moon and the stars and intermingled with these are the carved images of the triple Goddess, the Virgin, the Woman and the Crone.

All of these images are in constant motion, one fading into the other. Wind whips through the temple, moving through you as well.

You realize that you are awake and aware, here, in the temple of the Astral Plane, in Yesod, out of your body.

You have learned to open the eyes of your inner perception, that allow you to see clearly on this plane and yet have learned the art of maintaining a steady path forward, without being deceived by the astral forms perceived along the way.

The air is filled with the scent of jasmine and lily and you are filled with a sense of inner balance and harmony and a sense of the "rightness" in all things.

Now slowly, awareness of your physical body begins to return, as your consciousness returns back to this place and the present time.

But you bring back, as a part of yourself, all that you have learned and experienced.

And so ends the 32nd Path.

Path Journal

A. Record your emotional reactions to your path experiences here, immediately upon completion. Include any physical responses or sensations.

Date of completion: _____

Emotional responses: _____

_____

_____

Physical reactions: _____

_____

_____

What do you think these responses indicate? _____

_____

_____

B. Use this section as a diary of your experiences during the week following your completion of the path. Be sure to include how you react to things emotionally, as well as how you deal with any major issues that might arise.

Day 1: _____

_____

Day 2: _____

_____

Day 3: _____

_____

Day 4: _____

_____

Day 5: _____

_____

Day 6: _____

_____

Day 7: _____

_____

C. Review the week's experiences. How has the path affected the way you handled this week's issues? _____

_____

_____

_____

D. What special dreams has this path stimulated this week? _____

_____

_____

_____

Areas Path 32 Will Help You Work On

- "Lightness" - letting go of material things
- Gaining a proper perspective on the worth of "stuff"
- Seeing your material roadblocks more clearly
- Understanding the limitations you impose upon yourself
- Using assertiveness with balance
- The ability to view past lives and to discern the patterns in them that may affect the present
- The ability to astral travel and strengthening the astral body
- The ability to visualize things clearly
- Enhancement of dreams
- Opening the door to "oneness"
- Getting through your own resistance
- Overcoming your fear of losing control
- Rebirthing
- Learning the ability to tune into the elements (psychometry)
- Knowing and finding what you really want
- Disorientation leading to detachment
- The ability to deal with things of the physical plane
- Opening the psychic senses to other realities and developing your intuition
- Getting in touch with your roots
- Learning to do whatever is required without resistance or emotional upset
- Taking responsibility without grief
- Manifesting your creativity and productivity

- Manifesting work and payment for work

- The ability to be "invisible"

- Overcoming depression

Path 31

Correspondences

— Sphere of Malkuth —

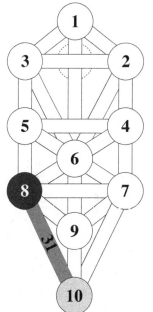

We commence our journey in the Sphere of Malkuth, the Kingdom.

The Hebrew Divine Name is Adonai Melek.

The Archangel of the Sphere is Sandalphon.

The Choir of Angels are the Ashim, the Souls of Fire.

The Planet that corresponds is the Earth, or Saturn.

Colors are all shadowed natural hues.

The element is earth.

The corresponding body parts are the feet and the anus.

The number is 10.

The tarot correspondences are the four 10s and the four princesses or pages.

The associated stones are onyx and granite.

Plants are Irish Moss, Hemlock, and Heart's Ease.

The musical note is "B".

The magical image is a young woman, crowned and throned.

The mythical correspondence is Hades, King of the Underworld.

The spiritual experience is an understanding of the four elements and the spirit that binds them.

— 31st Path —

The 31st path is known as the Perpetual Intelligence because it regulates the motions of the Sun and the Moon, keeping each in their proper order and orbit.

The Hebrew letter for the path is Shin, which means "tooth."

There is no planetary correspondence, but the element is given as Fire; although all four elements are present, they are transmuted through Fire.

The path corresponds to the Tarot Major Arcanum card Judgement.

The scent is olibanum.

The magical tools are the wand and the lamp.

The stone is fire opal.

The color is glowing orange-scarlet.

The spiritual experience of the path is a resurrection and rebirth through a letting go of the separateness of the personality.

Living beings are all of the phantasmal forms of the astral plane.

Guides encountered along the path include Arel, Ruler of Latent Heat, Samael, Ruler of Volcanic Fire, and Anael, Ruler of the Astral Light.

The musical note is "C."

— Sphere of Hod —

Our Sphere of Destination is Hod, Splendor.

The Hebrew Divine name is Elohim Tzabaoth.

The Archangel is Michael, Prince of Splendor and Wisdom.

The Order of Angels are the Beni Elohim, the "Sons of the Gods," or the "Elemental Kings."

The corresponding planet is mercury.

The number is 8.

The Tarot correspondences are the four Eight's.

The Sephiroh is symbolized by names and versicles and the apron, as well as by language and visual images.

It corresponds to systems of magic, science, religion and government.

The color is orange.

The symbolic creatures are two snakes entwined.

The metal is quicksilver.

Stones are opal and agate.

Herbs are fennel, cedar, cassia and cinquefoil.

The mythical figures include the Greek God Hermes, the Roman Mercury, the Egyptian Thoth and Chiron, the healer, teacher and warrior who was half God, half mortal.

Body correspondences are the loins and the legs.

The musical note is "D."

The magical image is a hermaphrodite.

Now close your eyes, and lay your mandala aside.

Invocation

"May we be encompassed by the name Adonai Malek and established in the temple of Malkuth, the Kingdom. May the portal of the 31st path be opened to us, and may we journey thereon in the power of the name Anael, ruler of the Astral Light, to the gate of the Sphere of Hod. And in the name of Elohim Tzabaoth may we be firmly established in the wonders of that Sphere."

Path

You open your inner eyes to behold a strange landscape.

Everything that you see is in shades of gray.

There is little difference between the gray of the land and the gray of the sky.

You do not see the sun.

You cannot tell if it is day or night.

An enormous cone-shaped mountain stands before you, the only peak to be seen rising out of a wide, flat plane.

Wind blows relentlessly across the plane and no plants or animals seem to be able to withstand its constant battering. The plane is barren, except for occasional large "standing stones" scattered across it, seeming like guideposts in a barren wilderness.

The only vegetation you see is on the mountain itself, where the folds and ravines of the rising slopes give protection from the winds.

Buffetted by the wind yourself, you make for the protected slopes of the mountain before you.

Just as you reach the lower slope, rain begins to fall, accompanied by powerful flashes of lightning.

The lightning becomes more and more frequent as you climb, shattering nearby stones and trees.

You have not yet found any clear path leading upward, or any safe haven. You briefly consider returning back to the plane beneath you, but you recall its barrenness and know that there is nowhere there that you would care to go.

But as you briefly look out across the plain, you realize that this electrical storm is centered around the mountain, as if drawn to it, of perhaps created by it.

There is no time to ponder this revelation. A bolt of lightning hurls into the earth within feet of you. You quickly move on, searching, now, for a clear path upward.

You find a footpath, and begin to run along it, lightning dogging your footsteps.

A little bit further, you keep telling yourself. Just a little bit further. But you know you cannot outrun the lightning. What is drawing it? Before you can arrive at an answer, you spot a cave opening on the slopes rising just above you. You leap across rocks, and grabbing the edge of the stone ledge just below the cave, you pull yourself up onto it.

Gratefully, you tumble into the cave, as another bolt of lightning smashes into the ledge, causing it to crumble away just as your feet leave it! Inside the cave it feels peaceful.

The crashing of the thunder is a distant echo. You pause to rest while your eyes acclimate to the darkness.

Again, you ponder the source of the lightning. Could there be some magnetic source in the mountain that is attracting it, like a magnet to a loadstone? Your eyes begin to adjust to the dim light; you realize that the cave is illuminated. Some kind of small luminescent lichen grows on the walls, giving off a soft light. In their dim light you see the glow of fire opals. You put your hand on the wall, expecting it to be moist and cool and are surprised to find it warm and very dry.

Where is the warmth coming from? Hand over hand you place your hands on the rock surface as you move back toward the rear of the cave, finding it getting progressively warmer. The wall at the rear of the cave is so hot that you have difficulty touching it.

You are so absorbed in your exploration that you are unaware of another presence in the cave until you hear a chuckle behind you.

Shocked, you quickly turn about, to behold a figure neither male nor female, but something of both. This androgynous being announces that its name is Arel. It holds a lamp in one hand and reaches out with the other to take your hand. You reach out, too, and as you touch the hand of this strange being you are amazed at the searing heat emanating from it.

Arel smiles in understanding and gestures as if to indicate that the heat coming through the cave wall and the heat emanated by its body are one and the same.

You begin to perceive that both are variations of latent heat. As you realize this, you feel your own body begin to become warmer, as if recognition of the latent heat in the cave and in Arel has released certain blockages to the energy flow in your own body. Your feet and your lower spinal area begin to get hot and to vibrate.

You remember how the thunderstorm outside seemed to be drawn to the mountain and you ask Arel about it. But Arel only smiles, then moves on, gesturing you to follow.

Arel moves into a tunnel you didn't see before. It leads upward, gradually moving in a spiral counter-clockwise.

The walls are smooth and they glow with the same latent heat that the rear wall of the cave did. You begin to realize that the walls are too smooth. This tunnel was not formed by the movement of rock, or by man's hands. The slick sides, roof and walls could only have been formed by the melting of rock at immensely high temperatures! You realize now why all the surfaces feel warm to you. You travel up an old lava-tube and you are inside of an active volcano! As if to give further support to your theory, the floor beneath your feet suddenly begins to shift and shake and far ahead of you a crack appears in the wall, cutting down from the roof toward the floor. Deep red lava - super heated rock, begins to seep from the crack and as you watch, pieces of the surrounding wall begins to fall away, allowing more and more fiery lava into the tube you follow.

You look to Arel for guidance, but your Guide merely watches the flow move toward you. Your first instinct is to run back down the lava-tube, but you know you can never outrun it. You watch, instead, to see what your Guide will do.

Arel seems to be undergoing some kind of a transformation. As you watch, you see the body seem to shimmer and undulate, as great heat is released. The color becomes progressively redder and it begins to glow. Little sparks of fire dance along the surface of its body.

It turns to motion you onward and you see that the features are no longer those of Arel. You look upon Samael, Ruler of Volcanic Fire.

In his right hand he holds a glowing wand, which seems on fire, like his body. He points it at you and fire flows out of it and arcs into your own! You move forward to follow him and find that your own body is also burning with volcanic energy; heat pours from you in waves. You realize that the latent heat is being released. You are learning to use your fiery energy. Your physical being is being transmuted by spiritual fire.

Samael moves forward into a realm of heat, lava and fire, but is untouched by it. You follow in his footsteps and also remain whole and unblemished. You walk upon the very flow of lava, following the lava tube ever upward and inward, toward the center of the volcano.

Finally, you walk out into a large central cone. Orange-red fire burns everywhere, lava flows outwards from a massive orifice in the crater floor. Heat waves fill the air and you know that if you were not in your transmuted form you would be instantly turned to ash.

The realm of earthly fire surrounds you and you see it as the realization of the fire that burns deep within you. You suddenly realize that it was not the mountain the lightning was attracted to, it was you! You, when you did not recognize the energy that was your own, allowing it instead to crackle around you, out of control. And you realize, too, that you are the mountain, and the volcano burns within you! With this realization, a humming sound begins around you, as you again begin to transmute to still a higher level of fire energy. The humming gets louder, and louder, as more and more energy builds up within you. You feel the heat mounting, as the air around you, and your own body too, becomes hotter, and hotter.

A shuddering sensation passes through you as the heat reaches a level of such intensity that it is no longer bearable even at this level. The whole mountain shudders as the volcano begins to erupt, and you are carried upward and out of the cone.

An icy coldness fills you, and a sensation of ecstasy! You have been again transmuted to a still higher form of fire, that of the Astral Flame. You look about for your Guide, as you free-float in this formless, Astral Light.

You see the space around you filled with cool, colored flames, of every imaginable color. Phantasmal forms, too, of all sorts float by. You see trees, plants, animal forms and human, too. You see them at all different points in their evolution. You even see forms that have not yet come into existence and you see others that have not appeared on our physical planet in millennia.

You are filled with a certain sadness as you realize how fleeting all forms are, yet this sadness is compensated by a new understanding that as your evolution and the evolution of your planet continues, you are changed, but never destroyed! Your Guide appears. Yet again, there is a difference. Your Guide, too, has transmuted and on this level of Astral Flame you see her as Anael, who rules the Astral Light.

You begin to hear the astral sound. You hear it inside of your head, in your mind. It fills you, and you perceive the Astral Flame with new eyes, seeing it as flashing, vital and everchanging! Anael shows you the way to ride the Astral Flame upward, rising higher, and higher, into the realm of pure Spiritual Fire.

You perceive a glow above, as you continue to rise.

Anael leaves you now, this is no longer her realm and she can go no further.

You rise upward into the realm of Spiritual Fire. You are blinded by brilliance so intense that you cannot see.

The space around you has become dry. Again, you feel a heat so intense it feels icy cold.

Your skin prickles all over. The space surrounding you continues to become hotter and the brilliance intensifies still more! You endure the radiance. You are thirsty. You crave shade. You wish for darkness, for a lessening of the brilliance, but it only intensifies still more. You endure.

You become aware of presences surrounding you. You can barely see them in the brilliance. They surround you in a circle. Both testing and protecting. These are the Elemental Kings, the Order of Angels of the Sphere of Hod and they watch your transmutation, as you endure ever greater heat and brilliance.

All resistance within you evaporates; in the extremity of your discomfort you accept, opening to the light.

Heat and light flash through you without hindrance in repeated waves. You experience wave upon wave of heat and wave upon wave of brilliance.

You begin to feel lighter as all attachments to form, to the physical, to the emotional, are burned away.

With each wave of heat you are purged until you feel emotionless.

You feel a new sense of freedom and liberation.

Purged of every emotion, your intellectual vision is intensified and you behold something of the eternal ordering of things. You see and understand all that you behold with clarity of thought never before possible for you.

As the blazing white fire consumes you, you reach into the heart of it; deeper and deeper.

You go deeper and deeper, until you find a place of total blackness and stillness. Icy coldness has replaced the heat. Your mind is still.

You wait.

And wait.

Finally, you feel yourself released and you feel yourself floating upward through the cool darkness.

You revel in the coolness after the intense heat you have experienced and realize that you are surrounded by water.

You begin to swim upward, toward a light shining from above.

Your head breaks the surface of the water, and you see that the light emanates from a temple floating upon a vast and quiet ocean.

You see a platform of black and white checked marble; eight agate pillars support a roof of orange opal. This is the temple of Hod.

You swim toward the temple. As you approach, you see the Elemental Kings who were your observers through your test more clearly. One stands at each quarter of the temple. The mighty Archangel, Michael, stands before the entrance, as if to invite you in.

You climb from the water and walk onto the platform. The atmoSphere surrounding you is crisp and clear. As you walk across the black and white checked marble you feel your mental acuity reflected and enhanced by the intuitive understanding of opposites they represent.

In the center of the temple stands a figure from which the light you saw is emanating. It is so brilliant that you cannot see its face, but you see that it is neither male nor female, but is a hermaphrodite. It holds a staff, around which you see two snakes intertwined.

It says nothing, but gestures you to be seated. You sit at the feet of this being, at the center of the temple and contemplate your experience in coming to this place.

You have discovered the latent energy potential within yourself and have learned to release it. You have learned to travel the Astral Flame and have come to some understanding of your place and the place of mankind in the grand scheme of things. You have passed the test permitting you access to the realm of Spiritual Fire and have had burned from you all lower emotion and attachment to the world of form. You have learned to look upon the outer world with a newfound mental clarity. You have learned to find your center.

The temple slowly fades away around you now, as you slowly bring your consciousness back to this time and this place. But remember, you can always find the peace and clarity of the temple of Hod merely by looking to that still point within yourself.

And so ends the 31st path.

Path Journal

A. Record your emotional reactions to your path experiences here, immediately upon completion. Include any physical responses or sensations.

Date of completion: _____

Emotional responses: _____

_____

_____

Physical reactions: _____

_____

_____

What do you think these responses indicate? _____

_____

_____

B. Use this section as a diary of your experiences during the week following your completion of the path. Be sure to include how you react to things emotionally, as well as how you deal with any major issues that might arise.

Day 1: _____

_____

Day 2: _____

_____

Day 3: _____

_____

Day 4: _____

_____

Day 5: _____

_____

Day 6: _____

_____

Day 7: _____

_____

C. Review the week's experiences. How has the path affected the way you handled this week's issues? _____

_____

_____

_____

D. What special dreams has this path stimulated this week? _____

_____

_____

_____

Areas Path 31 Will Help You Work On

- Increased energy

- Fortitude, the ability to keep moving forward under any conditions or circumstances

- Increased mental activity

- Objectivity

- Putting your emotions "in order," and learning to rise above them when necessary; freedom from "emotional fetters"

- Personal empowerment

- Unblocking energy channels; the arousal of the Kundalini energy

- Increased sex drive

- Opening more to higher guidance

- Development of automatic writing skills

- Increasing creative ability

- Enhancement of interest and skill in martial arts

- Seeing and understanding patterns in seemingly unrelated things and events

- Recognizing the inherent balance in all things

- Finding your "center"

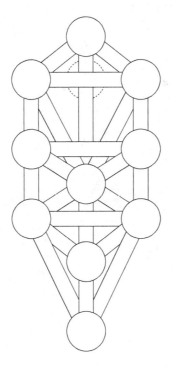

Path 30

Correspondences

— Sphere of Yesod —

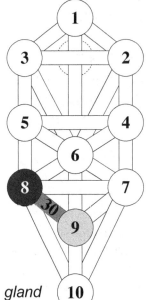

We commence our journey in the Sphere of Yesod, the foundation.

The Hebrew Divine Name is Shaddai el Chai, the Almighty Living God.

The Archangel of the Sphere is Gabriel, Prince of Change and Alteration.

The Choir of Angles is the Kerubim, the Strong.

The Planetary correspondence is the Moon.

The symbols are perfumes and sandals.

The color is violet.

The element is air, the Astral Light, or Akashic Fluid.

The number is 9.

The Tarot card correspondences are the four Nine's.

The corresponding body parts are the reproductive organs.

The chakra is the Sacral Center, located just below the navel; the gland that corresponds to this center is the spleen.

The stones are crystal, pearl or clear quartz.

The metal is silver.

Plants are camphor, jasmine, frankincense and white sandalwood.

The musical note is "C."

The magical image is a very strong, beautiful, naked man.

The mythological correspondences are the Greek Godess "Artemis" (the huntress), the Roman Pan and Diana, the Norse Loki and the Wiccan God and Goddess, Cernunnos and Selena.

The spiritual experience is a vision of the machinery of the universe.

— 30th Path —

The 30th Path is known as the Collecting Intelligence because Astrologers deduce from it the celestial signs from the stars and perfect their science by it.

The Hebrew letter for the Path is Resh, meaning head, for this is the highest Path of human intellect, and is the activating force of the personality.

The planetary influence on the Path is the Sun, supplier of both light and warmth.

The corresponding Tarot Major Arcanum card is the Sun.

The 30th Path is a composite of the four elements, being comprised of all of the planets and signs under the rulership of the Sun.

The Path symbols are the opposing energies of fertility and barrenness.
The stone is chrysoleth.
The color is orange.
The scents are cinnamon and rose.
Herbs are frankincense, angelica and rosemary.
The plant is sunflower.
The associated mythological figures are Adonis and Apollo from the Greek Pantheon of Gods and Ra, from the Egyptian.
The symbolic creatures are the lion, the sparrow-hawk and the phoenix.
The symbolic living being is the child.

— Sphere of Hod —

Our Sphere of Destination is Hod, Splendor.
The Hebrew Divine name is Elohim Tzabaoth.
The Archangel is Michael, Prince of Splendor and Wisdom.
The Order of Angels are the Beni Elohim, the "Sons of the Gods," or the "Elemental Kings."
The corresponding planet is Mercury.
The number is 8.
The Tarot correspondences are the four Eight's.
The Sephiroh is symbolized by the apron, as well as by language and visual images.
It corresponds to systems of magic, science, religion and government.
The color is orange.
The symbolic creatures are two snakes intertwined.
The metal is quicksilver.
Stones are opal and agate.
Herbs are fennel, cedar, cassia and cinquefoil.
The mythical figures include the Greek God Hermes, the Roman Mercury, the Egyptian Thoth, and Chiron, healer, teacher and warrior who was half God, half mortal.
The body correspondences are the loins and the legs.
The chakra is the Solar Plexus Center and the glands are the adrenals.
The musical note is "D."
The magical image is a hermaphrodite.
Now close your eyes, and lay your mandala aside.

Invocation

"May we be encompassed by the name Shaddai el Chai and established in the temple of Yesod, the Foundation. May the portal of the 30th Path be opened to us and may we journey thereon in the power of the name Jehovah Aloah va Daath to the gate of the Sphere of Hod. And in the name of Elohim Tzabaoth, may the gate of Hod be opened to us and may we be firmly established in the wonders of that Sphere."

Path

You open your inner eyes to a vision of peace and beauty.

You are lying on the ground in a lush, walled garden.

The scent of fertile soil and jasmine flowers surrounds you.

A hazy sunlight fills the air around you. The air glitters with a silvery sheen.

You hear the sounds of birds and small animals all around you and revel in the multi-hued beauty of dew-covered flowers growing profusely upon the enclosing walls of the garden.

An ancient structure, hazy, only half-seen, and overgrown with vines forms one end of the garden's enclosure. It looks to be an old mansion, or perhaps a castle of some sort.

You see a door opening onto a long and winding hallway. From where you lie the hallway seems as insubstantial as the structure. You can see that there are a myriad of rooms and connecting halls leading off from the main one. Each is shrouded in mist. This phantasmal structure draws you.

Your attention is fully on the building as you walk across the garden to begin your exploration of it. So fully are you focusing on the building, in fact, that you are surprised when you hear the laughter of children coming from the left side of it.

You look off toward the sound of the laughter and see two small children, a boy and a girl, laughing and playing together in the water spurting from a fountain. The fountain itself is a work of art; the statue of a man, naked and beautiful, stands atop a nine-sided crystalline prism, from which water flows outward, in a rainbow of color.

The sight is soothing; in fact, it brings back memories of your own childhood and, momentarily, you see yourself as a child again! As a child, you recall the intense curiosity you have always felt about everything around you.

It has never been enough to know that something is, you always needed to know why it is; it has never been enough to know that something worked; you always wanted to know why it worked.

Filled with an intensified sense of curiosity, feeling like an adventurer and a scientist all rolled into one and filled with a childlike sense of wonder at all that you see, you walk again toward the insubstantial structure at the end of the garden.

And immediately you are in a long hallway that seems to lead onward toward a distant and brilliant light. You cannot see your own feet, for a haze covers the floor and your feet disappear into it. You reach out to touch a wall, but your hand passes through it. Everything here seems insubstantial, unreal, yet the air pulses with energy! You are drawn to the light, yet also to the many rooms and other passageways branching off from the one you are on. Your curiosity wins out yet again.

You enter a room just to your left and find yourself in a vast library. You become fascinated by the volumes of books, by the wealth of knowledge contained in this one place.

The books are old and dusty with age; they seem almost on the verge of disappearing, but in your mind's eye you see this library new and filled with the comings and goings of people seeking its knowledge.

You move out into the hall again and are startled to see people passing you, all going about their business. It's as if you have moved back in time, back to when this place was thriving and young.

In fact, as you look down at yourself, you see that you are still a child! You move down the many corridors, exploring, and finally find yourself in a chapel. Several people are inside, praying at the altar and you see a Priest, in his vestments. You can't hear what he's saying, but you can see by the reactions and attention of the people he's talking to, that it is very, very important. You stay for awhile, hoping to learn what is so profound.

But soon your curiosity again gets the better of you and you find you need to move on, to continue your exploration.

You leave the chapel. Outside, you see two men carrying swords.

They look interesting, so you follow them into a yard area where there are many more men involved in mock battles with each other.

Some are using swords, some jujitsu and other forms of hand to hand combat and still others are using archery or pistols.

You watch, fascinated.

After awhile, the same two men you had been following, who were also watching this practice, leave. You want to stay and watch more, but you also want to know where they are going. Again, your curiosity wins and you follow them.

They lead you to a large room with a single round table in it.

Around the table sit many grown men who are all leaning forward studying a map. You move closer to see the map, and realize that it is a map showing deployment of troops. These men are discussing war strategy. Fascinated, once again, you sit back to listen. It all reminds you of an intricate game of chess.

Before long you begin to become bored with the seemingly repetitious scenarios of strategy and you look around the room to see one man dressed very strangely. He wears a robe that is covered from neck to toe with astrological symbols.

When he gets up to leave, you follow him, to see if you can learn anything new.

He begins to walk up a winding set of stairs and you follow.

He turns into a room on the left. You enter behind him and see another library, but this one has long workbench-type tables running through the center of the room. Upon them are all types of strange apparatus; beakers and tubes and turning wheels and steaming kettles.

You watch the Alchemist work for a time, eager to learn his trade.

When he leaves his experiments and exits the room, you follow him again, eager to see what he is about.

Again, he climbs another winding stair, winding counter-clockwise upward. But this time, it seems that the stair goes on and on and there are no side-passages or adjacent rooms. Finally, he opens a door at the top of the stairway and you find yourself on the roof of the building.

By now, it has become dark and you see the moon large and full, directly overhead. You seem to see the calm and serene face of a woman looking down at you from it.

The Alchemist takes up a telescope and begins to look through it.

Seeing your curiosity, he hands it over to you and guides you as you look through it at the heavens.

As you look through the lens of the telescope, it's as if you are drawn through it and up toward the very heavens you look at.

You seem to float through space, at first seeing nothing but total blackness all around you.

But then, as if from a distance, you perceive a great spinning disc of light.

You move closer.

As you move closer to the spinning disc, you see that it's not a disc at all, but is rather comprised of millions of tiny, brilliant dots of light. You realize that you are looking at the Milky Way, the Galaxy that is the home of our solar system.

You move closer still.

Soon you are surrounded by the stars, winking and blinking around you in their brilliance.

You move toward one particular star that glows with a yellow brilliance. It is a special star. It is our Sun.

You move closer and closer, until the gravity of a planet you are passing pulls you toward it. You move toward the Sphere of Mercury.

Turbulent air currents tumble you through the air as you roughly land on the surface. Intense heat wells up through the soles of your feet. You see the craters of active volcanoes all around you.

You kneel down inside the crater of a volcano and collect a bit of sulphur you find there.

The air currents lift you up again, carrying you up in a spiral and out into space once more, until you drift again into the gravity field of another planet.

You are pulled toward this new planet until finally you come to land on warm sand. From horizon to horizon all you see is desert.

The Sun, so close above, is blazing and hot. The desert is stunningly beautiful. The landscape around you is washed in a blaze of color.

Light in all shades glitters off of the sand. The path before you is hard to follow, because you keep losing it in the dazzling sunlight.

The air is so dry and so hot, that you begin to find the dazzling light oppressive. You feel the burning of the Sun upon the top of your head. Your mouth is dry. You become tired, and your walking mechanical. You begin to see mirages. You find you are no longer studying the beauty of this place.

As you move onward, you begin to have trouble telling your real path from the mirage path before you. But still, you move onward.

The Sun is a white hot blaze. You wonder, how can it sustain life, when it seems so hostile? You see an ocean in the distance. Is it real, or mirage? You move toward it and as you do, it seems that no matter how far you walk, you can get no closer to it.

Finally, you close your eyes and you call upon your Guide.

Gabriel, Archangel of the Sphere of Yesod, appears before you - and with him is the Alchemist from the beginning of your journey. The Alchemist bears a staff entwined by two snakes. With it, he touches your brow. You immediately feel as if you have just awakened from a deep sleep. All weariness, oppression and thirst dissappears. You feel a new consciousness of your own inner power and are filled with an understanding of natural forces. Radiance fills you.

Now, with an act of your Will, you will yourself to the ocean's edge, where you scoop up a handful of sea-salt; then, you follow the Alchemist upward as he soars into space, leading you onward toward the other planets.

In your new-found freedom you soar toward Venus and then past Earth and onto Mars. You circle around the martial planet and fly on to Jupiter. From there you move in a giant circle around the ringed planet Saturn and onward to Uranus and then Neptune and then the cold planet Pluto.

As you travel around and past each, you feel something of each planet in yourself. It's as if the energies of each are needed to complete the picture of who you are. Although you can't describe them, you feel their energies revitalized within yourself.

Through each of the planets you feel another energy pour out and into you.

It is the energy of each one of the 12 constellations, comprising the 12 signs of the zodiac.

You become aware, for a brief moment, of the vast order of the universe, of how everything within it is dependent upon everything else within it, from the smallest to the largest.

You have completed your flight through the solar system and again head toward the Sun.

As you head toward the Sun, you are again pulled into the gravitational orbit of Mercury. You land at the foot of a smoldering volcano. The Alchemist is waiting to guide you upward.

You begin to follow the Alchemist up a path that twists and turns, leading in a counter-clockwise spiral up and around the slopes of the mountain.

As you move upward, you see that many paths lead off from the main one, but that the Alchemist always chooses the most direct path.

At some junctures it is difficult to see which path is the correct one, yet the Alchemist never falters, his experience combining with analytical and intuitive powers to choose correctly each time.

You come to a point where you can look up and clearly see the peak of the mountain. You are surprised to see, curled around the very peak amidst the gases and occasional flashes of fire being belched from the mountain, a huge and powerful looking dragon.

As you watch, the dragon wakes, stretches and reaches upward, his jaws wide, as if waiting to catch something in them. You look around, to see what he could be waiting for and you see that the Sun is rising toward its zenith and that when it exactly reaches its zenith, the dragon will be perfectly placed to swallow it! You and your Alchemist guide begin to move faster, heading upward as quickly as you can.

As you move upward you hear voices calling you off of the path, but you ignore them.

You see flashes of color and light, but recognize these also as attempts to distract you from your objective.

Upward and around you move, faster, and faster.

Finally, you and the Alchemist are at the top of the mountain, at a level just below the dragon. The Alchemist stops. He takes off, from around his neck, a gold medallion imprinted with the symbol of the Sun. He holds it at an angle to perfectly reflect the Sun's rays at the dragon. The dragon is bathed in the rays of the Sun from above and by reflection from below. He closes his massive jaws and looks around just as the Sun passes safely overhead.

Before the dragon can react further, the Alchemist takes from his robe an ancient cup filled with pure water. Directing the reflected light from the medallion into the cup, he solarizes the water. He motions for you to put into the water the salt and the sulphur you have collected. Then he adds into it some mercury from a vial he is carrying. The liquid begins to glow with incredible brilliance! Quickly, he races to the crest of the volcano and pours the liquid from the cup down into it. You follow and are just in time to see the dragon dive into the mouth of the volcano after it.

A deep rumbling begins and the earth beneath your feet shakes.

You feel a tremendous build up of energy as the rumbling gets louder and louder.

Suddenly, out of the flames and smoke rising from the volcano's cone flies the mythical bird, the Phoenix. It is the dragon reborn through the action of the Alchemists formula and the burning fire of the volcano. As you watch, it begins a steady flight upward, straight toward the Sun.

You turn to find the Alchemist looking at you with a direct and steady gaze. You realize that you, too, must transform the dragon within yourself.

The Alchemist takes his staff and once again touches it to you; first he touches it to your spleen chakra, just below your naval, where you have felt the buildup of serpent-energy. At the wand's touch you feel an enormous release of energy, traveling up your spine toward your solar plexus chakra, at the base of your breast bone.

He touches his staff to you a second time, touching you at the solar plexus chakra, and you feel an even more powerful release. You feel energy traveling to all parts of your body, creating new channels never available before, for the carrying of life-force energy on a more subtle and higher level than ever before. You feel your very body being transmuted and transformed, like the Phoenix.

With this transformation, you feel yourself growing from the child, to the adolescent, to the adult. As the adult, you look toward your Alchemist-guide once again. He lays aside his staff and you watch it shimmer and disappear. He takes a step toward you and then another and another. Finally, you feel his being merge into your own and realize that from the beginning he has been an extension of yourself.

As you realize this, another release of energy enfolds you and you are lifted up in a flash of white light that comes from within yourself. You hear a succession of musical notes that mark your passing the Initiation of the Personality into the great source of inner light.

You float in this self-generated light for a time, and as it begins to fade you find that you are floating in a sea that stretches for as far as you can see. But this sea is not dark and gloomy, but rather has brilliance to it, as if reflecting the light of the Sun.

Using your Will to direct you, you move toward a distant source of light. As you approach you see an island floating in the sea. A well-tended garden surrounds an 8-sided temple. The light shines from a lamp hanging in the center of the temple.

You walk out of the water onto the shore. As you enter the garden you hear voices. You move closer to see two people, a man and a woman, in deep conversation with one another. The polarity between them is a power nearly tangible. They glow with a true love shared.

You see that they have achieved, through their unconditional love of one another, something that can otherwise be gained only through great skill, learning and personal transformation. As they turn toward you, you recognize the children you found in the garden at the beginning of the path. They too have grown up. You turn and walk up eight steps into the temple of Hod. The black and white marble slabs of the floor remind you of the polar opposites so inherent in this Sphere. These are the opposite polarities of male to female, of intuition and mental, of higher to lower self. The secret to resolving these opposites is contained here.

In the center of the temple, beneath the light, you see an altar.

On it is the staff the Alchemist used, the staff of Hermes, with its two intertwined snakes. As you look upon it, you realize that knowledge and study have brought you to this point of transmutation; but only through unconditional love can you gain the wisdom of how to use it.

And so ends the 30th Path.

Path Journal

A. Record your emotional reactions to your path experiences here, immediately upon completion. Include any physical responses or sensations.

Date of completion: _____

Emotional responses: _____

_____

_____

Physical reactions: _____

_____

_____

What do you think these responses indicate? _____

_____

_____

B. Use this section as a diary of your experiences during the week following your completion of the path. Be sure to include how you react to things emotionally, as well as how you deal with any major issues that might arise.

Day 1: _____

_____

Day 2: _____

_____

Day 3: _____
_____

Day 4: _____
_____

Day 5: _____
_____

Day 6: _____
_____

Day 7: _____
_____

C. Review the week's experiences. How has the path affected the way you handled this week's issues? _____
_____
_____
_____

D. What special dreams has this path stimulated this week? _____
_____
_____
_____

Areas Path 30 Will Help You Work On

- Alchemy - the transformation of one base element into another- in this case, a transformation of your physical body into a form that may accommodate a higher and more refined energy

- Shapeshifting - a variation on (1)

- Learning to navigate through the Astral Plane

- Astral traveling

- Opening of the Sacral, and Solar Plexus Centers, and stimulation of the Third Eye Center

- Disengaging from the "material mind"

- Gaining confidence in "knowing" what is necessary to do, and being able to follow your "knowingness"

- Peace of mind, and awareness of how to achieve it

- Overcoming your fear of unconditional "freedom" and the responsibility that entails

- Being able to gather sexual tension and direct it

- Resolving seeming opposites

- Gaining mental clarity

- Being able to access the "Akashic Records"

- Prophetic insight

- Gaining mental fluidity and an ease of detachment

- Aids the study of Astrology and any technical science

- Mental ecstasy and exhilaration

- Development of the Magical Will

- Diligence in acquiring a skill

- Learning to use your healing ability

- Visualization

- Artistic inspiration

- Finding, understanding, and accepting a soul mate

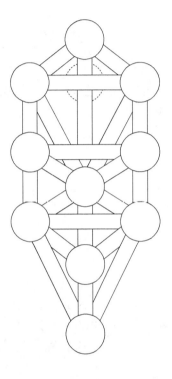

Path 29

Correspondences

— Sphere of Malkuth —

We commence our journey in the Sphere of Malkuth, the Kingdom.

The Hebrew Divine Name is Adonai Melek.

The Archangel is Sandalphon.

The Choir of Angels is the Ashim, the "Souls of Fire."

The Planetary correspondence is the Earth or Saturn.

The element is earth.

Malkuth is symbolized by a gateway, or sometimes a cavern entrance.

Its colors are all shadowed natural hues.

The stone of this Sphere is onyx or granite.

The metal is lead.

Plants are the red poppy, black helebore and belladona.

The number is 10.

The Tarot correspondences are the four Ten's and the Princesses or Pages.

Corresponding body parts are the base of the spine and the feet.

The chakra that corresponds is the Root Center.

The musical note is "B."

The magical image is a young woman, crowned and throned.

Mythological correspondences include the Greek God Hades and the Greek Goddess Persephone.

The spiritual experience is a vision of the Holy Guardian Angel.

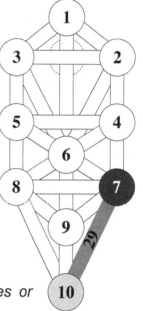

— 29th Path —

The 29th Path is known as the Corporeal Intelligence, because it forms every body which is formed beneath the whole set of worlds and the increment of them.

The Hebrew letter for the path is Qoph, which means "back of the head." The simple meaning of Qoph is "sleep."

The planetary influence on the Path is Jupiter.

The corresponding Astrological sign is Pisces.

The Tarot Major Arcanum card that corresponds to the Path is the Moon.

The symbols of the 29th Path are the magic mirror, the doe, the crayfish and the beetle.

The stone is pearl.

The scent is Ambergris.

Herbs are ash, elder, water iris, water lily and jasmine.

The color is crimson.

The musical note is "B."

Living beings are the dog, the wolf, a huntress and elemental beings of our own creation.

The mystical experiences include an understanding of your soul's organization into the physical body it inhabits, a "waking" from the sleep of the collective unconscious and a conquest of the phantoms reflected from the material world on to the astral plane, where you face and conquer the phantoms of the darkest recesses of your own mind, as well as those of your race.

Mythological correspondences include the Greek Hecate, Goddess of both the underworld and the overworld, Artemis, Greek Godess of the hunt and childbirth and Diana, her Roman counterpart, as well as the Egyptian Anubis, God of the underworld and resurrection.

— Sphere of Netzach —

The Sphere of Destination is Netzach, Victory.

The Hebrew Divine name is Jehovah Tzabaoth.

The Archangel is Haniel, Prince of Love and Harmony.

The Order of Angels is the Elohim, the Gods who are also called The Order of Principalities.

The corresponding planet is Venus.

The number is 7.

The Tarot correspondences are the four Seven's.

The symbols of Netzach are the girdle, the rose and the lamp.

The stone is emerald or turquoise.

The metal is copper.

The color is green.

The corresponding body parts are the loins, hips and legs.

The corresponding chakra is the Solar Plexus Center.

Living beings are the dove, the sparrow and the swan.

The symbolic creature is the lynx.

The musical note is "E."

The scent is rose.

Herbs are blackberry, cherry tree, dwarf elder and golden seal.

The magical image is a beautiful, naked woman.

Mythical correspondences are the Greek Goddess Aphrodite, the Roman Venus and the Norse Goddess Freya. All are Goddesses of love and of nature.

The spiritual experience is a vision of beauty triumphant.

Now close your eyes, and lay your mandala aside.

Invocation

"May we be encompassed by the name Adoni Malek and established in the temple of Malkuth, the Kingdom. May the portal of the 29th Path be opened to us and may we journey thereon in the power of the name Shaddai Al Chai to the gate of the Sphere of Netzach. And in the name of Jehovah Tzabaoth may the gate of Netzach be opened to us and may we be firmly established in the wonders of that Sphere."

Path

You open your inner eyes to look upon a natural scene of great beauty.

You stand in a clearing surrounded by ancient, giant trees; thick green grass interspersed with moss and wildflowers covers the ground all around you.

You hear birds, and, in the distance, the trickle of water.

You can't imagine a more beautiful place; you feel totally calm and comfortable with the natural environment around you.

At odd angles throughout the clearing you see standing stones.

You move closer to run your hands over the surface of one of these and you see etchings in the stone that are very nearly eroded by the action of wind and rain over the many centuries that have passed since the stone was placed here.

You discern the barely visible symbol of the moon and its eight phases, inscribed in a circle around a hunting horn.

You see that the moon phases are shown to correspond to the harvest cycle of planting, nurturing, harvesting - birth, death and rebirth again.

As you gaze at the hunting horn, you seem to hear the sound of a horn calling to you, as if from a great distance. It's a sound that arouses both fear and longing in you at the same time. You listen to hear it again, but all is quiet. You think that perhaps it was your imagination.

You move on, to explore the other stone shapes in the clearing.

Near the center of the area is a simple stone structure, with several steps leading down into it.

You go inside to discover that this is an ancient burial tomb.

Since you're already inside you look around.

You see a stone casket in the center of the tomb. Inscribed on its cover you see symbols depicting birth, death and rebirth.

Standing around the casket are tools and baskets of what look like the remains of food and other things a returning soul might need.

You look into the casket through a hole in the lid and are surprised to see only dust. The occupant is long gone! You contemplate again the symbols on the top of the casket.

And again you hear the hunting horn. It sounds once only, and then all is quiet as before.

You leave the tomb.

Just outside the door is a stone basin filled with water. You can't see the source from which the water comes, but it appears to bubble up from the bottom, overflows the rim and runs into the earth.

Flowers bloom profusely around the basin. A mother of pearl cup stands on its rim. You fill the cup from the basin and drink.

You immediately feel cleansed, as if all weariness has been washed away. You become aware again of the calls of the birds, the animal and plant life teeming in the forest around you. You seem to feel the very pulse of nature.

You drink again and feel a sense of unity with all that you see around you.

Again you hear the call of the hunting horn.

At the far side of the clearing you see two standing stones that support a third, in the form of an arch, or perhaps a gateway. The configuration fascinates you. You put the cup down and go to get a closer look.

You walk all around it, looking at the unlikely positioning of the stones.

You find it odd, that when you stand in front of the stones and look through their arch you can see nothing clearly; all you see is a blur.

You walk around them again and note that from the back you can look through the arch and see the clearing quite clearly.

You walk to the front again, but still the area under the arch is blurred, although the forest surrounding it is quite clear.

Fascinated, you step through the arch.

Immediately you note changes! It's as if you've moved into a different time, a different place.

A soft mist surrounds you and the light that filters down through immensely tall elder trees is soft and unreal, reminiscent of moonlight.

Again, you hear the hunting horn, but this time it's closer. You realize it belongs here, not in the solid world you came from! You see a path, barely discernable in the mist and begin to follow it. Orchids and lilies catch your eye.

The path twists and turns, like a maze winding through the thick and alien forest. You can see only as far as a few feet around you, the mist is so thick.

You do not feel comfortable here, as you did on the other side of the gateway.

You hear sounds, as of great creatures moving through the mists surrounding you and you stop moving forward, in fear of disturbing them.

No sooner do you stop, than the noises stop as well.

You begin to move again - and again you hear the sounds of under- brush snapping beneath large limbs.

You stop again. Again, the sounds stop.

Is something following you?   Stalking you? You begin to run. Crashing noises follow along behind you as you run, and run, and run, until your lungs burn and your legs will move no more.

Exhausted, you stop. Again, all sound of pursuit stops.

You wait. Surely, this creature that torments you will now appear! But nothing happens. No creature appears.

You decide to backtrack along your own trail, to catch this illusive pursuer.

As soon as you begin to move backward along your trail the sounds of pursuit begin again, but this time from the direction you had been heading, as if this creature had somehow gotten ahead of you and now follows you back! Your mind says,"This is impossible, I heard nothing!" and then a suspicion begins to form.

You pick up a pebble and throw it off the trail, into the mist.

Immediately you hear a similar sound reflected back at you from just beyond where you threw it.

You try it again and again you hear the "echo" of the pebble's passing.

You begin to laugh at yourself. You have been running from the echo of your own footsteps and the creature in pursuit was of your own creation.

You begin to move along the path more confidently now.

Up ahead of you, you see a silvery glow. You approach slowly, to see a beautiful woman kneeling in the brush just to the right of the path. She wears a girdle from which a hunting knife protrudes and is poised to shoot an arrow at a great stag. The glow emanates from her body.

As you watch, she places arrow to bow and sends a silvery shaft at the stag. You watch the beast fall and see its crimson blood flow. You feel a sense of sorrow and loss at such beauty destroyed.

Before you can react, the woman moves forward and removes her arrow from the carcass of the stag. It immediately jumps to its feet. No blood is apparent. Both the woman and the animal disappear.

The hunting horn sounds.

This time it sounds much closer and you begin to hear the baying of dogs.

The barking gets closer... and closer.

You begin to wonder what prey these dogs chase.

Soon the pack is so near they are nearly upon you.

A small animal hurls onto the path before you.

For a moment you see the panic and terror in its eyes, and then the dog pack is upon it.

You don't stay to see it slaughtered, but run as quickly as you can from the ripping and tearing noises of death, down the winding, ethereal paths flanked by ash trees.

You begin to slow, only to hear the sound of the dogs following you! They get closer.

In blind panic, you begin to run.

You have no awareness of where you are running to; breath coming quickly, filled only with naked fear, you are out of control.

Finally, in your panic, you slip and slide down the rough slopes of a stream bed and come to rest in the hollow of a dead tree adjacent to the flowing stream.

The bowl of the tree cradles you like a womb and the running water soothes your spirit.

The sound of the baying dogs dwindles into nothing.

Your breathing slows again and you regain control. You wonder if the dogs were actually following you, or if the echo effect from earlier had created the illusion of the chase.

The hunting horn sounds again and as it does, the beautiful woman you saw before appears before you. At her heels is a wolf and in her arms she carries the small animal you saw the dog pack chasing. You see that it is whole and healthy.

She smiles, and says, "The physical form may be destroyed, but the spirit always lives on, to be reborn into a form of its own choosing." She takes from her belt a magic mirror and holds it before your eyes; you look into it and it is as if you have returned back into your mother's womb, surrounded by the waters of the unborn.

You have no conscious awareness of self, only an awareness of "being." You have had self-awareness before, but now you are entering a pre-conscious period of "sleep."

You begin the process of forming a body to wear in this lifetime.

You organize all of its parts, its potential abilities carefully.

You are creating a vehicle which will perform in the best way possible for you, after your birth. You are establishing the basis for the replacement and maintenance of that body after you are born, through the proper regeneration of your body's cells.

You become aware, almost hyper sensitive, to every sensation and need of that body. Your five physical senses sharpen and your awareness to your physical needs intensifies.

You watch, in your mind, the growth of that body from the first tiny cell, into a ready-to-be-born babe.

You realize, now, that it is in the process of creating the body, your vehicle to travel through the physical plane, that your unity with all other beings is lost! You recognize anew your control over your own organic form and evolution, but you also see now, your need to experience a spiritual rebirth, to reach for the unity you have left behind.

With this realization, you find yourself sliding from the tree that has acted as mother's womb, into the water of the stream.

You begin to move through the water, sometimes walking, sometimes swimming. A gentle, cleansing rain begins to fall.

Soon others begin to join you. You see men and women of all ages and of all races and religions. You begin to see that they are also representatives of different times - some are cave men, wearing furs and skins, others are from some future era.

They begin to remove their clothing and soon there is no apparent difference among them.

All move forward, in the same direction as you. Some are laughing and talking, some are crying, some are serious and some are singing.

As you move forward through the water you begin to feel lighter.

You feel as if your very body is transmuting in some indeterminate way. But it feels good.

You begin to join hands with your fellow travelers as you continue to move forward. Soon you are singing and dancing through the shallows of the stream.

Moving in rhythm and harmony, you bathe in the shower of a waterfall.

Now animals of all kinds begin to join you, cavorting among you as you all move onward.

At this moment, you cannot tell yourself from the traveler next to you or from the beast at your heels. You are completely immersed in the group mind and the momentum of being carried onward. You feel a joyous freedom from ego.

At last you come into a wide lake and the group disperses, each taking with them a newfound unity with one another and with nature, each moving in the direction of their own growth and that of their race and culture.

You walk from the water into a volcanic area. Geysers spout streams of warm water under pressure and you see steam rising from pools of water that you walk by. The ground here is parched and cracked and you see trees blackening, their roots in tepid water.

As you move forward, you hear the sounds of baying hounds in chase. You banish it and it instantly stops.

You hear voices calling out to you in joy or in pain. You banish them, too. They were only voices dissuading you from your path. Now they are gone.

You see flashes of color and half-formed images both alluring and fearful. With a wave of your hand you banish them as well.

You have conquered your phantoms, those created by you yourself, as well as those imprinted in your mind by the culture you live in.

You revel in the new found power over yourself and over the power of illusion that you now have! You continue to travel through this volcanic landscape, until finally you come to a wall of flame.

This is not illusion. It is the wall of fire symbolizing spiritual rebirth through which you must pass to reach the Temple of Netzach.

Without fear, you move forward into the wall of fire. It feels almost familiar to you, as you allow it to burn from you all resistance. You feel yourself becoming clearer and somehow lighter, as you move through the fire. As you walk, the flames turn from scarlet, to orange, to violet and finally, to green.

You step through onto a platform floating on a sea of green flame.

The platform is a copper, inlaid with turquoise.

In the center of the platform is a Temple comprised of seven emerald pillars. Its floor is inlaid mother of pearl and freshwater pearls decorate the green columns on which you see roses of all colors climbing.

A single lamp, forever burning, hangs in the center of the temple.

Tiny specs of light float off from it in all directions and you have the impression of thousands of unconscious life sparks moving outward from the light of the group mind.

Haniel, Archangel of the Sphere, greets you. As he reaches out to touch your hand, you are filled with a wonderful feeling of love and universal harmony. For just a moment, your eyes are filled with all of the most wonderful and beautiful artistic creations possible and you hear the strains of beautiful music. Although you cannot see her, you have the impression of a most beautiful woman observing you with pleasure.

And so ends the 29th Path.

Path Journal

A. Record your emotional reactions to your path experiences here, immediately upon completion. Include any physical responses or sensations.

Date of completion: _____

Emotional responses: _____
_____
_____

Physical reactions: _____
_____
_____

What do you think these responses indicate? _____
_____
_____

B. Use this section as a diary of your experiences during the week following your completion of the path. Be sure to include how you react to things emotionally, as well as how you deal with any major issues that might arise.

Day 1: _____
_____

Day 2: _____
_____

Day 3: _____
_____

Day 4: _____
_____

Day 5: _____
_____

Day 6: _____
_____

Day 7: _____

_____

C. Review the week's experiences. How has the path affected the way you handled this week's issues? _____

_____

_____

_____

D. What special dreams has this path stimulated this week? _____

_____

_____

_____

Areas Path 29 Will Help You Work On

- Understanding reincarnation and that life does not end, but only changes form
- The ability to revisit past lives, and to find your "roots"
- The ability to perceive cycles
- Understanding unity and the "group mind;" gaining a feeling of belonging, and of "being home"
- Allowing self-recognition that you are wanted and loved by the Universal Mother
- Healing family disputes
- Spreading harmony among others
- Enhancement of visualization ability
- Further stimulation of the Third Eye
- Aiding clairvoyance and crystal gazing ability
- Increasing receptivity
- Increasing your ability to drop resistance and "go with the flow"
- Purging pain

- Increasing creativity

- Confronting your fears and understanding that they are nothing more than a reflection of yourself, created by you

- Being in touch with your own body and its needs

- Knowing that you are responsible for creating and maintaining your own body

- Self-healing

- Increasing contact with your Guides

- Enhancement of sexual enjoyment

- Increasing personal and group prosperity

- Aiding in work involving animals

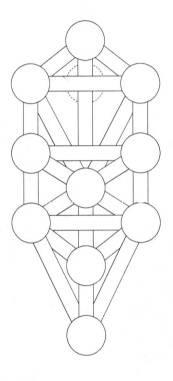

Path 28

Correspondences

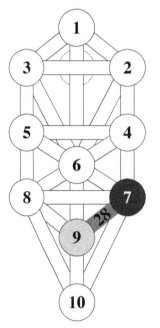

— Sphere of Yesod —

We commence our journey in the Sphere of Yesod, the foundation.

The Hebrew Divine Name is Shaddai el Chai, the Almighty Living God.

The Archangel of the Sphere is Gabriel, Prince of Change and Alteration.

The Choir of Angels is the Kerubim, the Strong.

The Planetary correspondence is the Moon.

The symbols are perfumes and sandals.

The color is violet.

The element is air, the Astral Light, or Akashic Fluid.

The number is 9.

The Tarot card correspondences are the four Nines.

The corresponding body parts are the reproductive organs.

The chakra is the Sacral Center, located just below the navel.

The corresponding gland is the spleen.

The stones are crystal, pearl, or clear quartz.

The metal is silver.

Plants are gardenia, jasmine, and heliotrope.

The musical note is "C."

Symbols are the horn and the cup.

The magical image is a very strong, beautiful, naked man.

The mythological correspondences are the Greek Goddess Artemis, the Roman Pan, the Norse Loki and the Wiccan God and Goddess, Cernunnos and Selena.

The spiritual experience is a vision of the machinery of the universe.

— 28th Path —

The 28th Path is known as the Natural Intelligence, so-called because through it is consummated and perfected the Nature of every existing thing beneath the Sun.

The Hebrew letter for the Path is Tzaddi, meaning "fish hook."

The meaning of the simple form of the letter is imagination.

The corresponding astrological sign is Aquarius.

The planet is Saturn.

The element is Air.

The metal is lead.

The Path corresponds to the Tarot Major Arcanum card The Star.
The symbols are the urn, the censor and the morning and evening star.
The stone is artificial glass.
The scent is galbanum.
Herbs are absinthe, fennel and buttercup.
The color is violet.
The musical note is "A#."
The magical weapon is the censor.
Living beings representative are the eagle, the peacock and man.

— Sphere of Netzach —

The Sphere of Destination is Netzach, Victory.
The Hebrew Divine name is Jehovah Tzabaoth.
The Archangel is Haniel, Prince of Love and Harmony.
The Order of Angels is the Elohim.
The corresponding planet is Venus.
The number is 7.
The Tarot correspondences are the four Seven's.
The symbols of Netzach are the girdle, the rose and the lamp.
The stones are emerald and turquoise.
The metal is copper.
The color is green.
The corresponding body parts are the loins, hips and legs.
The corresponding chakra is the Solar Plexus Center.
The living beings are the dove, the sparrow and the swan.
The symbolic creature is the lynx.
The musical note is an "E."
The scent is rose.
Herbs are blackberry, cherry tree, dwarf elder and golden seal.
The magical image is a beautiful, naked woman.
Mythical correspondences are the Greek Goddess Aphrodite, the Roman Venus and Diana and the Norse Goddess Freya. All are Goddesses of love and of nature.
The spiritual experience is a vision of beauty triumphant.
Now close your eyes, and lay your mandala aside.

Invocation

"May we be encompassed by the name Shaddai El Chai and established in the temple of Yesod, the Foundation. May the portal of the 28th Path be opened to us and may we journey thereon in the power of the name Jehovah Elohim to the gate of the Sphere of Netzach. And in the Name of Jehovah Tzabaoth may the gate of Yesod be opened to us and may we be firmly established in the wonders of that Sphere."

Path

You open your inner eyes to find yourself in a world where everything appears soft and unreal, covered in a silvery mist.

You are standing on a crystal platform in the lush, tropical garden of the Temple of Yesod.

The scent of jasmine, gardenia and heliotrope is almost overwhelming.

A strange sound, somewhat like a million voices all whispering at once, surrounds you, fading into a sound that could almost be a soft breeze.

The very air around you vibrates with energy and in the silvery glow you can see the pulsing of tiny points of light.

You recognize the Kerubim, the Choir of Angels of this Sphere, hard at work as they bring into magnetic harmony and balance all of the energies moving into and out of the material plane, working toward the perfection of each.

With each breath you take you feel yourself more and more energized by the air you breathe in; air energized by these tiny beings.

Looking up, you see the large, white Sphere of the full moon.

You see that it is this milky Sphere that acts as a two sided mirror, reflecting the realms of spirit into the physical plane below, but also reflecting upward the thoughts and creations of man.

You realize the difficulty for the unwary of telling the difference between the two! The crystal platform that you stand upon and the moon above, seem to be the only substantial part of this mystical garden that surrounds you, until you notice two giant fruit trees at one end of the garden.

You are not sure whether you have floated or walked to them, but no sooner do you notice them than you stand before them.

You see that the one on the left bears orange fruits of great beauty and the one on the right violet fruits of equally wonderful appearance.

Your mouth begins to water. You take a moment to decide which fruit to eat.

But then, you see the almost hidden form of a serpent entwining the branches of the one on the left.

You quickly pick a violet fruit from the tree to your right. You bite into it and a sweet, amazing flavor flows from it.

As you swallow the juice of the fruit you feel lighter and a feeling of joyousness overcomes you.

The garden around you disappears and you find yourself on the crystal platform again. But you are not alone.

A brilliant being stands before you. His silvery glow takes your breath away as you intuitively recognize the Archangel Gabriel.

He gestures to the fruit, which you still hold. You show him that it is the violet fruit that you have chosen and he smiles.

The violet fruit, you know now, is the fruit of the Tree of Life.

The orange fruit was of the Tree of the Knowledge of Good and Evil.

The joyous feeling you still feel comes from the feeling of union with all things that share the joy of life! The Archangel Gabriel takes from the folds of his cloak a horn and blows upon it.

The crystal platform begins to move and the air about you begins to shimmer and vibrate. Soon you are surrounded by a stream of forms passing you by in all directions.

As you watch the astral light flow about you, you recognize the undulations, or ripples that move through it as being akin to the currents in water, only much less dense.

You begin to pay attention to the various forms that you see and recognize some as people you have known who have recently died and are passing through this plane. You see Gabriel restoring and directing them.

You see still others that have been dead for a long time and those who seek a return to the physical. Gabriel is also directing, while the Kerubim work arduously to give their magnetic substance form.

You see all forms that leave and enter the physical plane passing through the touch of Gabriel.

You realize that not all of the forms moving upward on the planes are dead. Many, like you, are travelers. Some merely sleep, others dream or daydream and still others are, like you, consciously seeking enlightenment and must pass through the Astral Light.

It is your turn for Gabriel to show you the best way in which you may approach the divine energy within yourself.

The Archangel takes his horn and fills it with a clear, glowing liquid. You drink and are filled with an inner light. You feel the Kerubim, the Choir of Angels of the Sphere working within you.

You feel a release of the creative patterns within you as the liquid flows downward, illuminating your Sacral Center. You feel the free flow of creative and intuitive energy unleashed.

You are consumed by a crystalline light as the energy released from your sacral chakra is released up your spine and out through the top of your head.

When the light around you diminishes, you find you still remain on the crystal platform, adrift in the Astral Light, but Gabriel is no longer with you.

You are, however, not alone.

Sitting and standing, in groups and clusters, are others who, like yourself, travel this Path.

But you notice something strange about them. Each wears a mask; and each mask is exactly the same, made of peacock feathers.

You put your hands up to your own face and are surprised to find that you, too, wear a similar mask.

You all join hands to form a large circle and begin to dance to a rhythmic tune.

One couple breaks off to enter the center of the circle and spontaneously creates a beautiful dance of their own.

The musicians become so excited by this that they, too, begin to create new melodies.

You were hesitant to join the group at first, but the joy of participating in such wondrous creativity is enough for you to relax and become a part of it.

You all begin to add your own bit of individualism to the dancing and music, some singing, some playing, some clapping, some dancing new steps and somehow it all comes together in a beautiful, perfect whole! Finally, breathless, you all drop to the floor to rest. As you look about, you see that everyone still wears their mask, but strangely, all of the masks are different now, as if each reflects something of the person who wears it.

You feel good all over, in a relaxed, satisfied sort of way.

Soft music plays in the background as you all bask in the aftermath of creative energy released.

Some intuition causes you to look up. As you do, you see the huge, black tentacles of an astral creature closing over the platform you ride upon.

You cry the alarm and everyone looks up.

You know that this creature was drawn by the massive energy you have all released and is intending to feed upon it.

No sooner do you realize this, than you begin to feel a loss of energy, a draining upon you.

You look about you and see that all of the others with you experience the same weakening as the creature sucks at the life force within you all.

You close your eyes and call upon your Guide with all of your inner strength - and are surprised to see, instead of Gabriel, a virginal young woman appear.

She smiles as if to set your fears at rest, but tells you all that you must deal with this monster yourself, from within.

She shows you how.

No matter that you feel tired and drained, you must first concentrate on your breath, she says.

As your breathing becomes deep and regular you become aware that the sensation of being drained has stopped.

You look up to see that the monster still hovers over you and as your breathing speeds up, the sucking on your energy begins again.

Quickly, you bring your attention back to the young woman and continue to breathe as deeply and regularly as you can. The energy loss stops again.

The young woman begins to lead you in a mantra, giving sound to the breath. She says, "Soooooooooo, hummmmmmmm," over and over again, and you follow.

Before long your mind is still and you have forgotten your fear.

You feel centered once again and grounded, even though there is nothing of solid substance in the Astral realm.

You open your eyes to look up, and find that the creature is gone.

You gave it no resistance, no tension to grab hold of and it has gone on to seek easier prey.

You realize that this vampiric creature is a symbol of the people and situations in your daily life that sap your energy and now you know that meditation, centering and non-reaction are the ways to prevent this drain! You look around you and see that no one wears a mask now. The fear you have all experienced caused the masks to drop and the feeling of centeredness and strength you now feel makes it unnecessary to put them back on. You all see one another, now, as you really are.

The young girl walks with sandaled feet to the front of the platform and points upward.

You all look up, to see the bright Morning Star shining down from above. From it, seven rays of light in all of the rainbow colors stream down.

You feel an intense yearning toward the star, toward Venus, toward the Sphere of Netzach.

Your young guide motions you to sit. You realize that she wants you to meditate again, to open yourself to the higher energies within yourself.

Again you begin to breathe deeply, letting your mental nature come to a point of stillness where there is no thought.

You focus your attention on the morning star and nothing else.

Your will to move upward intensifies until there is nothing else.

You begin to feel a drawing sensation again. But this time, there is no loss of energy, rather a feeling that a vast energy source is drawing you upward.

You feel your own Higher Self active within you, pointing the way upward, energizing you, and giving you the means to reach up to the Sphere of Netzach.

The platform begins to be drawn upward, higher, and higher, through the Astral Light.

The air around you begins to become turbulent, the platform is tossed about and you have to hold tightly to avoid being thrown from its surface.

The Astral winds howl and you again see all sorts of strange forms all about you, all threatening your upward journey, but your Will remains focused and the drawing power of your Higher Self remains firm and you continue upward.

The star appears closer now, but in the turbulent space around you, you begin to see brief flickers of fire.

The flickers become larger and more frequent and you seem to see faces and forms in the fire.

Soon, your platform is being drawn upward through an ocean of fire.

Visions begin to flash before you; your perceptions are expanded.

You begin to envision other realities.

Finally, you pass into the heart of the violet flame.

A deep pervading sense of stillness fills you. You feel an inner "knowingness" at the core of your being that springs from the unfoldment of your highest intuition. Your mind is clear and still.

Eventually you feel a burning in your solar plexus chakra as the fire takes hold and spreads throughout your being. You are filled with exaltation.

Suddenly you find yourself stepping out of the fire and on to a hillside of green flame.

A structure with seven columns entwined in roses stands before you.

You recognize the temple of Netzach and walk toward it. You realize now that the single lamp burning within it is none other than the Morning Star itself.

The light coming forth from it is so very intense that you cannot look directly at it.

You notice in the lush gardens surrounding the temple every type of animal you can imagine. A lynx tamely rubs against your legs and leads you into the temple.

As you enter, an eagle with wings wide spread takes off, flying upward into the light.

Inside, you notice this time that the walls, ceiling, supporting pillars and even the floor, are covered with the most beautiful works of art imaginable.

Wonderful music fills the air.

You see a statue of a woman holding a babe. You move closer, only to see that it is a statue of the young woman who was your Guide.

She is a Goddess of the Sphere of Netzach and we are all her children.

You feel as if you have come home and sit at her feet to meditate.

And so ends the 28th Path.

Path Journal

A. Record your emotional reactions to your path experiences here, immediately upon completion. Include any physical responses or sensations.

Date of completion: _____

Emotional responses: _____

_____

_____

Physical reactions: _____

_____

_____

What do you think these responses indicate? _____

_____

_____

B. Use this section as a diary of your experiences during the week following your completion of the path. Be sure to include how you react to things emotionally, as well as how you deal with any major issues that might arise.

Day 1: _____

_____

Day 2: _____

_____

Day 3: _____

_____

Day 4: _____

_____

Day 5: _____

_____

Day 6: _____

_____

Day 7: _____

_____

C. Review the week's experiences. How has the path affected the way you handled this week's issues? _____

_____

_____

_____

D. What special dreams has this path stimulated this week? _____

_____

_____

_____

Areas Path 28 Will Help You Work On

- Meditation and the ability to "still" the mind
- Opening the Sacral Center and freeing your energy
- Energizing yourself and others
- Recognizing the physical reality you live in
- Applying yourself to your studies
- Developing intuition in Astrological or other technical work
- Career planning and finding suitable work
- Problem solving
- Development of physical ability and martial arts skills
- Enhancement of dreams and understanding dream symbols
- Recognizing vampirism and your own inherent strength to resist it
- Learning to become a "pane of glass" that lets disharmony "pass through" you

- Learning to deal with your astral fears, visions, and worries by withdrawing your attention from them, by centering yourself through deep breathing
- Becoming more secure in dealing with your problems; recognizing that there is always an answer
- Gaining knowledge of what is needed for you to move toward your own perfection
- Applying your Will toward your own evolution
- The ability to know who you really are, and to see others as they truly are
- Understanding that everything and everyone about you is a reflection of yourself
- Understanding the power of the group mind
- Being able to both nurture and receive nurturance
- Strengthening your connection to your Higher Self
- Improving your higher intuition and "knowingness"
- The ability to protect yourself psychically, as well as physically
- Finding inner peace
- Opening the Solar Plexus Center
- Increasing creativity
- Increasing your ability to detach

Path 27

Correspondences

— Sphere of Hod —

We commence our journey in the Sphere of Hod, Splendor.
The Hebrew Divine name is Elohim Tzabaoth.
The Archangel is Michael, Prince of Splendour and Wisdom.
The Order of Angels is the Beni Elohim, the "Sons of the Gods."
The corresponding planet is Mercury.
The number is 8.
The Tarot correspondences are the four eights.
Symbols are language and visual images.
This Sephiroh also corresponds to systems of magic, science, religion and government.
The color is orange.
Symbolic creatures are two snakes intertwined.
The metal is quicksilver.
Stones are opal and agate.
Mythical figures include the Greek God Hermes, the Roman Mercury, the Egyptian Thoth and Chiron, healer, teacher and warrior who was half God and half mortal.
The body correspondences are the loins and the legs.
The chakra is the solar plexus, the gland is the adrenals.
The musical note is "D."
The magical image is a hermaphrodite.

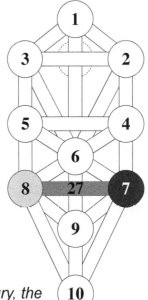

— 27th Path —

The 27th Path is known as the Active or Exciting Intelligence because through it every existent being receives its spirit and motion.
It is called the "House of God" or "Lord of the Hosts of the Mighty" - Elohim Gibor Tzabaoth.
Many know it as the "Path of the Flaming Sword."
The Hebrew letter is Peh, which means mouth.
This letter is a "double" letter, showing that this is one of the "Gateways of the Soul" with two possible directions we may follow.
It is through this Path that the higher energies are brought in to energize the personality.
It is the first of the three major "initiations" you will experience on your journey "up" the Tree.
The Planetary influence is Mars.

The corresponding Astrological sign is Scorpio.

The Major Arcana Tarot card that corresponds is the Tower.

The magical weapon is the double edged sword.

Symbolic living creatures are the horse, the bear, the wolf, the scorpion and the lobster or crayfish.

Other symbols are the pentagram, the cross and the tower.

The stone is ruby.

The color is scarlet red.

The musical note is "C."

Scents are benzoin, sulphur and tobacco.

Herbs are cayenne pepper and dragon's blood.

Plants are poppies, poplars, pansies and yew.

The associated mythological figures are the Roman God Mars, the Greek Athena and the Hindu Kali.

The spiritual experience is one of transformation through crisis and renewal through suffering.

The primary lesson on the Path is that old forms must pass before new ones can exist.

— Sphere of Netzach —

The Sphere of Destination is Netzach, Victory.

The Hebrew Divine name is Jehovah Tzabaoth.

The Archangel is Haniel, Prince of Love and Harmony.

The Order of Angels is the Elohim, the Gods who are also known as the Order of Principalities.

The corresponding planet is Venus.

The number is 7.

The symbols of Netzach are the girdle, the rose and the lamp.

The stone is emerald or turquoise.

The metal is copper.

The color is green.

The corresponding body parts are the loins, hips and legs.

The corresponding chakra is the Solar Plexus Center and the gland is the adrenals.

Living beings are the dove, the sparrow and the swan.

The symbolic creature is the lynx.

The musical note is an "E."

The scent is rose.

Herbs are blackberry, cherry, dwarf elder and golden seal.

The magical image is a beautiful, naked woman.

Mythical correspondences are the Greek Goddess Aphrodite, the Roman Venus and the Norse Goddess Freya. All are Goddesses of love and nature.

The spiritual experience is a vision of beauty triumphant.

Now close your eyes, and lay your mandala aside.

Invocation

"May we be encompassed by the name Elohim Tzabaoth and established in the temple of Hod, Splendor. May the portal of the 27th Path be opened to us, and may we journey thereon in the power of the name Elohim Gebor to the gate of the Sphere of Netzach. And, in the name of Jehovah Tzabaoth may the gate of Netzach be opened to us and may we be firmly established in the wonders of that Sphere."

Path

Let your breathing slow and your mind drop down into a deep reverie.

Release it from all thoughts of the material world through the power of your will.

Let yourself drift freely, your mind and consciousness rising ever upward through the various levels of being, to arive finally at the temple of Hod.

The temple is familiar and comfortable, with its black and white marble floor and its eight surrounding agate pillars supporting the roof of orange opal.

You recognize the four elemental kings standing at each corner of the temple and you feel the presence of the mighty Archangel Michael surrounding you.

Upon the altar you see something glowing and, looking closer, you see that it is the staff of Hermes, entwined with its two snakes.

You move forward to pick it up, but then you hear the voice of the Archangel say, "No; that is not the weapon you will need upon this Path." You turn, to behold Michael, clad as a warrior in burnished armor.

He holds a flaming sword in his hand. He moves toward you, offering you the sword.

You turn away. Why do I need a sword? I am not a warrior," you think. You look back and Michael has disappeared.

You look toward the Beni Elohim at the corners of the temple to see what they thought of your choice. But in their eyes and demeanor you see no reaction.

Apparently, here, your decisions are to be all your own.

You walk from the temple into a landscape that is stark and barren. The smell of something burning is in the air.

You look about you and see that there are cities studded across the land that you look at, smoke and sulphurous fumes polluting the air about each one of them. It is that smell that reminds you of something burning.

You realize that you are looking at a scene from an alternate reality to our own, but one which is possibly a vision of our future.

Nothing grows, or lives anywhere on this barren land. Those living in the cities have consumed all, leaving the land desolate and dead. The tall spires of the cities throw their shadows over the dead land.

You begin to cross this plain, heading north.

As you walk, the angle of light from above throws you first into light, then shadow, then light again. The alternating of light and shadow goes on and on, until at last you no longer notice it. You keep walking.

As you get closer to one of the cities, you see the walls the inhabitants have erected to separate themselves and possibly protect themselves from the other occupants of the plain.

You keep walking.

The sun is high overhead now and you are beginning to tire. Your mouth is dry.

You see another traveler on the way; you see that he carries many skins of water piled on the red horse he leads. You ask for a drink of his water.

He immediately refuses, telling you he intends to sell it in a city ahead, where water is being rationed.

You offer to pay. He looks at you, sees that you carry nothing of great wealth and he laughs. Before you can say more, he is moving on.

You hear the distant howl of a wolf. Shivers go up your spine; you feel the premonition of some disaster.

You continue to move on toward the nearest city, hoping the people there will be more generous.

As you get closer to the city you begin to truly appreciate its towering structures. Even from this distance you can see people bustling about in all sorts of activity. You aren't yet sure, but it looks like many of them are carrying armaments of some kind.

You see something lying in the road a short way ahead and move faster to see what it might be. As you come up to it, you recognize the shape of a human body. You roll the body over, to see the face of the water merchant. His throat has been cut and he has been robbed of all he had.

The wolf howls in the distance again and another shiver goes up your spine. You look about you, no longer feeling so safe! You begin to wish, that you had taken the sword Michael offered you.

You continue to walk on.

The nearer of the cities is now quite close and you see that indeed, the people are all carrying arms. You see children in rags and diseased beggars in the streets; but the wealthy in their finery pay them no heed.

As you approach, a guard at the gate demands to know your business. You tell him you seek water and perhaps a place to rest.

He laughs and tells you that no strangers are allowed in the city and that there is certainly not enough water for you when his city is in the midst of mounting an attack on its neighbor to obtain their water rights to the river! He asks what religion you are. When he hears your answer, he says, "Well then, I can't let you in anyway. We don't allow any of 'you' within our walls!"

The wolf howls. This time you do not shiver. You walk on; you don't really want to enter this place and hope your luck will be better at the next city.

As you continue your trek, you come across an old hermit who remembers this plain, fertile and green, before the cities blocked off the water supply for their exclusive use. You are not surprised to learn that the city you have just left is attacking the other city now only because they have finally succeeded in polluting their own water beyond usage.

You thank the hermit for his bit of information and begin to walk on, when a bear appears behind him. You cry out in warning, but he only laughs and strokes the bear. You move forward and the bear reaches out its nose to be stroked. You are amazed.

The hermit says, "I have one more thing I would share with you before you go." He leans forward and whispers a word of power into your ear. This word is personal. It is yours alone. When you hear it, a tremor begins in your body and you feel a tremendous force, as of universal Will, moving through you.

The hermit says, "Being unarmed here in this place is a danger to you. Use this word of power I have given you only in time of great need and use it well."

You begin to move on. After a few steps, you look back and are surprised to see that the hermit and his bear are gone, as if they have faded into the earth itself.

You continue your journey.

After a time, you hear the muffled sound of many voices, and coming over a rise, you see a military troop setting up camp for the evening.

As you get closer, you begin to hear their conversation. You realize that each has a separate and individual reason for participating in the battle to come. All of the reasons are stated with an equal intensity approaching obsession.

One says, "They have no right to the water, they have abused their use of it and taken what should be ours!" Another one answers, "The last time we fought them, my uncle was killed and my sister raped. They do not deserve to live!" Still another says, "My mother left my father to marry one of these fiends. Kill them all!" You hear another voice say, "They practice a religion in that place that is an evil against the one faith. It is right that our leaders are finally attacking!"

Another says, "Their city is wealthy beyond imagining. The spoils will be ours!"

Still another says, "There will be a great deal of money to be made on the heels of this war!" As you pass the men setting up camp you hear one final voice say, "I can't wait to see what a real battle is like! My girl will be so impressed she will definitely marry me when I get back!"

Feeling somewhat depressed, you walk onward. Soon you realize you are passing the command tent. You move closer and hear the officers in discussion.

"How do the odds look?" a muffled voice asks. "We'll probably lose at least a quarter of our force on the first run, but losses on the other side will outweigh that sacrifice," a second voice answers.

The first voice goes on, "Let's make it a quick run in and out then; I want to wrap this up and get back in time to put my vote in on that new land owner's law. I only wanted this assignment for the bonus - I'll need it quickly once they start throwing out the share-croppers." Feeling disgusted and somewhat dirty, you again move on, thankfully leaving the army encampment behind.

As you walk you think back over the conversations you have heard.

Each soldier who spoke was fighting for what he believed and was even willing to die for it. But you find yourself questioning the beliefs and values themselves, if not the men's single-minded determination to force them upon the world.

You wonder if having or winning anything could possibly be worth the pain and sacrifice these men are about to make! As you walk the sun disappears below the horizon and you are left to walk through the long night with your dark thoughts.

You begin to realize the power of the spoken word, as you come to see how all of the men were affected by their own words as well as those of their officer's.

You begin to see how your own values and your belief system has been shaped by the words of those around you and even how your own words have affected the actions and attitudes of those very same people! You remember the times you have obsessed over things or people you needed or wanted to have, to own, or to control, or to change to your way of thinking.

Perhaps, you think, I am not so different than these men who fight! You walk on.

Before long you see that you have come to a wide but shallow river.

A diseased smell rises from the river, which is brown and oily with pollution. You look at it with distaste.

You need to cross it to get to the destination you seek. You walk along searching for the narrowest point, or a bridge, but finally you conclude you must wade across.

The sun rises as you begin your crossing.

You wade out ankle deep and the slime clings to your legs.

Forcing yourself to move on, you move to the center of the river where the water is chest deep. The odor of decay is overwhelming.

You look up at the opposite shore and see an army gathered there, poised to charge across the river. Looking back to the shore behind you, you recognize another army gathered there also about to charge.

You hear a horn and both armies jump into the river, moving toward one another and you.

As they converge around you, you hear them all yelling and screaming battle calls intended to incite fear and strengthen themselves.

You see the single-minded determination in the eyes of the men of both forces and you realize that they fight for the same mixed reasons you have heard.

As you watch, bodies are cut, blown apart and dismembered. No one gives any quarter.

The river runs red with blood.

You watch one of the officers on the bank raise his weapon and take his own life as he realizes his force will not win.

As you watch you realize there can be no winner here! Sick with nausea and grief, you look up toward the sun, now high overhead once again and you utter your own word of power that the hermit gave to you.

Immediately, you perceive the river as the vertical bar of a cross and the Path you have been traveling as the horizontal bar, with you standing at the point where the two meet, in perfect balance.

You feel the power of the four elements supporting and converging upon you through the arms of the cross. Above your head ruling the East is Tipareth, below your feet is Yesod ruling the West. To your right is Hod ruling the North and to your left is Netzach, ruling the South.

You hold your arms out sideways from your shoulders forming a cross with your own body.

You hear the word ATOH and you touch your forehead.

You hear the word MALKUTH and you touch your breast.

You hear the word VE-GEVURAH and you touch your right shoulder.

You hear the word VE-GEDULAH and you touch your left shoulder.

You hear the word LE-OLAHM AMEN and you clasp your hands together at the breast.

You feel that you are uplifted, cleansed. The river of blood and the plane it crosses have disappeared.

You feel the heat of clean fire coursing through you, burning away the fear, the despair, the ugliness you have seen.

You focus on the fire.

It gets more and more brilliant. Soon all you can see around you are the clean flames of the astral fire.

You seem to see the tiny forms of elemental creatures in the fire and they are drawing you, leading you toward a central point.

You see a brilliant, blazing point of light; it is within your own breast.

It is the blazing sword of Michael. You put hand to breast and take up the sword. As you hold it up in front of you, you see that it blazes with a light almost unbearable.

The voice of the Archangel comes out of the astral fire all around you. He says, "Yours is the Path of the Flaming Sword, and to follow it successfully, you must become the Flaming Sword yourself. You must be willing to do battle, but choose your battles wisely!" Your body begins to cool and the brilliant light fades.

You find yourself standing again on the barren, windswept plain.

But now there is no river, there are no cities, no soldiers.

The only structure you see is a tall tower and it stands directly before you.

Intuition tells you that this tower is of your own creation, built stone by stone of your own values, beliefs, obsessions, needs and limitations.

You would like to be anywhere else in the world at this moment, but as you look at the flaming sword burning in your hand and feel its counterpart in your breast, you know that it is time to conquer the tower.

You see only one entrance. It leads down into darkness.

Overcoming your own resistance with difficulty, you enter.

The air inside smells dank and musty and there is a distinctly metallic scent in the air as of old blood.

Your blazing sword illuminates a dark dungeon. You see old instruments of torture and pain scattered all about, many with bits of flesh and blood still clinging to them.

You are both revolted and fascinated. You look at these objects more closely and suddenly realize they all have one thing in common.

They are instruments of self-torture.

You are suddenly cast into a memory of a time when you entered into a situation knowing it was wrong for you. You stayed too long; you wallowed in the pain; you loved the pain; and finally you became immune to the pain and it had no further use for you.

You look around the dungeon again and see only old discarded tools, long forgotten.

The sword flares brilliantly.

You walk up a set of stairs winding counter clockwise, that end in a large chamber. The air is damp and musty and you see that the humidity in the chamber comes from a fountain in the shape of a scorpion. The waters it spews forth are blood red.

You walk to the fountain and find a cup with a phoenix engraved upon it sitting on the edge.

You are still thirsty, so you fill the cup and drink. The red water tastes of salt.

Immediately, all of your past sorrows rise up before you. You feel the pain of rejection a thousand times over; you feel the dashing of your hopes all over again. You feel a deep sense of loss connected to the destruction of home, family, or loved ones. You feel the fear of facing these sorrows.

As all of these emotions arise, you feel the counterbalance of the flaming sword within your breast. Its fire pushes outward with strength and fortitude new to you.

You find that you can accept the sorrows and losses of your past and that they strengthen, rather than diminish you! The sword flares brightly once again! Straightening your shoulders, you move up the next set of stairs, still moving counter-clockwise, to the third floor.

Here, a pool of water is set into the floor.

You go over and look in. As you do, you see that this is a magic mirror, showing what was, what is and what will be.

You see the plain you recently walked, but as it must have been a long time ago, lush, green and beautiful. You see settlements form and grow, living in peace and harmony. But as they grow, you see that each consumes more and more of what nature has provided to sustain it, until you see the beginnings of the eventual destruction you experienced.

As you watch, you feel frustrated and angry. So many wrongs - murder, rape, theft, lies, total destruction of land and people - how can a just God allow this, you think. You see even the well-meaning making blunders and mistakes with far reaching consequences! Your anger, your feeling of helplessness in the face of overwhelming wrongs that cannot be changed and undone, mounts.

The sword flames brightly and the image in the pool fades.

A new image appears in the waters of the pool, showing the Sun rising over the plane; in its light you see the remnants of people from the two dead cities working together for survival. You see one individual teaching a way to survive, a way to overcome. You recognize yourself. You see a new society forming - one without walls. You see that its birthing has not been painless.

The sword flares again! You mount the stairs to yet a fourth floor and see a room empty, except for a single orchid growing upon a dead log.

You realize that out of death comes life, out of loss comes renewal, out of pain comes joy.

You smell the sweet scent of the orchid and your third eye tingles with the hint that if it were fully open, you could indeed see all.

You proceed to the fifth and final level. The room is empty and there appears to be no way out. You begin to hear the sound of drums.

You resist the urge to move to the beat.

Soon, your very resistance has become pain. You begin to feel your body swaying and bouncing in spite of your attempts at resistance.

Your imagination brings a melody, words, to the beat. Soon, there is an overwhelming chaos of noise in your head.

Unable to stop it, you relax into it and it sorts out into the single sound of drumming.

All resistance is gone. You are one with the beat. You have become the pattern.

The walls of the tower you created begin to shake and crumble.

The sword flares anew as the tower falls.

Its fire surrounds and protects you, giving you the courage and fortitude to pass through any change and remain balanced.

You find yourself walking upon a sea of liquid flame toward the temple of Netzach.

You recognize the lush green gardens surrounding the temple with its seven rose entwined pillars.

You step onto the path leading toward the temple and are met by a red-haired wolf. He looks familiar to you as he looks at you with his sly grin. He leads you to the temple. An eagle looks down at you from its perch on the roof.

Inside, you are not surprised to see statues and paintings and countless other art forms all depicting death, birth and rebirth. At the center of the temple you see a statue of the

3-fold Goddess; She who gives birth, She who nurtures and She who cuts the cord to life.

You sit down to contemplate.

And so ends the 27th Path.

Path Journal

A. Record your emotional reactions to your path experiences here, immediately upon completion. Include any physical responses or sensations.

Date of completion: _____

Emotional responses: _____

_____

_____

Physical reactions: _____

_____

_____

What do you think these responses indicate? _____

_____

_____

B. Use this section as a diary of your experiences during the week following your completion of the path. Be sure to include how you react to things emotionally, as well as how you deal with any major issues that might arise.

Day 1: _____

_____

Day 2: _____

_____

Day 3: _____

_____

Day 4: _____

_____

Day 5: _____

_____

Day 6: _____

_____

Day 7: _____

_____

C. Review the week's experiences. How has the path affected the way you handled this week's issues? _____

_____

_____

_____

D. What special dreams has this path stimulated this week? _____

_____

_____

_____

Areas Path 27 Will Help You Work On

- Facing your greatest fears
- Letting go of useless patterns and shedding useless values
- The ability to meet out justice and to understand it
- The ability to avert arguments or to achieve skill in debates
- Learning about your powers of endurance
- Understanding that to lose what you have been afraid of losing is to gain your freedom
- Learning that there is nothing to lose
- You are not a victim
- Suffering is useless, unnecessary, and self-imposed

- Frustration and a desire to be done with your own sense of futility

- Love triumphs over obstacles

- Dealing with the unexpected, and an improved ability to handle crisis situations

- Having faith in yourself

- Understanding that fighting is always significant of insecurity

- Dissolving greed and me-ism

- Generosity

- Overcoming small-mindedness in yourself and others

- Understanding your need for love, understanding, encouragement, and unconditionalness

- Understanding your right to defend yourself, but also the requirement not to impose yourself on others

- Overcoming inertia

- Understanding the statement, "what goes around, comes around"

- Finding a suitable partner or mate

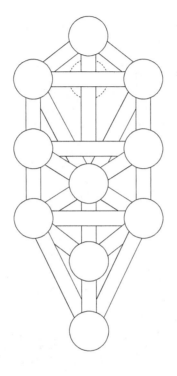

Path 26

Correspondences

— Sphere of Hod —

We commence our journey in the Sphere of Hod, Splendor.
The Hebrew Divine name is Elohim Tzabaoth.
This is known as the Absolute, or Perfect intelligence.
The Archangel is Michael, Prince of Splendor and Wisdom.
The Order of Angels are the Beni Elohim, the "Sons of the Gods"
   or the "Elemental Kings."
The planet is Mercury.
The number is 8.
The Tarot correspondences are the four eights.
Symbols are the apron, language, and visual images.
Hod corresponds to systems of magic, science, religion and
   government and to the mental processes themselves.
Its color is orange.
The symbolic creatures are two snakes, intertwined.
The corresponding animal is the monkey.
The metal is quicksilver.
Stones are opal and agate.
Herbs are fennel, cedar, cassia and cinquefoil.
The mythological correspondences include the Greek Hermes, the Roman Mercury, the
   Egyptian Thoth and Chiron - healer, teacher and warrior who was half God and half
   mortal.
The body correspondences are the loins and the legs.
The chakra is the solar plexus, the gland is the adrenals.
The musical note is "D."
The magical image is a hermaphrodite.

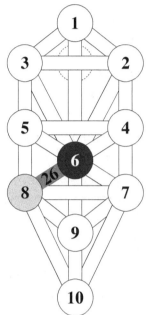

— 26th Path —

The 26th Path is known as the Renovating Intelligence, because the Holy God renews
   by it all the changing things, which are renewed by the creation of the world.
Its esoteric titles are the Lord of the Gates of Matter and the Child of the Forces of Time.
The Hebrew letter is Ayin, which means eye.
The simple letter is "mirth."
The corresponding astrological sign is Capricorn.
The planetary influence is Saturn.
The Major Arcana Tarot Card is the Devil.

The color is indigo.

The stone is black diamond or hematite.

The magical tools or weapons are the "secret force" and the lamp.

Symbols are the Philosopher's Stone and the Elixir of Life.

Symbolic living creatures are the dragon, the monkey and the crocodile.

The musical note is "A."

Scents are musk and civet.

Herbs are absynthe, rue and lambs tongue.

Associated mythological figures are Pan and Chiron, both born of one celestial and one human parent.

The spiritual experience is a transmutation of power, a release from the limitations of matter.

The 26th Path is known as the Hermetic Path; its reward is raw power and the ability to manipulate Astral currents.

— Sphere of Tiphareth —

The Sphere of Destination is Tiphareth, Beauty.

The Hebrew Divine name is Jehovah Aloah Va Daath.

It is known as the Mediating Intelligence or Influence.

The Archangel is Raphael, Prince of Brightness, Beauty and Life. He is the Archangel of Healing.

The Order of Angels is the Melechim, the Angelic Kings called the Order of Virtues, Angels and Rulers, who are responsible for creating and maintaining perpetual balance and harmony in all things.

The corresponding planet is the Sun.

The number is 6.

Symbols of Tiphareth are the Calvary Cross, the Rose Cross, the Truncated Pyramid and the Cube.

The stones are topaz and diamond.

The metal is gold.

The color is yellow.

The corresponding body part is the breast.

The corresponding chakra is the Heart Center and the gland is the thymus.

Living beings are the lion, the child and the phoenix.

The symbolic creature is the sparrow-hawk.

The musical note is "F."

The scent is aloe, cinnamon and clove.

Herbs are angelica, almond, frankincense and myrrh.

The magical image is a Majestic King, a Child, or a Sacrificed God.

The mythical correspondences are all of the Sacrificed Gods, including the Egyptian Osirus, the Indian Krishna and Buddha and the Christian Jesus.

The spiritual experience is a vision of the Harmony of things and of Healing and Redemption.

Invocation

"May we be encompassed by the name Elohim Tzabaoth and established in the temple of Hod, Splendor. May the portal of the 26th Path be opened to us and may we journey thereon in the power of the name Adonai Malek to the gate of the Sphere of Tiphareth. And, in the name of Jehovah Aloah Va Daath may the gate of Tiphareth be opened to us and may we be firmly established in the wonders of that Sphere."

Path

You are surrounded by the sound of ocean surf as you open your inner eyes.

You are lying upon a beach and you see children playing in the surf and water birds fishing in the shallows.

Picknickers laugh and talk together nearby.

You languish in the warmth of the Sun. Its warmth upon your skin intensifies. Soon your skin is burning with its heat. The sun is intense, penetrating, demanding.

You stand up and look for some shade.

Overlooking the beach is a huge eight-pillared structure, with an orange roof and checkered floor.

You immediately recognize the Temple of Hod, with which you are quite familiar now.

Without hesitation, you walk into it. As you enter, the sounds of the beach fade away and are replaced by the familiar ones of the temple.

You move directly into the temple's central room, looking for the Archangel of the Sphere, Michael. However, you see only his armor, lying near the black and white onyx altar.

Upon the altar lies the Staff of Hermes, with its black and white intertwined snakes surrounding the central staff of yew wood. As you look at the staff, the snakes seem to come alive and to pulse and glow to some unknown beat, first white, then black, then white, then black and so on. The central staff seems to hold them in a balance you cannot quite fathom.

As you continue to watch, the snakes slither into a new pattern, joining together head to tail, as if seeking to swallow one another and you see that their form around the central staff now is a figure eight.

You reach out toward the staff, which seems to be alive, but as soon as your hand touches it, it becomes again the inanimate yet powerful Staff of Hermes, with its intertwined twin serpents.

You hear a few short notes piped on a flute and twirl about, only to see the God Pan laughing behind you. He says, "Nothing is what it seems!" and disappears.

You turn back to the altar, but it and the Staff, have also disappeared! The temple is empty, except for the Elemental Kings, who are the Choir of Angels of this Sphere.

You approach the first of these, whose element is earth. He reaches out to embrace you and as he does, the temple disappears too and the Elemental Kings with it.

You look down at yourself. You are a child. You wear only a ragged apron and you are hungry.

You are standing outside a shop window; inside you see people dressed in all sorts of finery, eating and drinking, making your mouth water.

You aren't jealous; you simply see all of these wonderful things that are available and you want them, too! You turn away from the window with a new goal in life and you set out to accomplish it.

You see a man in the marketplace who is careless of his wallet and so you lighten it for him.

This buys you a meal that gives you the energy to do some intense planning.

You evaluate all of the different ways that you can imagine to better your situation.

You see yourself stealing, as you did the money from the wallet, until you have enough to set yourself up in some business.

You see yourself gaining your aim through the art of begging.

You see yourself acquiring a wealthy benefactor who supports and sets you up.

You see yourself using the money you have now to improve your appearance enough to get a bottom level job of some kind. Maybe you can work upward.

Soon you have used one of your plans to better your position in life and you now find yourself in an upwardly mobile position and frequenting the same places you had earlier only dreamed about.

But now you see that there is so much more to aspire to; so much more to have and to do.

Before long you have acquired a top-level position and along with it a big house, servants, the best quality transportation available.

You have a family now and you find that they want things, too.

So you continue to work upward, until you can purchase your own company.

Now, the needs of your company begin to multiply, so that you find it easier to buy and operate the companies that supply your raw materials, than to be dependent upon their schedules.

Your company expands, and expands.

Soon you no longer know the names of the people who work for you.

You hire other people to manage them.

A whole town grows up around your businesses. Everyone knows you.

You are elected Mayor.

Your life passes in this fashion, until you are wealthy beyond imagining, having acquired all of the material possessions and accompanying respect these can command.

Finally, upon your death bed, you review your life and are surprised to feel a sense of something missing.

You realize that you have never been able to trust others, for fear they would undermine or take what you have amassed.

You realize that you have never had the camaraderie of your family and friends, since all of your time, effort and interest, went into building your empire.

You realize that the material possessions you sought to own and control ultimately have controlled and dominated your life.

After your death you watch the struggle of family and friends over your "empire" and you watch it fall apart in the inept hands of those who followed.

You realize that nothing is forever. You remember Pan's advice that nothing is what it seems.

You hear the sound of a piping flute and find yourself back in the Temple of Hod. You realize, as he releases you, that all of this time you have been in the embrace of the Elemental King of Earth.

You move to the Elemental King of Air next and as he embraces you, you hear the sound of wind as the temple disappears and he carries you into the lower astral plane of strong emotions.

Again, you see yourself as a child growing into adulthood. But this time you see yourself constantly interacting emotionally with other people.

You see yourself enjoying the fullness of a happy family, feeling the love and support of parents, brothers, sisters. You see the type of emotional life this support leads to as you approach adulthood.

Then you see yourself striking out at them, hurting them, to force their love and attention. Again, you see the type of life this emotional beginning has led to.

You see yourself involved in the throes of first love. You again feel the joys, the excitement of discovery.

Again you feel the sense of rejection, the sorrow of loss, when love ends.

You see yourself later in love, in a triangle, when your lover loves someone else. You feel the pain, the jealousy, the betrayal again.

You see yourself in another love triangle, but this time it is you who loves another.

You see how you have made your children emotionally dependent upon you and how you have been emotionally dependent upon them.

You see yourself in every possible emotional situation, interacting with all of the people you know, until finally you realize that there is nothing in your life that is not emotion or rooted in emotion. You see how your emotional attachments have inhibited not only your own ability to grow, but that of others as well! You see how each emotional situation you have been in, whether good or bad, has led eventually to dependency and limitation, because you have tried to control it.

Again you hear Pan's pipe and you find yourself back in the Temple of Hod, stepping back from the embrace of the Elemental King of Air.

You move on and step into the arms of the Elemental King of Fire.

The temple disappears again.

Once again, you are a child. As a child, you find yourself involved in a world of sensation and feeling.

It feels good to play at sports and so you play and excel and learn that it also feels good to win. So, you dedicate your life to this until you are at the top of your form and technique - renowned and successful.

Then you discover that age has caught up with you and that you can no longer excel, but you have nothing else in life to fall back on.

Again, as a child, you excel in the arts and music. You are talented, perhaps a genius. Your work is beautiful and brings joy to others and so you do more and more, pushing yourself to the furthest of your limits. Your accomplishment brings acclaim, honor, and satisfaction. You are happy.

But again, upon your death's bed, you have the feeling that something is missing.

A child again, you submit to a world of sensation and feeling, and become immersed in the drug culture. Soon, nothing exists but the drug that gives you release and you realize that even in release, in running away, there can be bondage.

Seeing yourself as a child again, you become obsessed with the sensual feelings of sex. You confuse love and sex again and again until you learn that your yearning for the self-annihilation at the moment of orgasm is actually a yearning for union with a higher part of yourself.

You hear Pan's pipes again and find yourself back in the Temple of Hod. You step from the embrace of the Elemental King of Fire and into the arms of the Elemental King of Water. The Temple disappears.

You find yourself in the realm of mind and you are a child again.

You see yourself, as a child, curious, and interested in the workings of everything in the universe around you.

Your childhood guide is a monkey whose curiosity mirrors your own.

You pursue a higher education and you learn all that you can in the special field of your interest.

You excel in that field, working your way into the topmost echelon of achievement.

You see your inventions and work carried out to the benefit of society and the demand for your work and insight increases.

With each new discovery and with each new insight, whole vistas open before you, each needing further study and more time.

You begin to realize, as you grow older, that not in one lifetime, nor even in a thousand lifetimes, can you complete the intellectual exploration you have begun.

You have found the limitation of mind. Locked into time and form, mind can only endlessly pursue an endless succession of thoughts and ideas.

The Pan pipes sound again and again you are returned to the Temple of Hod, as you step from the embrace of the Elemental King of Water.

You realize that these Elemental Kings are each responsible for the building up of forms according to the nature of their own element and without them the physical and astral planes could not exist, evolve or improve. But you have also learned that each of these forms ultimately leads to entrapment into the world of form and time.

It is usually at the peak and the most intense point of the experience where we have the opportunity to perceive its limitation and the need to grow beyond it. It is at this peak moment that we gain a moment's insight into a higher purpose.

With this new insight burning within you, you realize that it is by power of mind that you have created every single aspect of your life, though until now, you have been unaware of it.

It is by the power of higher mind that you will be able to gain control of the raw forces of the astral plane acting in your life and thereby surmount the limitations of both time and form.

You remember back to the experience the Elemental Earth King showed you and realize that if the man who raised himself from street urchin to wealthy magnate had shared with others what he had amassed, that he would not have been limited by it.

You remember the experience the Elemental Air King showed you and realize that if you had not expected others in your life to meet your emotional expectations, you would have been released from the limitations those expectations and counter expectations placed upon you.

You remember the experience the Elemental Fire King showed you and realize that to be totally immersed in any goal, desire, belief, experience or sensation to the exclusion of all else ultimately becomes self-limiting.

Finally, you remember the experience the Elemental Water King showed you and realize that although the powers of mind may help you to understand and work with and through the forms of the material world, the mind itself is also a product of the astral plane and must be transcended to higher mind before its limitations can be surmounted.

The Archangel Michael appears before you and hands you a vial from which smoke rises. It is the famed elixir of life. You drink deeply and perceive one more truth. It is only through sacrifice that the limitations of the Sphere of Hod may be surpassed.

You exit the temple and move toward a tremendous crater in the earth, appearing as an eye surrounded by a coiled dragon.

When you look into it you see only darkness.

You feel a sucking sensation from the eye.

You feel this vast hole drawing upon your energies.

You become aware of others around you. Not all are human.

All are engaged in various activities that engage their total concentration.

Some are working, focusing only upon their own efforts.

Some are playing and partying with others.

Some are musicians, some are artists, some are scientists, some are merchants and some are derelicts.

Some are with their families.

Some are having sex, some are dancing, some are arguing; some are engaged in magic or religious ritual.

You can see that all are releasing an energy that is being absorbed into the black eye at the center of the activity.

You look toward the outer limits of this huge gathering and see the Elemental Kings looking on, as if guarding the activities.

Each is in his animal form - bull, eagle, lion and scorpion.

The energy consumed by the eye intensifies; you see and feel more and more flowing into it.

A tension begins to build... and build.

Finally, there is a tremendous release of sound and light from out of the eye.

You are engulfed by light.

It flows all around you and through you.

A burning sensation begins at your solar plexus and moves upward toward your Heart Center.

When it reaches your Heart Center another explosion occurs.

Light in all of the colors of the rainbow bursts from your Heart Center and flows outward in all directions. You are able to perceive the flow of the astral light and know that with minor adjustments of the rainbow flow pouring outward from you, you can control it.

The flow seems to go on and on and on.

Light flows into the top of your head and moves down to your chest and blends with the energy moving up from your solar plexus.

You feel as if you stand balanced within a column of light.

The light burns away your fears. It burns away all of the limitations you have, in your life, placed upon yourself.

A new "eye" opens within your heart and you can now see clearly what you have brought into creation in your life. You can see that what you have thought to be real is not. What you have not thought reality may yet be real. You feel a momentary sense of loss as your sense of reality and perceptions of self are adjusted. The light intensifies as the intense energy of Tiphareth begins to reach you, supplying the higher intuition necessary for this adjustment.

You feel yourself rising... higher... and higher.

A light shines down from above you. As you look through it, you see that its source is a red, spherical stone.

You feel your Heart Center expanding as the light from the stone flows through you, its qualities already yours.

But then the stone begins to turn white and the energy pouring into and through you starts to burn, creating and expanding channels that are new.

As the stone becomes more and more brilliant, so does the light moving through your heart, until finally, there is another glorious explosion.

When the explosion is done, the brilliant white stone is gone, but a speck of it remains within your breast.

You find yourself floating in brilliance.

You feel perfectly balanced, in perfect harmony with yourself.

You feel a strong inner desire to go out and to share, to teach and to give to others all that you have experienced here and in your life.

As this feeling fills you, you recognize that you have begun the Hermetic Path on the Tree of Life.

The light fades so that you can begin to see your surroundings and you see, standing about you still, the Kings of the four elements that you had to master to arrive here.

As you watch, they fade and you see that they have covered the Malakim, the Angelic Host of the Sphere of Tiphareth. You see that these energy beings are responsible for your newfound balance and harmony, for as you move and alter, they make constant adjustments to maintain your inner balance and harmony.

The Archangel of the Sphere, Raphael, appears before you. Taking you by the hand, he leads you into the golden brilliance of the Temple of Tiphareth.

An absolute stillness permeates the temple. Everything about you is bathed in brilliance and beauty. Through the intense light you can barely see six golden columns supporting a roof glittering like the finest diamonds.

In the floor at the center of the temple is a huge diamond eye, surrounded by a circle of topaz.

As you move to look into it the diamond speck of light within your breast begins to vibrate and you realize that the omniscience of the Sphere of Tiphareth lies within you now and that in the stillness, balance and harmony of your deepest self you can see and know all that concerns you and yours.

The light within your breast becomes a brilliance that expands to surround you once again. You sit down at the center of the Temple to meditate.

And so ends the 26th Path.

Path Journal

A. Record your emotional reactions to your path experiences here, immediately upon completion. Include any physical responses or sensations.

Date of completion: _____

Emotional responses: _____
_____
_____

Physical reactions: _____
_____
_____

What do you think these responses indicate? _____
_____
_____

B. Use this section as a diary of your experiences during the week following your completion of the path. Be sure to include how you react to things emotionally, as well as how you deal with any major issues that might arise.

Day 1: _____
_____

Day 2: _____
_____

Day 3: _____
_____

Day 4: _____
_____

Day 5: _____
_____

Day 6: _____
_____

Day 7: _____

_____

C. Review the week's experiences. How has the path affected the way you handled this week's issues? _____

_____

_____

_____

D. What special dreams has this path stimulated this week? _____

_____

_____

_____

Areas Path 26 Will Help You Work On

- Detachment, and sublimation of emotions
- Overcoming your tendencies to be over-dominating
- Overcoming feelings of selfishness and conceit
- Gaining a sense of calmness and centeredness
- Opening the Heart Center
- Increasing your energy
- Understanding that controlling the "carrot" for others to chase yields no fulfillment
- Understanding that you cannot grow beyond anything that you continue to pursue
- Knowledge that obsession comes from the desperate need to avoid opening the heart and giving up control
- Understanding that the only way to overcome our self-imposed limits and fears is to go deeper into them
- Recognizing that nothing is what it seems
- Recognizing that you are controlled only by that which you attempt to control

- Knowledge that whatever you build will eventually block your progress when you outgrow it; it will trap you until you discard it
- Understanding that nothing is forever
- The ability to see things as they are
- Improving perspective
- Tolerance for others, especially your partner(s)
- Increasing your spirit of generosity
- Understanding that you create your own reality with your mind
- Understanding that you have the right to protect your home, and you have the means to do it
- Exorcism
- Being able to open your heart and give up control
- Letting your Guides in
- Disengaging from patterns of over or under achievement
- Acquiring the drive for achievement and balanced growth
- Improving organizational ability
- Choosing your own goals, and being able to accomplish them
- Moderation
- Dealing with time

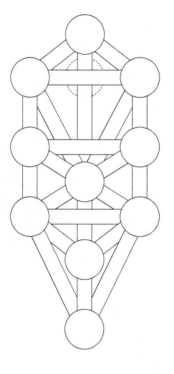

Path 25

Correspondences

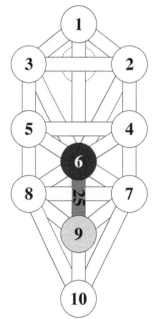

— Sphere of Yesod —

We commence our journey in the Sphere of Yesod, the Foundation.

The Hebrew Divine Name is Shaddai el Chai, the Almighty Living God.

The Archangel of the Sphere is Gabriel, Prince of Change and Alteration.

The Choir of Angels is the Kerubim, the Strong.

The Planetary correspondence is the Moon.

The symbols are perfumes and sandals.

The color is violet.

The element is air, the Astral Light, or Akashic Fluid.

The number is 9.

The Tarot card correspondences are the four nines.

The chakra is the Sacral Center, located just below the navel.

The corresponding gland is the spleen.

The stones are crystal, pearl or clear quartz.

The metal is silver.

Plants are gardenia, jasmine, and heliotrope.

The musical note is "C."

Symbols are the horn and the cup.

The magical image is a very strong, beautiful, naked man.

The correspondence in the physical body is the reproductive organs.

Mythological correspondences are the Greek Goddess Artemis, the Roman Pan, the Norse Loki and the Wiccan God and Goddess, Cernunnos and Selena.

The spiritual experience is a vision of the machinery of the universe.

— 25th Path —

The 25th Path is known as the Intelligence of Probation, because it is the primary temptation, by which the Creator trieth all righteous persons.

The Hebrew letter for the Path is Samekh, meaning, "Prop."

The meaning of the simple form of the letter is anger.

The corresponding astrological sign is Sagittarius.

The planet is Jupiter.

The element is Fire.

The metal is tin.

The Path corresponds to the Tarot Major Arcanum card "Temperance."

Symbols of the Path are vibration, the "womb preserving life," the tunnel, the archer and the arrow.

The stone is Jacinth.

The scent is lignum aloes.

Herbs are balm, betony, fig and spagnum moss.

The color is blue.

The musical note is "G#."

The magical weapon is the arrow.

Living beings are the dog and the horse.

The symbolic being is the Centaur.

The spiritual experience is to experience the enormity of the "Great Work," wherein the Personality may make first contact with the divine light, to experience an alchemical change within the body wherein the whole is made greater than the sum of its parts. The experience is one of ecstasy and enlightenment.

This Path is the "Path of the Mystic" and it completes the second segment of the Path of the Arrow, which goes straight up the Middle Pillar.

— Sphere of Tiphareth —

The Sphere of Destination is Tiphareth, Beauty.

The Hebrew Divine name is Jehovah Aloah Va Daath.

It is known as the Mediating Intelligence.

The Archangel is Raphael, Prince of Brightness, Beauty and Life; the Archangel of Healing.

The Order of Angels is the Melechim, the Angelic Kings called the Order of Virtues, Angels and Rulers who are responsible for creating and maintaining perpetual balance and harmony in all things.

The corresponding planet is the Sun.

The number is 6.

Symbols of Tiphareth are the Calvary Cross, the Rose Cross, the Truncated Pyramid and the Cube.

The stones are topaz and diamond.

The metal is gold.

The color is yellow.

The corresponding body part is the breast.

The corresponding chakra is the Heart Center and the gland is the thymus.

Living beings are the lion, the child, and the phoenix.

The symbolic creature is the sparrow-hawk.

The musical note is "F."

The scent is aloe, cinnamon and clove.

Herbs are angelica, almond, frankincense and myrrh.

The magical image is a Majestic King, a Child or a Sacrificed God.

The mythical correspondences are all of the Sacrificed Gods, including the Egyptian Osirus, the Indian Krishna and Buddha and the Christian Jesus.

The spiritual experience is a vision of the Harmony of things and of healing and redemption.

Invocation

"May we be encompassed by the name Shaddai El Chai and established in the temple of Yesod, the Foundation. May the portal of the 25th Path be opened to us and may we journey thereon in the power of the name El to the gate of the Sphere of Tiphareth. And, in the name of Jehovah Aloah Va Daath may the gate of Tiphareth be opened to us and may we be firmly established in the wonders of that Sphere."

Path

All around you is darkness.

In the dark you become aware of the beating of a heart.

It is your own.

You are surrounded by nurturing warmth that encloses and supports you. You feel safe. You feel totally relaxed.

You are in the womb.

Suddenly a rushing sensation surrounds you, gentle hands grasp you and draw you forth and you find yourself looking upward into the lovely face of Diana, Goddess of the Moon and the Sphere of Netzach.

She smiles.

Surrounding you is the beautiful astral garden of the Sphere of Yesod.

In the violet mist you see the natural beauty of great ash trees.

Jasmine flowers bloom profusely about you, their scent intoxicating.

You look about you to see forms of all sorts, some familiar, some not, barely discernable through the swirling mists.

All are in a state of change and transformation, from one form into another; all around you is constant change and activity.

You watch, in fascination, the Archangel Gabriel and the Choir of Angels as they bring forms into and out of existence in the material world of Malkuth.

As you watch, you grow from an infant into a child.

Soon you are tired of the experience the Astral Garden of Yesod provides and you begin to look for something more.

The astral forms that until now had excited and amazed you now appear old and worn.

Like a child putting away toys you have outgrown, you begin to look for a way to move beyond the Sphere of Yesod.

Through the mists you can discern three paths leading from the upper end of the Garden and one from the lower end. You look to Diana for some insight as to which Path you should take.

She only smiles again.

You move toward the upper end of the Garden, where you can see the three paths there more clearly.

Two paths lead off to either side of the Garden, twisting and turning as they go. A third path leads straight upward from one end of the garden, between the other two.

Somehow, the very directness of the middle path, being in its way so very different from the hazy and changeable formlessness of your present surroundings, attracts you.

You make your choice. Without hesitation you move to the middle path.

As soon as your feet touch the path, Diana releases a shining white arrow from her bow. You follow the flight of the arrow up the path, straight and true, as far as your eye can see.

As the arrow travels it illuminates the space around it and when it reaches its distant target far above, an intense flash of light is released.

The light flows downward and all around you. It fills you with a feeling of inspiration and excitement. For a brief moment you gain a flash of insight into the meaning of things. You are filled with an inner "knowingness" that there IS a higher power, there IS something "more!" As quickly as the flash of light filled you, it was gone. In its absence you enter into a deep and total darkness. The Garden of Yesod and Diana and Gabriel are gone.

All around you is darkness. But this is not the nurturing darkness of the womb; it is a darkness that stretches on and on before you, a tunnel of blackness through which you must pass to reach your destination. A tunnel of darkness made so much blacker by your very knowledge of the light you experienced.

You begin to move forward through the dark. Slowly a feeling of loss overcomes you. Where is the light? The darkness presses in upon you and you become aware of how very alone you are. You hear nothing, see nothing, feel nothing, yet still you move ahead. The darkness gives you no guide posts or signs to see your direction, or to offer you hope.

You begin to sink into despair. Sorrow and loss and a deep sense of emptiness well up inside you. You sink to your knees and begin to crawl forward.

There is nothing and no one to help you. Finally, you stop moving. Despair envelopes you.

But you remember the light. In desperate hope you begin to force yourself to crawl onward.

As you begin to move you become conscious of a faint speck of light within yourself, within your heart.

You concentrate on it.

It is the light of your faith.

As you focus all of your attention upon it, it begins to get brighter and brighter. Finally, it is bright enough to illuminate the darkness of the tunnel.

You rise to your feet and begin to move on upward through the tunnel, in confidence, surrounded by your own illumination, arising from your own faith.

The tunnel leads on, long and straight.

Before long, you come across a fellow traveler, who, like you, is traveling this path. But you see that the traveler has not yet found the faith to light his own way.

Without hesitation, you offer to share your illumination.

Together you move forward on your upward journey.

You are uplifted by the joy of sharing and the heady feeling of companionship following on the heels of your previous loneliness.

A feeling of love and faith fills you and you and your companion want to share this with others.

You and your companion reach out to all of the others you meet and gradually you create a following. All bask in the light of your faith.

You begin to preach. Your followers begin to worship you, instead of the light you are directing them toward. A center is built and you begin to enter into and to direct changes in the lives of your countless followers.

Gradually, you are pulled further and further from your Path.

Soon, your inner light dims. You are again plunged into darkness, this time, the darkness is even deeper than before.

You lose all sensory perception. Your followers are gone. Your friend is gone. You are totally alone again.

The darkness surrounding you is nearly tangible, as your senses search outward and still find nothing.

Then you seek inwardly for the spark of light you found before.

There is no trace of it.

Having no choice, you begin to walk onward and upward in darkness, carried forward by faith and trust alone.

Your faith becomes like an arrow that you have shot upward toward the light in your memory and you now follow the faint path it has left in your mind.

You stumble onward, no longer confident, no longer arrogant, but a searcher with an inner belief that carries you forward, always looking for that faint sign, that half-felt verification, that you follow the Path of the Arrow.

As you move onward through the darkness you hear the sound of hoof beats.

You are overtaken by a centaur that carries a lantern. As the light washes over you, you feel a sense of relief and a desire to stand forever in its beam.

The centaur laughs and motions you to follow him as he races down a passageway to the right.

You are sorely tempted by both his lightness of heart and the light his lantern provided you. You pause in indecision.

As you pause, an inner pain and sense of loss begins to overwhelm you.

You go back to following your Path.

As soon as you turn back to your Path you are overwhelmed by another flash of blinding white light.

You are filled with a momentary sense of the "rightness" and "harmony" of things. Before you can fully understand what you see, the light dims.

But you are left with a spark within your breast to light your way once more.

You journey onward again. As you continue to move forward and upward, others come to you for advice, wisdom and insight. You seem to have gained a greater ability, now, to interpret the signs and symbols of life. Although you give your advice and share your insight freely, you take no direct control or action in the lives of those who come to you.

You are offered positions of leadership and power, but remembering the absolute darkness following your last fall into temptation and, still feeling the allure of the light you seek, you refuse, and continue on your way.

As you progress along your Path, you continue to make friends, but each time the friend continues his or her journey in a direction different from your own. Although tempted to follow, each time you choose to follow your own Path. You become more and more alone.

Still, you move forward and upward, illuminating your own way with the light of your faith, following the remembered Path of the arrow.

You come to a juncture on the Path where you see an orgy in progress.

You stop to watch. You feel the stirrings of sexual desire as you watch male and female bodies moving together in complete harmony and abandon, performing endless acts of physical pleasure. Those who notice you wave you forward to join them.

As you teeter on the edge of submission to your desires, the light within your breast shrinks and dims, nearly extinguished.

Plunged into near darkness again, the writhing bodies moving in rhythm before you no longer appear special, exotic, or even desirable.

You turn from them, to continue your Path again.

As you do, a light again flashes in the darkness around you.

As it dims, a part of it remains, illuminating your energy centers.

An intense vibration begins at your Root Center; your Sacral Center begins to vibrate and expand as you experience a massive release of sexual force that pushes energy upward through your body.

Your Solar Plexus Center explodes upward creating a tremendous pressure in the center of your chest.

The pressure mounts.

Finally, your little mind of personality can no longer hold the force of the building pressure.

The energy shoots up through your Throat Center into your Third Eye Center and from there to your Crown Center. Finally, a fountain of light pours out and upward from the top of your head as the gates to your Higher Mind burst open! You feel a supreme force lifting you upward, upward. The light you have carried within you becomes brighter and brighter still, until there is nothing surrounding you, or within you, except light.

You feel your Higher Mind expanding and reaching outward. Your awareness is heightened to Superconsciousness.

You begin to perceive higher truth through direct intuition and perception.

You are filled with a direct understanding and insight into all that has happened in your own life and those lives of people close to you. That understanding and insight extends, until you perceive with direct clarity the "Truth" behind all that concerns you in the universe in which you live.

This sharpness and clarity can only last but a moment, but you know that you have created new pathways for this higher thought to be translated into lower mind so that you may understand and express it to others.

As the light dims you find that you are no longer in the tunnel.

You stand atop a high, flat-topped mountain. Beneath your feet you feel the soil and the rock and the very roots of the mountain that stretch far into the earth beneath. Your heightened senses reach deep into the earth as you feel yourself in the mountain and it within you. Slowly, you begin to fully comprehend the element of earth.

Slowly you pull your consciousness out of its immersion in earth, as you feel the force of a high wind whirling about you. Using your new heightened sensitivity you let your being merge into the wind, into the very air; as you become the air, you feel it ebb and flow in currents like water; you feel it compress and explode; you feel it act upon and shape the earth. Gradually, you begin to fully comprehend the element of air.

Again, you slowly pull your consciousness out of its merging with air as you become aware of a gentle rain falling upon you. The rain becomes fiercer and harder, demanding attention and again you use your heightened senses to merge with a single drop of water. You land with it upon the surface of the mountain and flow with it down the mountain, gradually merging with streams and eddies util it forms a rushing torrent. You are the water, flowing over the land, forming caverns and oceans. Gradually, you begin to comprehend fully the element of water.

But again, your consciousness is drawn back, this time by the superheating of the earth beneath your feet. Where the rain falls upon the mountain top it begins to sizzle and turn to steam. You feel a rumbling beneath your feet as licks of fire begin to erupt upward. Before long, the fire is all around you, is enveloping you.

You don't resist. You become the fire. You feel yourself as intense heat and flame. You begin to fully comprehend the element of fire.

The rain continues to fall upon you, and as the water meets the fire, you begin to mold the two elements within your own being, merging them one into the other until a perfect balance has been achieved and a new element emerges.

A shaft of golden light bursts forth from your heart and carries you upward, into the temple of Tiphareth.

The temple is constructed of shafts of multi-colored light in the shape of a truncated pyramid. At its center stands a crucifix, upon which you see the Sacrificed God of the Sphere of Tipareth.

You watch as his eyes open. You meet his gaze, and are immediately filled with the intense energy of healing and redemption.

You realize that nothing is ever lost, for each sacrifice you made released energy that became something more on a higher plane.

With this insight, the energy of healing that is filling you begins to radiate outward, flowing out from the Temple of Tiphareth and bathing everyone and everything about you in the pure clean energy of healing, redemption and love.

And so ends the 25th Path.

Path Journal

A. Record your emotional reactions to your path experiences here, immediately upon completion. Include any physical responses or sensations.

Date of completion: _____

Emotional responses: _____
_____
_____

Physical reactions: _____
_____
_____

What do you think these responses indicate? _____
_____
_____

B. Use this section as a diary of your experiences during the week following your completion of the path. Be sure to include how you react to things emotionally, as well as how you deal with any major issues that might arise.

Day 1: _____
_____

Day 2: _____
_____

Day 3: _____
_____

Day 4: _____
_____

Day 5: _____
_____

Day 6: _____
_____

Day 7: _____

_____

C. Review the week's experiences. How has the path affected the way you handled this week's issues? _____

_____

_____

_____

D. What special dreams has this path stimulated this week? _____

_____

_____

_____

Areas Path 25 Will Help You Work On

- Balancing your emotions and centering yourself
- Energizing yourself
- Maintaining a positive attitude
- Joyousness
- Developing inner faith
- Trusting your inner guidance
- Belief in yourself
- Recognizing and overcoming temptation
- Overcoming spiritual egotism
- Coming "home" to your "Self"
- Learning to carry your "home" within yourself
- Detachment and objectivity
- Being able to give unconditionally
- Developing your teaching ability

- Alchemical transformation. Channeling higher levels of energy

- Realizing and releasing the innocence of your inner child-self

- Understanding the statement that "I become the way, and light the way"

- Developing the "strength" of gentleness

- Transmuting your own sexual force to achieve higher consciousness

- Developing self-responsibility. "You are on your own, and must make your own choices."

- Letting go of your resistance to higher forces

- Reclaiming your Self

- Healing yourself and others

- Dream interpretation

- Assumption of "God" forms – i.e. letting a higher force focus through you

- Astral projection

- Attracting higher "protection" while traveling; traveling physically or on the astral, or even journeying toward a goal intellectually or spiritually

- Learning to "invoke" your Guardian Angel

- Beginning to develop the higher forms of psychism

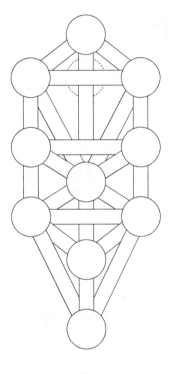

Path 24

Correspondences

— Sphere of Netzach —

We commence our journey in the Sphere of Netzach, Victory.
The Hebrew Divine name is Jehovah Tzabaoth.
The Archangel is Haniel, Prince of Love and Harmony.
The Order of Angels is the Elohim, the Gods who are also called the Order of Principalities.
The corresponding planet is Venus.
The number is 7.
The symbols of Netzach are the girdle, the rose and the lamp.
The stone is emerald or turquoise.
The metal is copper.
The color is green.
The corresponding body parts are the loins, hips and legs.
The corresponding chakra is the Solar Plexus Center, the gland is the adrenals.
Living beings are the dove, the sparrow and the swan.
The symbolic creature is the lynx.
The musical note is an "E."
The scent is rose.
Herbs are blackberry, cherry tree, dwarf elder and golden seal.
The magical image is a beautiful naked woman.
Mythical correspondences are the Greek Goddess Aphrodite, the Roman Venus and the Norse Goddess Freya. All are Goddesses of love and of nature.
The spiritual experience is a vision of beauty triumphant.

— 24th Path —

The 24th Path is known as the Imaginative Intelligence, so-called because it gives a likeness to all the similitudes, which are created in like manner similar to its harmonious elegances.
The Hebrew letter for the Path is Nun, meaning "fish."
The meaning of the simple form of the letter is movement.
The corresponding astrological sign is Scorpio.
The planetary influence is Mars.
The Tarot Major Arcanum card that corresponds is Death.
Symbols on the Path are water plants, lurid colors, carnivorous plants and sea creatures and all objects of desire.

Living creatures are the scorpion, the wolf, the turtle and the lobster or crayfish.

The symbolic creature is the Phoenix.

The stones are snakestone, carnelian and malachite.

The scent is benzoin.

Plants are cactus and houndstongue.

The color is greenish-blue.

The musical note is "G."

Mythological correspondences are the Mara, Goddess of the Mystic Sea, Hecate, Greek Goddess of the overworld and underworld and Athena, Greek Goddess of War and Home.

— Sphere of Tiphareth —

The Sphere of Destination is Tiphareth, Beauty.

The Hebrew Divine name is Jehovah Aloah Va Daath.

It is known as the Mediating Intelligence.

The Archangel is Raphael, Prince of Brightness, Beauty and Life.

He is the Archangel of Healing.

The Order of Angels is the Melechim, the Angelic Kings called the Order of Virtues, Angels and Rulers, who are responsible for creating and maintaining perpetual balance and harmony in all things.

The corresponding planet is the Sun.

The number is 6.

Symbols of Tiphareth are the Calvary Cross, the Rose Cross, the Truncated Pyramid and the Cube.

The stones are topaz and diamond.

The metal is gold.

The color is yellow.

The corresponding body part is the breast.

The corresponding chakra is the Heart Center and the gland is the thymus.

Living beings are the lion, the child and the phoenix.

The symbolic creature is the sparrow-hawk.

The musical note is an "F."

The scent is aloe, cinnamon and clove.

Herbs are angelica, almond, frankincense and myrrh.

The magical image is a Majestic King, a Child, or a Sacrificed God.

The mythical correspondences are all of the Sacrificed Gods.

The spiritual experience is a vision of the Harmony of things and of healing and redemption.

Invocation

"May we be encompassed by the name Jehovah Elohim and established in the temple of Netzach, Victory. May the portal of the 24th Path be opened to us and may we journey thereon in the power of the name Elohim Gebor to the gate of the Sphere of Tiphareth. And, in the name of Jehovah Aloah Va Daath may the gate of Tiphareth be opened to us and may we be firmly established in the wonders of that Sphere."

Path

You experience intense warmth upon your skin and a sensation of being propelled upward.

You open your inner eyes and see only green flame surrounding you.

You are being lifted upward on the astral currents of the green flame of Netzach, to the Temple of Netzach.

The flame burns inward as it lifts you and the intense heat passes through your whole body.

Wherever the green flame has touched, you are left with a feeling of cool receptivity.

The beauty of the flame is breathtaking.

Finally, the flames begin to die away from around you and you step out onto the Path leading to the Temple.

You look down, to see a scorpion at your feet. You quickly move on.

As you move up the Path you see all manner of bird, animal and plant life abounding in the gardens surrounding the Temple.

Roses grow profusely everywhere, in every color imaginable. You lean forward to catch the scent of one and are immediately scratched by a hidden thorn.

Rubbing the scratch, you continue on your way.

Outside the Gateway to the Temple, you see a fruit tree growing and you move forward to pick a fruit. As you part the branches to select a piece of fruit, movement catches your eye.

Looking closer, your eyes meet those of a serpent slithering gracefully along the branch of the tree. Making as few sharp movements as possible so as not to disturb the creature, you carefully reach for the fruit.

No sooner do you reach forward, than the serpent slithers forward, wraps itself around your arm and slides its way up to your shoulder where it raises its head and looks deeply into your eyes.

You are surprised by the enormous feeling of power and intensity radiating from the creature. You feel no sense of malice or intent to do you harm, rather that it wishes to confer some insight upon you.

But you cannot seem to fathom what the serpent is trying to tell you.

It slowly wraps itself around your body and slithers downward around and around you until it reaches the ground.

In a few moments, you lose sight of it as it disappears into the undergrowth alongside the Path.

You remember the fruit you were about to taste. Reaching forward again and encountering no further inhabitants in the tree, you grasp the fruit, yank it free and bite firmly into it.

A wonderful sweetness fills your mouth and a strong scent seems to overwhelm you.

You feel an immediate lift in your spirits and a sharpening of all of your senses.

You become aware of many sounds and smells in the garden that you had not noticed before. Your eyes drink in the intensified colors of the flowers and foliage surrounding you.

In a remote corner of your mind you realize that the fruit must have been a mild narcotic, but you have trouble even holding onto that thought.

You become overwhelmed by your heightened sensitivity and begin to wander in the gardens surrounding the temple.

You are incapable of thought; you only want to feel; to feel everything.

You stumble over the roots of a tree and land squarely on the ground. The scent of the soil is rich in your nostrils as you gather great handfuls of dark earth in your hands and sift it between your fingers.

The earth is moist and alive and you feel its fertility as an almost tangible need.

Looking around, you see a seedling growing up from between two flagstones, where it will undoubtedly wither and die.

Almost of their own accord, your hands dig a deep hole in the fertile soil. With each scoop of soil, you revel in the feel of the cool dark earth, feeling its total receptivity as if it were your own.

The hole is dug. You gently remove the seedling from its unhealthy home and with infinite love and care, spread its roots in the hole and softly pack the rich earth around it.

As your fingers grasp the stem to stabilize it, you actually begin to feel the loving force of the earth flow upward into the tiny plant, strengthening it, nurturing it, supporting it, totally receptive to its every need.

You watch the plant begin to grow. The stem widens and lengthens, until you feel real bark beneath your fingers and with your heightened sensitivity, beneath the bark you can feel the life energy coursing strong and true as your seedling grows beneath your hands into a tree.

You feel the energy of the tree as something totally different than the energy of the soil, yet both fill you with aliveness.

In the energy of the tree beneath your hands you begin to feel a sensation of need. You focus in on that need. It is a need to merge; a need to be part of another.

You watch as the tree begins to bloom profusely; then you wait with it patiently for the strong wind that will carry its pollen to another of its species.

When the wind comes, you fly with it as it carries your tree's pollen across the garden to another like it. You watch as the pollen settles upon the flowers of this tree and gently slides down the stamen petals. You feel the need of each tree for the other. You feel the merging of the essences of each tree, one with the other.

You feel the joyous beginning of new life as the cycle begins again.

You begin to wander further into the garden. As you go, you see all manner of creatures engaged in loving acts of all sorts.

You pass a pair of Lynx combing and grooming one another.

You see two tigers coyly leading one another on in the endless game of courtship.

You see two wolves copulating, oblivious to everything but one another.

You see two stags fighting over a doe.

You pass a nest where a swan sits upon her eggs, her mate solicitous to her every need, knowing she cannot, will not leave her nest.

A sparrow flies by you, carrying some insect that it brings to its young.

You see an insect laying her eggs, then solicitously guarding them and then patiently laying down to die as the newly hatching young begin to feed on her. She willingly, even eagerly gives her life that in the cycle of birth and death her young might live.

You see a rabbit pretending lameness to draw a hunting hawk from her nest of younglings. You feel her fright and her determination as the hawk begins its dive, her pain as the beak of the hawk strikes her leg, her relief as she barely makes it to a dense clump of shrubbery to hide. You share in her patience as she waits the hawk out and in her anguish as, truly lame now, she returns to her young.

All of these things you can see feel and otherwise experience with great vividness that surpasses your ordinary senses. It is as if you do not merely observe, but actually see the energy and emotions generated by each thing you see.

You begin to truly appreciate the force of love in all of its many forms and to understand, on its deepest level, the constant interplay of energy at work, always moving between polarities, based on the need of one individual for the other.

You perceive the nurturing, protective need of those who have more for those who have less; but you see as well that this chain is unending, for those who need love and nurturing grow, they become those who do the loving and nurturing and those who have given all come to a time of need wherein they must be the recipient of these gifts.

This knowledge flows into you freely, without interference of mind. It is a simple insight, a new understanding of the interaction of the forces of life and death.

You continue your walk through the garden.

As you move onward you see people, some single, some in groups, ministering to one another's need for love on all levels; some of the people you see are making love with one another, others are merely touching one another. Some are listening to their loved ones; some are talking and sharing their dreams with them. Some are sharing their activities, their creative endeavors.

In every contact you see, you see the same polarity at work; you begin to actually feel the energy flowing back and forth on all of its various levels, from the physical, to the emotional, to the mental, to the spiritual.

Shortly you come to a shrine, unlike anything you have ever seen before.

An ancient oak tree with the face of a Goddess carved into it in base relief leans over a shimmering pool of water.

Before the tree, you see a supplicant of this nature-Goddess. She takes from her girdle an offering of freshly cut roses, laying them on a flat stone beneath the tree. As the offering is received, a wind blows up and the branches of the tree give a sighing voice to their delight in the acceptance of her gift.

She prostrates herself before the shrine and as you watch, she pricks her finger and allows a few drops of her blood, ruby red, to drop into the pool of water.

You seem to see a shimmering in the air around the tree as this offering, too, is accepted. You feel the love of the girl for her Goddess as a nearly tangible thing and, too, you feel in the shimmering aura around the tree the presence of something infinitely greater than the tree, a presence of power nearly electric, that sends love back equally to the girl.

You perceive that the love of the girl has brought this very elemental female aspect of the God Force into existence on this plane and that once manifested here, that Force can and does generate an equally loving energy back to her, an energy that will manifest in the fulfillment of her need, or in the raising of her consciousness! Your whole body begins to vibrate as the energy flow between the girl and the Goddess envelopes you.

The vibration intensifies.

You see brilliant colors flashing all around you and then you find yourself inside the Temple of Netzach.

Cool green light surrounds you. You look toward an emerald studded altar at the center of the temple and see that the green light emanates from the light hanging above it.

You kneel before the altar and as you do, the naked figure of a stunning woman appears before you. You recognize the features you last saw carved into the oak tree and feel the same intensely magnetic "presence."

As you watch, the Goddess squats to give birth to a tiny boy child whom she holds to her breast and suckles in joy and love.

Before your eyes the child grows and you can feel the enormous love growing between them.

The boy becomes a man and the loving feeling projected between the two develops the intense overtones of sexuality.

The man grows to his prime and you see perfect union taking place, as between two halves of one whole.

Then the man begins to grow old and feeble. Again, the Goddess nurtures and ministers to him.

Finally, he dies in her arms.

You cry her tears of loss with her. You feel her total emptiness.

You let go of life with she who cannot die.

Finally, you look up at her to find her smiling. Her belly bulges large with child again.

She says, "Know you, that this is the mystery!" and points you toward the open door of the Temple.

You feel as if you have passed some kind of test, have been initiated into some form of the "Mysteries," but have no words with which to explain the feeling.

You walk out of the door.

The Temple has disappeared.

You find yourself floating adrift in a large, boundless ocean.

There is no land in sight. You see only the brilliant Sun, high overhead, its reflection shimmering on the water.

A fish, shimmering with incandescent green scales, leaps from the water just in front of you, passes over your head and reenters the water behind you.

A few moments later, it leaps over you again.

It swims back toward you, this time close to the surface so that you can see it; you begin to realize that the fish is to be your Guide.

You begin to follow it, swimming along on the surface of the water, watching it going deeper and deeper.

Soon you realize that if you don't go beneath the surface of the sea you will lose your Guide entirely.

Taking a deep breath, you dive beneath the water.

You are immediately astonished by the stillness and the silence of this underwater world.

The water is cool on your skin and the blue-green water is crystal clear and amazingly refreshing.

You see your Guide as a glittering and glowing green streak moving through the water before you.

You follow as the fish leads you deeper into the sea.

The pressure of the water bearing down upon you intensifies and your chest begins to burn.

Still, the fish continues its dive.

You begin to look up toward the surface of the water with despair. You know that it's too late to head back to the surface already. "Oh, why did I do this?" you ask yourself.

But there is no path available now except that which leads onward, into the depths of the sea, behind the one who guides you.

You cannot hold your breath any longer, you can bear the pressure no longer.

You let go. You relax. You breathe in.

Instead of water, your lungs are filled with the astral flame, which is the ocean through which you swim.

Adrenaline flows through you along with relief and in joy you swim after your fish-guide.

Now, you begin to notice details of the "sea" through which you swim.

Beautiful green grasses grow up from the sea bottom, but when you go down to investigate them, you quickly become entangled in their strands. With some difficulty, you untangle yourself and move on.

You are attracted to the brilliant red bloom of a plant that seems to float in the water; as you approach to investigate, your fish- guide races back to divert your attention.

When you turn back to the beautiful flower, you see that an unsuspecting denizen of the sea has already gotten too close to it.

The poor thing has been impaled upon its long bristles and is slowly being digested as it is drawn into the cavernous mouth of the flower.

Shuddering, you turn from the spectacle realizing it could have been you if not for your Guide.

You look for your Guide and find that he has moved far ahead.

You begin to follow him, but are attracted to some glittering stones you see on the ocean bottom. You swim down to investigate instead.

The emeralds, turquoise and snakestones you see lying there are beautiful, but as you begin to gather them, you realize their weight will hold you down. Again, you begin to swim after your Guide.

But he is nowhere to be found.

Frantic, you swim toward a cave to see if he has gone in.

You approach the opening. A long serpent like the one in the garden swims out of the cave directly toward you. Not really interested in knowing if it is the same one, you quickly swim away.

It follows you.

Panic grips you as you find you cannot out-swim it. You swim on desperately, not realizing that you have entered a strong current.

The current gets stronger and stronger.

You try now to get away from both the serpent and the current, but no matter how hard you strive, you are carried onward.

Finally, exhausted, you stop your struggle. The current still carries you forcefully on and now the serpent is almost upon you.

You give only a last feeble struggle as the serpent reaches you and slithers up and around your body.

You are surprised as it moves to act as a support for you. "My strength is your strength," it whispers.

You are totally relaxed, ready for whatever follows, as the current carries you onward and into a torrential whirlpool.

The water spins around and around, faster and faster, pulling you downward into a deep pit at its center.

You look downward into the depths of the whirlpool and behold a face looking back up at you, just before you are sucked into the final blackness of oblivion.

You float in total blackness.

You feel nothing, hear nothing, and see nothing.

You are completely empty of all thought and sensation.

All resistance is gone. All desire is gone.

Even the desire to live, or the desire to die, has no meaning.

You float.

Gradually, you become aware in the stillness of a glorious sound; it is a music that has been with you all along, but that until now was so subtle that even your heightened hearing could not have heard it. It is within you.

You begin to follow the music in your head and as you do, you begin to see the beautiful outline of a Temple created of beams of light. It is the Temple of Tiphareth.

You walk victoriously into it and move to stand at the center of a six-pointed star of gold located at its center.

Rays of light explode outward from you in every direction and with them go your expanded senses. Momentarily, you feel yourself a part of all things in this earthly plane, as you feel a part of them in yourself.

You recognize the cycles of life and death and understand the meaning of the old proverb that "To live is to die and to die is to live!"

Your upward-searching senses touch upon new realms of consciousness not yet open to you and you are filled with joy that you are truly a part of this wonderful universe.

And so ends the 24th Path.

Path Journal

A. Record your emotional reactions to your path experiences here, immediately upon completion. Include any physical responses or sensations.

Date of completion: _____

Emotional responses: _____
_____
_____

Physical reactions: _____
_____
_____

What do you think these responses indicate? _____
_____
_____

B. Use this section as a diary of your experiences during the week following your completion of the path. Be sure to include how you react to things emotionally, as well as how you deal with any major issues that might arise.

Day 1: _____
_____

Day 2: _____
_____

Day 3: _____
_____

Day 4: _____
_____

Day 5: _____
_____

Day 6: _____
_____

Day 7: _____
_____

C. Review the week's experiences. How has the path affected the way you handled this week's issues? _____
_____

D. What special dreams has this path stimulated this week? _____

_____

_____

_____

Areas Path 24 Will Help You Work On

- Feeling that you are a part of everything, and that everything is a part of you

- Universality

- Increased interest and awareness of plants, nature, gardening, and nurturing the environment

- Increasing the sensitivity of all of your physical senses

- Increasing sensitivity of the psychic senses that correspond to the physical five senses

- Recognition that momentary desires are only diversions

- "Surrendering" to a "calling"

- Facing and passing through your own death wish

- Letting go of the mind

- Resurrection; insight into the interplay of life and death

- Knowledge of the power within you, and that it is appropriate for whatever you have to do

- Intensification of your energy and creativity

- Intensification of receptivity

- Learning to yield to the cycles of life and death, and utilizing this understanding to determine your direction

- Accepting your feminine side

- In letting go you get a surge of energy; Spiritual Orgasm

- Understanding that love is a need to give of your Self

- Understanding that the "urge to merge" or find a "soul mate" and be absorbed into that mate is an urge to return to the soul

- Letting go of physicality

- Astral travel

- Overcoming your fear of death

- Confronting your fears and conquering them

- Assimilating grief

- Insight into solving your own inner conflict

- Understanding and insight into other's inner conflicts

- The arousal of kundalini energy through sex

- Being able to deal with whatever comes out of your unconscious mind

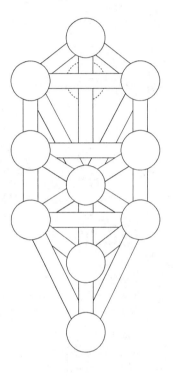

Path 23

Correspondences

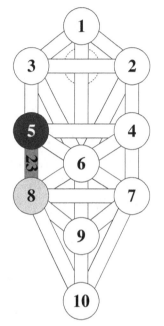

— Sphere of Hod —

We begin our journey in Hod, Splendor.

The Hebrew Divine Name is Elohim Tzabaoth, God of Hosts and Armies, of Mercy and Agreement, of Praise and Honor; God of Multitudes.

The Archangel is Michael, Prince of Splendor and Wisdom.

The Order of Angels is the Beni Elohim, the Sons of the Gods.

The color is orange.

The corresponding planet is Mercury.

The number is 8.

It corresponds to the four eights of the Tarot deck.

The element is water.

The metal is quicksilver.

Stones are agate and opal.

The musical note is "D."

Symbols are the octagon, the scepter and the apron.

The scent is clove, lavender or cinnamon.

Living beings are the swallow, the ibis, the monkey; also, two snakes intertwined and the scorpion.

Herbs are vervain, mace, storax, fennel and styrax.

The body parts are the loins and the legs.

The chakra is the Solar Plexus Center and the gland is the adrenals.

The magical phenomenon is mentalism, psychism as clairvoyance and sensory deprivation.

The spiritual experience is a vision of splendor.

The magical image is a hermaphrodite.

Mythological correspondences are Hermes, Greek messenger of the Gods and both Egyptian Thoth and Greek Chiron who taught the arts of civilization and war.

— 23rd Path —

The 23rd Path is known as the Stable Intelligence, so called because it has the virtue of consistency among all numerations.

The Hebrew Letter is Mem, which means water.

The Esoteric title is the Spirit of the Mighty Waters.

The element is water.

The color is deep blue.

The musical note is "G#."

The astrological sign that corresponds to the Path is Libra.

The Planet is Venus.

The Tarot Major Arcanum Card is the Hanged Man.

Body parts that correspond to the Path are the lower back, the kidneys and the renal system.

The stones are chrysolite and jade.

The scent is aloe.

Living creatures are the elephant and the tortoise.

The Spiritual Experience on the Path is one of suspicion, testing and consistency.

The magical phenomenon are the "mirror" of oneself, meeting the Goddess in her three forms, a baptism of water, drowning, unity, trance and the mystery of the crucifixion.

Symbols found on the Path consist of mirrors, the Maltese cross, the Sacrificed God, the Tau cross and the cross above the triangle.

— Sphere of Geburah —

The Sphere of Destination is Geburah, Strength.

The Hebrew Divine name is Elohim Gebor, God of Might.

It is also called Pachad, meaning Terror and Fear.

The Archangel is Kamael, Prince of Strength and Courage.

The Order of Angels is the Seraphim, the Flaming Ones who are also called the Order of Powers.

The corresponding planet is Mars.

The number is 5.

It corresponds to the four fives of the Tarot deck.

The color is scarlet.

Symbols are the pentagon, the five-petaled Tudor rose, the sword, the spear, the scourge and the chain.

The body part is the right arm.

The chakra is the Throat Center and the corresponding gland is the thyroid.

The incense is tobacco or dragon's blood.

Herbs are oak, nettle and aloe.

The stone is the ruby.

The metal is iron.

The living beings are the horse, the wolf and the bear.

The magical image is a mighty warrior in his chariot.

The magical phenomen is a Vision of Power.

The spiritual experience is one of energy and courage versus cruelty and destruction.

The Mythological correspondences are the Roman God Mars and Goddess Athena, the Indian Kali and the Norse Thor and all other Gods and Goddesses of War.

Now, please close your eyes, and lay your mandala aside.

Invocation

"May we be encompassed by the power of the name Elohim Tzabaoth and established in the palace of Hod, Splendor. May the portal of the 23rd Path be opened to us and may we journey thereon in the power of the name Jehovah Tzabaoth to the gate of the Sphere of Geburah. And in the Name of Elohim Gebor may the Gates of Geburah be opened to us and may we be encompassed by the wonders of that Sphere."

Path

You open your inner eyes to find yourself in the by now familiar temple of Hod.

Beneath your feet the floor is of black and white squares and the roof overhead is a familiar glowing orange.

As you look about you, you count eight arches in the walls and you note that eight pillars support the high ceiling.

The temple itself you notice for the first time is an octagon.

You are drawn to flames that burn at the center of the Temple. They erupt from a crucible that burns with a mixture of cinnamon and aloe wood while filling the Temple with a yellowish-white light.

The scent has the affect of clearing your mind and leaving a feeling of crisp alertness.

Upon the altar lies the Staff of Hermes with its two intertwined snakes and you see a large carved statue of a Hermaphrodite, magical image of this Sephiroh, standing beneath one of the arches.

You move closer to examine the figure and the arches. You find opals and agates imbedded in the stone, in patterns depicting various scenes. You have to stand back to see them more clearly.

The first depicts a giant crowned king astride a great bear. He carries in one hand a spear and in the other a sword. He is surrounded by a pack of dogs as he hunts.

In another scene you see the same king with a beautiful and innocent young man. You see them as teacher and student.

You continue to wander around the Temple studying these life-size glittering murals, until you come to a large arched doorway that you had not seen before, supported by orange pillars.

You feel comfortable in this place and yet you know that you must move beyond the Temple of Hod to follow the 23rd Path.

You look up to see the Egyptian God Anubis, the conductor of the dead to judgment. He is perched upon the arch, as if guarding the gateway to this Path.

As you move through the arch, his eyes follow you, but he makes no move to stop or to encourage you on your way.

On the other side of the gateway you find yourself surrounded by a hazy mist. With difficulty, you discern a path that wanders off into the mist. You begin to follow it.

It begins to twist and turn and is crossed again and again by other paths that look exactly the same.

You come to a fork. You make your choice and then proceed onward.

Before long you come to a dead end.

Frustrated with your choice, you double back along the path while intending to pick up the first path where it forked from this one.

But there are so many intersecting paths that it now seems almost impossible to tell whether you have arrived back at the same fork.

You begin to discern that you are in a maze and that your only course is to continue to wander in it until by some stroke of fortune you are able to recognize where you are.

As you wander, the mist thickens to fog so dense that you can barely see a few yards in front of you. Here and there you walk through patches of rain, so that your clothing is soon soaked through. Your very senses are muffled by the fog and rain.

And still you wander.

Wandering in the smothering dampness and mist, your senses stretch outward, searching for something of solidity to hold on to, to focus upon.

You hear a swallow call and move in the direction you think the sound came from, only to find yourself further lost in the mist.

You smell the scent of lavender and of vervain and yarrow, but again, you cannot locate the source of the scent.

In loneliness you begin to imagine being a part of a large group of people. As you do, you hear many voices drifting toward you through the dense fog. You move toward the voices.

Suddenly, you stumble into a clearing filled with tents and wagons of brightly painted colors.

After walking through the fog, wherein your senses were all muffled, the assault on your eyes and ears is overwhelming.

You see hawkers selling their wares, musicians playing their instruments, street performers doing their routines and all sorts of vendors selling various kinds of food.

As you walk among the stands and displays you come upon a small tent set somewhat aside from the others.

A crowd is gathered around it.

You wander over to it to see what everyone is looking at.

You peer over the shoulders of those in front of you to see an old woman bending over a bowl of glittering water, seeming to be in some sort of a trance. You realize that the glitter is caused by quicksilver floating in the water.

As you take in this whole panorama you begin to realize that you have traveled here by the power of your mind. Your loneliness and need for people has brought you to this noisy gathering and your intense desire to find your way has led you to this crystal-gazing gypsy.

As you move closer you find yourself listening to what she is telling those who come to her for insight into their futures. You have no way of knowing if what she is saying is true or false.

As you watch those who visit her, you see them all believing and agreeing with her. You consider asking about yourself.

Suddenly a scorpion falls on your foot. You quickly shake it off.

You begin to realize that influencing people through communication is a power by itself.

In your mind, you begin to take that power and follow its possibilities.

You immediately realize and understand the uses of power of persuasion in business, commerce, academics, government and as you mentally follow this path of power, you find yourself transported to a place outside of an important government building.

You are about to use your new found powers of persuasion and communication to influence a group of people whose resources you will need. Your concern is not the truth, but only with using your influence to gain your desires.

As you pause outside the building to gather your thoughts under an oak tree you hear a sound from above and look up to see a monkey in the branches overhead. Distracted from your thoughts, you turn your full attention to him and realize that he is pointing upward. He seems to be telling you something.

Slowly, while his words penetrate your mind, you hear that the proper place to use your power is in magic and religion through surrendering your desires to higher values.

As you ponder these words the monkey vanishes before your eyes.

You turn your thoughts inward and immediately you find yourself floating in nothingness. With your senses deadened, you continue to float as a strange satisfaction comes over you. You feel that you have no need for action. You float... effortlessly.

Soon, the Archangel Michael appears to you in a vision of splendor. Surrounding him is the Beni Elohim – the Quoir of Angels of this Sphere. Their singing envelopes you as you feel cool water gently being poured over you.

Gradually, you realize that you are standing in a pool of deep blue water, surrounded by aloe plants.

As you relax, your breathing becomes deep and regular.

You look toward the shore, only to see the monkey standing upon the water's edge pointing toward the rocks along the water crisscrossed with veins of chrysolite and jade. He seems to be acting as your Guide.

You cross to the rocks, so that you may see them more clearly. You see that the glittering veins form a single word – MEM - pointing to a path that leads from the water.

You climb out of the water and begin to follow this Path.

No sooner are you out of the water than your feet sink ankle deep into mud like quicksand. You attempt to walk, but as you try to lift your feet the mud turns your own force against and you fall headlong into it.

It seems that the more you struggle to release yourself from the muck, the deeper you dig yourself in.

Finally, exhausted, you stop your struggle.

Your eyes come to rest on a tortoise near you, who is just digging himself out of the mud following his long hibernation.

You watch and learn from his slow and deliberate movements. He applies a gentle yet constant strength as he moves each leg while gradually pulling himself clear of the mud. Each time that a predator appears, he pulls back into his shell and waits out the danger before moving slowly and steadily onward.

You begin to pull yourself from the mud again and this time, as you apply all of your strength with firm and gentle constancy, you succeed.

Finally, the Path leads away from the water, where in the distance you can see a herd of elephants. "Elephants? Where am I?" you say to yourself.

After a moment of disorientation you realize that you have arrived here, again, by the power of your own mind.

As soon as you realize this, the ground falls away from beneath your feet and you find yourself plummeting downward through water.

You sink down, down, down, so deep that there seems to be no bottom.

Gradually, you begin to feel your whole being melting into the water.

Becoming the water, you lose awareness of your individual self. There is only the water.

Although you have no awareness of where you are, the first feeling you are cognizant of is of hands gently washing your body amidst the smell of scented soaps and oils.

In your half-aware state, you cannot tell if the hands moving over your body are your own or if they belong to another person. Nevertheless, you bask in a soothing and enjoyable feeling.

Eventually, you open your eyes to see a beautiful young girl leaning over you while washing you. Her face is ageless and full of wisdom.

You feel as if the weight of many years has been washed from your breast. You feel clean and regenerated.

Soon, she gently takes your hand and leads you out of the water and into a village of small huts where you see the people of a culture that you do not recognize. In not being familiar with this culture, it is easy for you to be objective. Because of this you see the truth of all that passes before you.

You see people carrying out their trade, following their family traditions, pursuing their desires and working with their government.

You watch them acting on their beliefs, following their religious practices and consulting their Shaman for guidance.

You watch the Shaman performing magic rituals.

Although none of these methods are of your culture or religion, you realize that through watching them, you understand yourself, your culture and your own people. You see yourself in all of them! You are filled with the deepest empathy, compassion and understanding for all that you see, and yet, with your new-found knowledge, you withhold any action.

Suddenly, as this new way of perceiving life fills you, you find your whole body hanging extended, upside down, with your head pointed toward the ground and one foot tied overhead.

You are held motionless, suspended in air. In this reversed position you begin to realize some important principles.

There is action in inaction.

There is freedom in bondage.

From this seemingly paradoxical reasoning you realize that your new awareness comes from your unexpected change in perspective. Waves and waves of prior experiences begin to wash over as you make the connection with your new understanding.

Suddenly, you realize that torrents of rain are washing over you as you hang suspended by one foot while the other crosses your knee.

You are, slowly, becoming soaked through and through.

Soon, you become aware of a matronly woman kneeling on the ground before you. She appears to be worshipping, as if at a shrine.

In the act of seeing her, you experience a double consciousness.

You realize that it is not you, but the Christ who hangs here in symbolic death and that you are both the woman and the Christ.

He and you are one! The woman's hands comfort you as she holds you to her breast.

She is both woman and Goddess.

As you sleep upon her breast, you realize that you and she are also one! Again, you wake, but this time, you find yourself floating upon a great sea.

As you float, out of the water arises a powerful, dark figure of a woman - strong, tall, ageless and wise - wise beyond knowing.

She points toward the shore. It appears as if to be an eternity away, yet you begin to swim, and as you do you feel your body filled with buoyancy. You feel her power carrying you through the water.

As you approach the shore, you find the water filled with the fiery serpents who are the Choir of Angels of the Sphere of Geburah.

Each gives off an electrical charge as steam rises from the water all around them.

You would seek to avoid these creatures and yet your Path leads through them. With courage, you continue. Soon, you reach the group.

As you swim among them you realize that you and they are of one consciousness and that they will not harm one of their own.

Relieved, you pass among them unharmed.

Finally, you reach the distant shore and as you climb on to the land, the serpents sense the change in your consciousness as no longer the same. They start to pursue you.

As they climb on to the land, you here a crack.

A mighty warrior appears. He stands in a chariot and the crack is the sound of his scourge in the air.

Sparks begin to fly and as they do the fiery serpents all scatter.

This warrior of incredible strength raises his right arm with his hand clenched in a fist.

He gestures for you to follow.

Without looking to see if you do, he turns his chariot and drives off.

You immediately begin to follow and yet, because you are on foot, you swiftly lose sight of him. Soon, you find yourself in trouble again! You are surrounded by spear carrying serpent people! At first, they are threatening. They surround you. They seek to spear, swallow and overwhelm you, and again, you do not resist.

Rather, you merge your consciousness with them and as you do they immediately disappear.

No sooner have these beings disappeared from sight than the mighty Archangel Kamael glides down and lands before you.

You hear the sound of drums and a mighty red horse appears. He is flanked on one side by a wolf and on the other by a bear.

The mighty Archangel mounts the horse and begins to guide you, moving slowly so that you may follow.

You come to a five-sided Temple, a pentagon.

You mount five steps of iron.

You feel yourself moving through tremendous resistance and as you feel it, you merge with it. You become the resistance.

As you do this, the resistance dissipates.

At the top of the steps you see five pillars and five lamps.

A five sided altar, of deepest ruby, lies within.

You seek to enter and yet again, you feel great resistance.

More and more the resistance builds. Yet, resolutely, you move forward, while melting into the resistance.

As you do this the resistance weakens. Lightning flashes. Fire dances all around you. You know that any ounce of deception, on your part, would lead you to burn beyond tolerance.

Throughout all adversity, you have learned to remain constant and unchanging; outwardly blending while remaining true to yourself at the core.

As you see the Archangel Kamael, his eyes look through you like a lazer looking for any indication of deception and faltering values.

As his gaze passes through you and continues, you breathe a sigh of relief in knowing that you have prevailed! Finally, you pass into the Temple of Geburah. Fire dances on the five walls around you, forming a pentagon of flame. At the center of the temple stands the mighty warrior in his chariot.

You stand in awe as the sense of absolute power this being radiates washes over you. You are filled with the raw power of intense energy projected at you.

Your Solar Plexus Center expands as you take a deep breath and a shaft of pure force flashes up toward your Throat Center. As you continue to breathe, energy, with such power of will as you have never felt before, fills you with a force beyond imagining.

You realize that the lessons that you have learned on this path are necessary to the right use of that will.

And so ends the 23rd Path.

Path Journal

A. Record your emotional reactions to your path experiences here, immediately upon completion. Include any physical responses or sensations.

Date of completion: _____

Emotional responses: _____

_____

_____

Physical reactions: _____

_____

_____

What do you think these responses indicate? _____

_____

_____

B. Use this section as a diary of your experiences during the week following your completion of the path. Be sure to include how you react to things emotionally, as well as how you deal with any major issues that might arise.

Day 1: _____

_____

Day 2: _____

_____

Day 3: _____

_____

Day 4: _____

_____

Day 5: _____

_____

Day 6: _____

_____

Day 7: _____

_____

C. Review the week's experiences. How has the path affected the way you handled this week's issues? _____

_____

_____

_____

D. What special dreams has this path stimulated this week? _____

_____

_____

_____

Areas Path 23 Will Help You Work On

- The ability to overcome resistance, adversity, and trials through tenacity and strength of purpose

- Knowing when to take and when not to take action
- Understanding that the observer is also the observed
- Unity - your inner and outer worlds are the same and are only reflections of one another
- The power of your mind, coupled with your will, gives conscious control of action
- Awareness that you have the power to use your will either for evolution, or for abuse
- Understanding the power of communication and the power of silence
- Honesty and self-honesty
- Understanding the principle of vacillation
- Recognizing changes in energy flow - energizing or de-energizing
- Overcoming resistance by merging with the object of resistance, yet being able to remain unchanged yourself, at your core
- Peace
- Objectivity
- Overcoming your fear of not being able to control your own power
- Cleansing and baptism
- Understanding that "you can never go back" to innocence or ignorance
- Opening the Throat Center
- Understanding that control of the breath helps you to control yourself, and that deep breathing helps you let go of your resistance
- Learning the proper balance of power and will
- Understanding the adage, "99% is a bear; 100% is a breeze!"
- Learning to "go with the flow"
- Gaining objectivity to the structure of society gives insight and understanding into it
- Fortitude and strength to accomplish any endeavor
- The art of invisibility
- Astral travel
- Healing ability

Path 22

Correspondences

— Sphere of Tiphareth —

We commence our journey in the Sphere of Tiphareth, Beauty.
It is called the meditating intelligence.
The Hebrew Divine Name is Jehovah Aloah Va Daath.
The planet is the Sun.
The Archangel is Raphael.
The Order of Angels is the Michalim, or the "Kings."
The spiritual experience is a vision of beauty and the mysteries of
    the crucifixion.
The elements are air and spirit.
The symbols are the warrior, the truncated pyramid, the cube, the
    lamed, the Rosy cross and the Calvary cross.
The metal is gold.
Stones are diamond and yellow topaz.
The symbolic creatures are the lion and the phoenix.
Magical phenomenon include a vision of the self made perfect, a
    manifestation of the day star, the balance of the four elements and
    the unity of the spirit.
The magical images include a majestic King, a child and a sacrificed God.
The body part is the breast.
The chakra is the Heart Center.
The corresponding gland is the thymus.
Mythological correspondences include all of the sacrificed Gods.

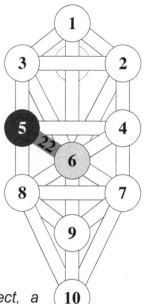

— 22nd Path —

The 22nd Path is called the Faithful Intelligence, so called because by it spiritual virtues
    are increased and all dwellers on earth are nearly under its shadow.
The Esoteric Title is the "Daughter of the Lords of Truth; the Ruler of the Balance.
The Hebrew letter for the path is Lamed, which means ox-goad, or whip.
The meaning of the simple form of the letter is work.
The corresponding sign is Libra.
The planet is Venus.
The corresponding Tarot Major Arcanum card is Justice, the ruler of balance and a
    personification of abstract law, justice and equality.
The color is either emerald green or blue.
Herbs are the rose, fennel or vervain.

The perfume is galbanum.
The metal is copper.
Stones are emerald and turquoise.
The musical note is "F#."
The symbolic creatures are the sparrow, the swan and the dove.
The mythological correspondence is Matt, Egyptian Goddess of Truth, who measures out both happiness and misery, both positive and negative "karma" earned on the wheel of life. It also corresponds to all other Gods and Goddesses representing truth and balance.

— Sphere of Geburah —

The Sphere of destination is Geburah, the Radical Intelligence. The Hebrew Divine Name is Elohim Gebor, the Mighty God.
It is also sometimes known by the name Pachad, which means Terror and Fear and is the Clarifier.
The Archangel is Kamael, Prince of Strength and Courage.
The Order of Angels is the Sepharim, the fiery serpents or Flaming Ones, who are called the Order of Powers.
The Magical Image is a Warrior in His Chariot.
The planet is Mars, who is also the God of War.
The Spiritual experience is a vision of power.
The color is red.
Symbols are swords, pentagrams and the five-petaled Tudor rose.
The stone is ruby.
The metal is iron.
The corresponding body part is the right arm.
The corresponding chakra is the Throat Center.
The gland is the thyroid.
The plant is oak.
The element is fire.
The musical note is "G."
The mythological correspondences include all Gods and Goddesses of War.
Now, close your eyes, and lay your mandala aside.

Invocation

"May we be encompassed by the name Jehovah Aloah Va Daath and be established in the Sphere of Tiphareth. May the Portal of the 22nd Path be opened to us and may we journey thereon in the power of Jehovah Tzabaoth to the gate of the Sphere of Geburah. And in the name of Elohim Gebor may the gate of Geburah be opened to us and may we be firmly established in the wonder of that Sphere."

Path

Your physical eyes are closed and you find yourself drifting freely.

You begin to rise. Higher and higher you go.

You pass above the airy clouds and soon you've left the material world behind you.

You are moving upward through the darkness, past spirits and phantasms.

You float up through the realms of dreams, of desires, of hopes and passions.

Finally, you begin to feel the warmth and brilliance of clear light.

The light is more powerful than a thousand Suns.

It streams through your body. You feel energized, cleansed and purified.

Gradually, your ascent slows and then stops. You feel your feet coming to rest on a firm base.

You open your inner eyes to find yourself in a great circular bowl of white marble.

Six evenly spaced white pillars surround the temple. They stretch up so high that you cannot see the roof of the temple. You have a sense of peace, of warmth and beauty.

Through openings high above your head the morning sunlight streams into the hall from all directions, drenching you with warmth and satisfaction.

The hall is brilliant from the Sun's light reflecting ever around the room and yet you find its brilliance no trouble.

You feel balanced and are filled with a sense of pure well being.

You turn slowly, looking at your surroundings.

Gold leaf inlays of flowers and gentle scenes decorate the walls around the temple.

At the center of the hall, the floor is raised and in that area is an altar.

Upon the altar you see a truncated pyramid and a crystal bowl filled with diamonds and yellow topaz.

Between each pair of great pillars is a door and there are six doors all together.

As you again face the altar, you see that one door behind and left of the altar is open and inviting.

As you move closer to the door, you feel the autumn breezes gently flowing inside.

The air is refreshing and pleasant.

You continue through the door and out onto the long path leading through the outer countryside.

The path moves onward into the distance, following the waving contours of knolls, plateaus and valleys.

The autumn breezes are warmed by the midday Sun.

As you move up the path you begin to hear a great thunderous sound.

The earth below your feet trembles.

You look around you and you see a cloud of dust, following behind on the path and approaching very rapidly. With each passing moment the shaking of the earth increases, the sound intensifies.

You can hear the hooves of powerful horses and a commanding voice coming from that direction.

The distance between you now is only a few yards. You see a tremendous warrior standing upon a mighty chariot. The chariot is sheathed with iron. Its front is covered with copper inlays. It is drawn by two mighty horses, one black and one white.

The animals seem experienced, yet anxious, each with his strong will controlled by the warrior-driver.

He motions you into the chariot, but before you can quite secure your footing, he sets off at a full gallop.

You hang on to the chariot with all your strength, as the ground rushes by beneath you.

You ride over hills and through unfamiliar terrain. The Path is ever upward, yet consistently veers to the left.

The driver does not like altering his course and wants to go straight and ever upward, yet obstacles continually move him to the left. Speed and direction are the only interests of this warrior-charioteer.

Ahead on the path is a large fallen tree. Instead of changing direction the driver continues on straight. The horses madly pull to avoid the tree, but he drives them and the chariot directly over the fallen tree.

The force is so great that you are thrown from the chariot.

You roll, and tumble out of control down a steep sided hill. It is not apparent if the driver wished you to be thrown, or if he's even aware that you are no longer with him!   Finally, you come to a stop at the base of the hill. You're in a battle ridden valley.

Around you are men and horses lying dead and dying. Smoke rises around you from the charred and bloody earth.

Flags, spears, swords and all manner of weaponry clutter the country side.

Far behind you, you can see the remaining half of an army regrouping.

Far in front of you, you see another army coordinating its groups of soldiers, cavalry and bowmen, preparing for yet another assault.

Over to your left is a small pond, which up until now has remained untouched by the battle. Clear blue waters, cool and placid, are topped by a pure white swan floating peacefully and dreamily in the midday Sun.

Upon the hilltop you see your charioteer raise his right arm, lifting his great sword up toward the heavens.

Suddenly, the armies begin to charge and clamber at each other once again.

In great Spheres of smoke and clouds the armies approach each other.

All sight of the pond and the swan is lost as the men blindly and courageously charge across the field.

The sound is so great that you cover your ears. As the battle begins to rage all around you, you become so tense that you crouch, covering both eyes and ears to shut out the fray.

Suddenly, you find yourself in utter darkness. It is very quiet.

You open your eyes slowly and see yourself back on the Path.

You are high above the raging battle.

You look down and see men from both armies still fighting. But the swan still floats serenely on the still waters of the lake.

You continue along now, on up the Path. Up ahead you see a fence with a gate.

Beyond the gate is a courtyard with flowers growing in profusion and in all colors, shapes and sizes - reds, greens, blues and yellows.

A small ornamental pond holding fish and lotus blossoms stands in the middle of the garden.

From the shadows comes a young woman, hardly more than a girl.

She wears a dress of pleated linen. Her black hair falls thick and straight to her shoulders. She wears a headdress that holds a single pearl colored feather.

She stops before you and invites you to sit with her.

You sit in the grass, beside the wild vervain and myrtle flowers.

Doves and sparrows play and call in the tree branches above you.

Her face, though so young, shows an ageless wisdom. But it is her eyes that hold you enthralled. For no one can look into the eyes of Maat, whose eyes are truth, and tell a lie.

You feel very comfortable and at ease here. She softly explains that you need not fear, since no one is ever asked to go beyond what they feel comfortable with.

She questions you about yourself.

She asks about your life and you answer all her questions without holding back. It seems very natural to speak of your deepest fears and of your sorrows, of your failures and lost dreams and of secrets you hold inside.

As you speak, you know that the words are heard by her alone, those who may be around you do not hear what passes between Maat and those with whom she speaks.

After some time of contemplation she rises, and as she turns to leave, she bids you a farewell.

You rise and look out into the distance. The sky is clear blue, the rolling hills reflecting deep, emerald green.

You start up the Path once again.

You move only a short distance along and you see a line of the dead. You recognize some who have just lost their lives in the battle you so recently witnessed.

Each stands quietly and patiently in line with neither hope nor fear. In their hands, each one holds his own heart, waiting for it to be weighed.

The person at the front of the line extends his arms. He gives the heart to a tall dark figure holding a scale in the left hand.

You move closer and you recognize again the Goddess Maat, with whom you have just spoken.

As you watch, she places the heart of the first man on one side of the scale; on the other side rests the feather from her headdress.

She weighs the heart to see if it is light enough to balance the feather. Then she raises her arm and directs him along the path he is to follow.

As he moves on, the next one in line approaches the balance.

You continue to watch this scene for a while. Maat sees you and points in the direction you are to go. You move along up the Path to the left, as she has told you to.

After a time you see before you a five-sided temple all in red and surrounded by massive oak trees. Their branches stretch far up into the sky.

The Sun is moving lower, deepening the color of the afternoon sky, with shades of somber violet, red, orange and pink.

Around your feet are fallen oak leaves, turning red and brown from the cool fall day.

A sudden gust of wind blows more leaves from the tree and they swirl by your face, rustling down to your feet.

You feel as if the wind is rushing you on toward your destination. You move on toward the temple, climbing the five steps.

Inside, near the door, are piled swords and spears and all manner of weapons from battles long past.

The temple is filled with reliefs of battles and action, showing courage and fortitude.

The walls shine with inlaid rubies.

You behold at the center of the temple Mars, the God of War.

He holds upraised in his right hand a great iron sword. He looks straight at you, with neither malice nor compassion, only an understanding of your experience; truth being found, justice being delivered, punishment being dealt.

His clear blue eyes look into yours and you understand that balance requires adjustment; that whatever is necessary to bring the organism into adjustment and equilibrium will be done. This is a process, which, as the symbol of the sword tells us, is not always pleasant.

The blueness of his eyes penetrates and fills you with lightness and balance, and as he disappears from your view you find yourself still looking mentally into those same eyes and bringing the understanding of this balance into yourself.

You sit and contemplate.

And so ends the 22nd Path.

Path Journal

A. Record your emotional reactions to your path experiences here, immediately upon completion. Include any physical responses or sensations.

Date of completion: _____

Emotional responses: _____

_____

_____

Physical reactions: _____

_____

_____

What do you think these responses indicate? _____

_____

_____

B. Use this section as a diary of your experiences during the week following your completion of the path. Be sure to include how you react to things emotionally, as well as how you deal with any major issues that might arise.

Day 1: _____

_____

Day 2: _____

_____

Day 3: _____

_____

Day 4: _____

_____

Day 5: _____

_____

Day 6: _____

_____

Day 7: _____

_____

C. Review the week's experiences. How has the path affected the way you handled this week's issues? _____

_____

_____

_____

D. What special dreams has this path stimulated this week? _____

_____

_____

_____

Areas Path 22 Will Help You Work On

- Turning away from brutality, death, lack of sensitivity, and the glorification of war
- Dealing with feelings of abandonment

- Dealing with feelings of frustration

- Overcoming disorientation and a tendency to stray from your chosen path

- Overcoming your insecurities

- Realizing that letting go of your emotional ties results in a feeling of relief and overall purging

- Opening the Heart Center

- Understanding that your own thoughts, actions and reactions set in motion the external forces which act upon you to bring change

- The ability to deal with loud and obnoxious people

- Understanding that strife and peace are two halves of a single whole

- The ability to see a "cause" for what it is, and know whether you want to be a part of it

- Understanding that life is a "double-edged" sword, and how you live it is a test of your balance; the trials you experience throughout life force you to continually make adjustments until you have attained balance

- Cutting away useless parts of your Self

- Understanding that there is a reason for everything

- Insulation from life is equally as futile as total immersion in emotional strife

- "I'm O.K." - gaining feelings of acknowledgement from a "higher source"

- Knowing that it's O.K. to "do it your own way"

- Understanding that every action attracts its equal and opposite reaction

- Recognizing that when truth is spoken, there is no need for war

- Increasing your energy

- Improving your organizational ability

- Learning to let go of your own "expectations" of yourself and others

- Helping to understand and resolve issues involving legality and fairness

- Resolving karma - good and bad

- Letting go of your regrets

- Understanding what you need to gain or eliminate in order to achieve balance within yourself

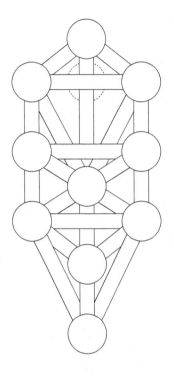

Path 21

Correspondences

— Sphere of Netzach —

We commence our journey in Netzach, Victory.

The Hebrew Divine Name is Jehovah Tzabaoth, God of Hosts and of Armies, of Triumph and of Victory, ruling the universe in Justice and Eternity.

The Archangel is Haniel, Prince of Love and Harmony.

The Choir of Angels is the Elohim, the Gods who are also called the Order of Principalities.

The element is fire.

The number is 7.

The Tarot correspondence is the four sevens.

The musical note is "E."

The planet is Venus.

The color is green.

Stones are malachite, blue topaz and crystal and amber.

The mineral is copper.

Plants are all fragrant and blossoming flowers, especially rose and cypress.

The incense is rose or benzoin.

The body parts are the hips and loins.

The chakra is the Solar Plexus Center and the gland is the adrenals.

The mythological correspondences include all Goddesses of Love and Nature.

The magical image is a beautiful, naked woman.

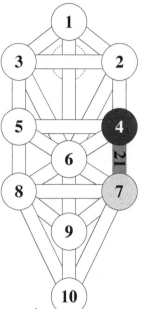

— 21st Path —

The 21st Path is called the Intelligence of Conciliation because it receives the divine influence, which flows into it from its benediction upon all and each existence.

The Hebrew Letter is Caph, which means fist. It is a double letter, which describes the opposites of riches and poverty.

The Esoteric Title is the Lord of the Forces of Life.

It is the connecting Path between the higher self and the personality.

The Tarot Major Arcana card that corresponds to the Path is the Wheel of Fortune.

The color is violet.

The planet is Jupiter.

Stones are sapphire or amethyst.

The metal is tin.

The incense is horehound.
Herbs are clove, oakmoss and sage.
The musical note is "A#."
Symbols are the fist, symbolizing he who grasps comprehension, or the circle; also, the wheel of karma, symbol of life, birth, death and rebirth.

— Sphere of Chesed —

The Sphere of Destination is Chesed, Mercy. It is sometimes called Gedulah, Magnificence and Glory.
The Hebrew Divine Name is El, the Strong and Mighty God, ruling in Glory, Magnificence and Grace.
The Archangel is Tzadqiel, Prince of Mercy and Beneficence.
The Choir of Angels is the Chasmalim, the Brilliant Ones, who are also called the Order of Dominions or Dominations.
The planet is Jupiter.
The color is blue.
The stone is amethyst.
The incense is cedar.
Herbs are olive and shamrock.
The body part is the left arm.
The chakra is the Throat Center and the gland is the thyroid.
Symbols are the pyramid, the square, the orb, the equal-armed cross, the crook and the scepter.
The mythological correspondences are all of the "illuminated ones" who are the Kings of the Gods.
The magical image is of a fatherly King upon his throne.
Now, please lay your mandala aside and close your eyes.

Invocation

"May we be encompassed by the name Jehovah Sabaoth and established in the Sphere of Netzach. May the portal of the 21st Path be opened to us and may we journey thereon in the power of the name El to the gates of the Sphere of Chesed. And in the name of El may the gates of Chesed be opened to us and may we be firmly established in the wonders of that Sphere."

Path

Your inner eyes slowly open and you find yourself in a garden.

Plush emerald green grass is beneath your feet and the fragrances of beautiful flowers are all around you.

The morning Sun is nice and warm, the grass is so soft and the blooming roses, violets and lilies are intoxicating.

At the center of the garden stands a building. There are two cypress trees on each side of it. When you look at the front you see a copper door.

You open the door and you step inside. You look around. The walls are made of rose quartz, the floor of malachite and marble. There are seven flaming torches warming the air to create a beautiful and relaxing atmoSphere. This place warms your blood in a very sensuous way.

As you enjoy this warm and peaceful feeling, you are reminded of a place you've been and still may long for. This is the way home should be. You feel so much at home here; warm and safe, clean and orderly.

But more than all this, is a feeling of being surrounded by love.

You know by pure emotion and instinct that you are home now.

This is home and this love and peace is what you have always wanted and needed. You know that this is your natural birthright, this peace and love that you are enjoying right now.

You feel completely satisfied, enjoying this feeling of bliss; yet there is still a yearning in your heart.

It's as if in spite of the wonderful way you feel, something is missing. There's something else, still, that you are looking for.

You don't know what it is, yet in your yearning you decide to venture out of this beauty, even though at this very moment you have everything that you have always wanted.

Not knowing where you are going, what you will see or experience, you open up the back door.

In front of you, you see a pathway paved with violets and nutmeg and wildflowers. The sun is bright and golden.

Happily, you follow the Path.

You come to a sea shore on which lie pebbles and sea shells in all colors. Floating on the waters is a sailing ship. She is waiting for you! You look for a means to get to her.

You see a white rock, and from behind it steps a beautiful woman.

She is dressed in a shimmering garment. Amethyst and sapphire adorn her wrists and neck. She smiles and signals you to follow her.

She walks across the water with you following and steps into the ship. Sails unfurled, the ship sails off.

The Sun is by now high in the sky as you pass by coast after coast and a myriad of islands, separated from one another by endless miles of sea.

You experience the sea in all its moods, calm, playful and stormy.

For what feels an eternity to you, you just continue to move on, until finally you see the sun setting. The huge orange globe of the Sun fills up the whole horizon, toward which you sail. The water reflects every single ray of light. You are absorbed by the magnificence and glory of the sunset.

No one seems to care which way you are going, in the vast sea of unconsciousness. You consciously elect to "let go" of control and simply flow with the current, letting "fate" be your Guide. You let your faith carry you onward.

Night arrives. The warmth of the Sun gives way to the chill of the night. The brightness gives way to total darkness.

The sun is gone, but the moon soon comes up to take its place.

It illuminates the sea with speckles of gold and silver, bathing all before it in a milky white light. The sea reflects the moon like a mirror and you see that it reflects you as well. It reflects every breath and every action that you take, like an echo in stillness.

You look and you find that you are the moon, you are the stars, you are the sea and you are the very breath that you take and that you are everything there is.

Soon the Sun again rises and your ship comes to shore.

You step onto the sands, waving goodbye as the ship returns across the vast ocean, continuing its ever repeating journey.

Soon you are surrounded by local villagers. They are cheerful and friendly. Most are farmers.

They take you back to their homes, where you decide to stay with them for awhile, to learn and work with them.

You pass the first of several seasons with them.

It is spring and you help them to plant the seed for their crops in neat rows.

As spring turns into summer, you see how the seeds that you helped to plant grow and turn into beautiful and leafy plants.

You stay through the fall to share its rewards as you help to harvest all the plants that you helped to sow and to grow.

Winter comes and you feel the stillness of outer calm, where nothing seems to be happening, yet everyone around you is recuperating and planning for the next spring planting.

Finally, spring is here again. As the farmers return to the fields again to continue their cycle of planting, you realize it is time to move on.

You express deep thanks to everybody.

One of the people you visit in your leave-taking is an old man, infirm and bound to his bed. He's been sick for such a long time, but he is glad of your visit.

He is struggling and gasping for every breath he takes. His death is near.

You say your goodbyes and move to another room, to also say goodbye to the lady of the house.

Again, you hear the gasping and struggling of someone in great stress. But this time, it is a woman in the throes of childbirth.

You would like to wait, but at this moment your Guide comes to you and indicates that you must move on.

As you are leaving the house, you hear an explosion of noises; the cry of a newborn, the voices of a loving family raised in rejoicing at the new birth, but also, the grieving voices of people letting go of a loved one as the old man dies.

You feel deeply for all of them... you say prayers both to celebrate the birth of a new soul and the liberation of another! You leave the village now and continue onward.

Your Guide leads you up the Path and then disappears, leaving you before a giant wheel, which blocks your way completely.

The wheel has twelve spokes and on its very top sits a giant sphinx.

Since there is no other route to follow, you realize that you must climb through the wheel in order to continue on your Path, which you see continues straight onward, on the other side of the wheel.

Very carefully, so as not to disturb it, you climb onto the wheel.

But as soon as your feet touch its surface, it starts to spin.

You try to run faster, to beat it and jump free, but the faster you run, the faster it spins, allowing you no opening to get off! Then you slow down, so maybe by some chance you can find an opening to climb out the other side.

But, although it slows down with you, it offers you no opening to get off.

It continues turning and turning.

It's a sequence of rotation. The movement begins and ends; then it begins and ends and begins and ends, again and again, and again.

It's just endless.

You notice, finally, that the spinning of the wheel is merely a reaction to the energy that you have generated yourself.

Every time you move, the wheel begins a cycle of spinning in reaction to your motion.

It spins at any angle, no matter how crazy-seeming, following your motions.

This perpetual movement of the wheel obviously is caused by you.

It is not the result of chance or accident! You're getting so tired; you feel you can't move on any more.

You're getting dizzy.

You reverse direction, but the wheel merely continues its perpetual spinning in the opposite direction.

You don't want to go through this endless cycle anymore.

You're out of breath; you're tired; you're bored.

You look up, for guidance.

You call for help.

Then you look upward at the sphinx.

You notice now that the sphinx is itself not inside the circle of the wheel! It sits on the outer rim of the wheel and while the wheel turns, the sphinx remains still! It is removed from the wheel entirely! You see that there is one spoke of the wheel directly under the sphinx and recognize, finally, a way to get out of this endless cycle.

You take a deep breath and come to a halt directly beneath the sphinx and the spoke leading up to it.

Now, very careful to keep the pressure on your left and right feet equal, you slowly climb up the central shaft of the wheel, careful not to overbalance the wheel in any direction! Suddenly, just like the sphinx, with its knowledge that comes through balancing the four elements of the physical plane, you are out of and above the wheel! Meanwhile, the sphinx looks at you. As your gaze locks with its own, you grasp the deep understanding that you were unable to go beyond the wheel because, before deciphering the lesson of the wheel, you needed its protection! You jubilantly raise your arms, hands clenched in a fist, knowing that you now comprehend a higher realm that is open to you at this moment! In front of you now, is the most magnificent and beautiful amethyst pyramid.

The four sides of it clearly indicate to you Chesed, the Temple of Foundation.

It is the foundation from which we may rise to the highest point and the foundation from which all beneath gains strength and wisdom.

Olive and shamrock surround the pyramid and its door is open to you.

You enter.

Sitting on an amethyst throne you see a mighty King, in a blue robe.

He appears kind and loving and he holds an ankh and an equal armed cross in one hand. In his other hand is a scepter.

Law, order, justice and love all surround him.

He is the one who establishes the underlying framework that all matter is built upon.

In his eyes are deep knowledge and wisdom.

You approach more closely and see reflected in those eyes your own innermost self, your Guides and your teachers.

An echo of the foundation of your own being resonates just beyond your grasp, yet it is close enough that you sense the possibility of grasping it.

You are surrounded by the love and leadership and joyous acceptance of this ancient King. He is ready to disclose to you the magnificence of the aspect of the Divine intelligence, as seen through this temple of Chesed, which you are now ready to explore! You open your heart and mind to the wisdom, knowledge, insight and understanding that can only come through when you make a vessel of yourself waiting to be filled.

And so ends the 21st Path.

Path Journal

A. Record your emotional reactions to your path experiences here, immediately upon completion. Include any physical responses or sensations.

Date of completion: _____

Emotional responses: _____

_____

_____

Physical reactions: _____

_____

_____

What do you think these responses indicate? _____

_____

_____

B. Use this section as a diary of your experiences during the week following your completion of the path. Be sure to include how you react to things emotionally, as well as how you deal with any major issues that might arise.

Day 1: _____

_____

Day 2: _____

_____

Day 3: _____

_____

Day 4: _____

_____

Day 5: _____

_____

Day 6: _____

_____

Day 7: _____

_____

C. Review the week's experiences. How has the path affected the way you handled this week's issues? _____

_____

_____

_____

D. What special dreams has this path stimulated this week? _____

_____

_____

_____

Areas Path 21 Will Help You Work On

- Neutrality
- Non-attachment
- Unconditionality and acceptance
- Calmness and peacefulness; being centered
- Getting "out of the rut by breaking old patterns
- Cleansing your spirit
- Gaining release from being hyperactive or a "type A" personality
- Overcoming the tendency to overcompensate

- Understanding that the only way to win is not to play

- Anticipating change, not dreading it

- Being able to make new beginnings in your life

- Understanding the cycles of birth and death, that for each birth of a person or thing or even experience in your life, there must be a death – something must be let go of

- Understanding that what keeps you in a pattern is the security of knowing the pattern

- Understanding that in order to grow, you must take risks

- Being able to "time" your change through your understanding of the patterns involved

- Through awareness, hold to the productive and discard the monotonous

- Being able to see the large in the small and the small in the large

- Trusting in your "higher" self

- Developing the instinctive and intuitive mind

- Getting off the "wheel" that is your pattern enables you to see cause and effect objectively

- Releasing your energy blocks

- Contacting your Guides and your Higher Self

- Making a "vessel" of your Self

- Trusting in faith and "going with the flow"

- Opening the Throat Center

- Passing from student, to teacher, to being a channeler of truth

- See beyond the "wheel" and outgrow the need for its guidance and protection

- Healing

- Seeing and understanding the interconnectedness of all things

- Gaining mental clarity

- Improving grounding and the ability to "root"

- Dealing with "Dad"

- Being your own creator

- Channeling, especially clairaudience and automatic writing

- Dreaming and dream interpretation

- Increasing creativity and artistic ability

Path 20

Correspondences

— Sphere of Tiphareth —

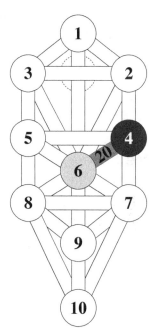

We commence our journey today in Tiphareth – Beauty, known as the mediating intelligence.

The Divine name is Jehovah Aloah Va Daath.

The corresponding planet is the Sun.

The Archangel is Raphael; manifested beings are the Christ & the Buddha The order of Angels is the Michalim or Kings.

The spiritual experience is a vision of beauty, the Christ consciousness.

The elements are air and spirit.

The metal is gold.

Minerals are diamond and yellow topaz.

The magical phenomenon is a vision of the self made perfect.

The body part is the breast.

The virtue is devotion to the great work.

The vice is pride.

The scents are cinnamon and clove.

— 20th Path —

The 20th Path is known in Hebrew as Yod, the intelligence of will.

It's symbol is the open hand.

The corresponding sign is Aries.

The Tarot arcanum is the Hermit, the first of the three great initiatory cards corresponding to the sign Virgo.

The intelligence of the 20th Path prepares all created beings so that the existence of the primordial wisdom may become known.

The God-concept would include Chiron, Mercury or Hermes and the created beings Moses and other spiritual leaders of their people.

The color is green to yellowish-green.

Herbs are Narcissus, lotus, storax, cedar, mint and cinnamon.

Metal is quicksilver.

Minerals are peridot and chrysolite.

— Sphere of Chesed —

Our Sphere of destination is Chesed.

The Hebrew Divine name is El.

The Archangel is Zadkiel.
The order of angels is the Chasmalim.
The planet is Jupiter.
Body part is the left arm.
The stone is amethyst.
Incenses are cedar and cinnamon.
Plants are olive and shamrock.
Symbolic animals are the eagle and the peacock.
The symbolic mythical creatures are the unicorn and the dragon.
Living beings are the Christ, Buddha and all the illuminated ones.

Invocation

"May we be encompassed by the name Jehovah Aloah Va Daath and be established in the Sphere of Tiphareth. May the portal of the 20th Path be open to us and may we journey thereon by the power of the name Elohim Saboath to the gate of the Sphere of Chesed. And in the name of El may the gate of Chesed be open to us and may we be firmly established in the wonders of that Sphere."

Path

A bright light in the shape of a glowing ball is above you.

It grows larger as you are surrounded by its brilliance and heat.

Stay here a moment and feel the heat and brilliance surround you.

The light and heat of the sun becomes so intense that your skin tingles and burns.

You feel you clothing fade away in the rays of the sun.

The rays of hot white light penetrate your flesh and melt away all that gives you weight and density. You are being transmuted by the light of the growing sun.

It surrounds you and you feel one with it. You are transparent and then, finally, invisible.

A group of people pass you. You wave. There is no response.

Remember... You are invisible.

The sun draws you upward to it. Your consciousness merge with the very air and space you travel through.

Swiftly ascending, upward, still rising, you are absorbed into the sun's incandescent brilliance.

Then suddenly, with a blinding flash you are caught up into a supreme and imageless brilliance. Slowly, you become aware in this suspension of a gradual turning on a vertical axis.

Gradually, a sense of your surroundings begins. The turning slowly stops and you find yourself in a temple.

The walls appear to be made of shafts of light from the brilliance you have just experienced.

You are facing the East and you can see that the walls and floor of the temple are actually crystalline topaz, studded with shimmering diamonds.

The temple glows and sparkles around you.

There is a soft mist and a strong fragrance of cinnamon and cloves.

Sweet and heavy, the fragrance hangs in the air.

Facing the eastern wall you notice a cross of gold, with the Christ figure on it.

It is not clear in the mist and haze of the incense and the flashing of the diamonds from the walls around you and so you are drawn to the cross to get a better look.

As you approach more closely, you are pulled right through the cross and even the wall itself, to find yourself standing outside.

The temple is gone.

You are standing in a desert. The sky is blazing and clear blue.

Your feet are bare. You can feel the hot sand beneath them.

You begin to walk slowly. There is a dry wind from the east that pushes against and through you. You notice a river in the distance, of shimmering aquamarine and lined with soft narcissus flowers. The sweet fragrance is carried on the dry wing to you, even though you are far away.

Slowly, you walk, and wonder where your path through the desert will take you.

Suddenly, from nowhere, a huge black creature appears, charging toward you. As it gets closer, you see it as a fierce and growling dog, with three heads. Panic strikes you, fear moves you, and you begin to run across the sand.

Your panic rises to a crescendo, and then in your amazement, the creature overtakes you and passes through you! Totally amazed, you stop dead in your tracks and laugh explosively as you finally believe that you ARE invisible! You no longer are controlled by or have attachments to the physical world.

Suddenly, your chest heaves and a tremendous explosion emanates from your heart. The explosion coalesces into a figure standing before you.

It is an ancient and wise man, clothed in a brown tattered robe and holding an ash wood staff in his right hand.

His piercing dark eyes look through you as you shudder with excitement as he holds out his open hand to you and moves it toward the east, intending for you to follow! Illuminated by the light emanating from his hand though the wind moving all around you is kicking up the sand so that it is difficult to see, you follow. You know that he is the only way to your goal.

As you follow, a massive swarm of locusts appears, covering the desert. They devour the flowers and the fruit along the river banks.

They cover you as well. You run forward in sudden fear.

Why did this come upon you? There is darkness on the desert and the sky is black with the swarming locusts.

You look to your Guide for help and then remember that you are invisible, no longer controlled or motivated by material concerns.

The fear abates and from the west, a hot, dry wind sweeps over you, pulling the locusts off of you and sweeping the desert, the fruit and flowers and pushing the locusts into the river in the distance.

Relieved, you travel onward, following your Guide and his light, to your unknown destiny.

You notice that your general direction is toward the sea. As you walk through the sand a flash of lightning brightens the sky and thunder crashes around you. Huge hail stones descend upon you. It beats at your body as it beats at the desert sand around you. You run toward your Guide for mercy and help and again you remember that you are invisible and the rain and hail pass harmlessly through you.

The flashes of lightning stop as quickly as they appeared.

Again, the desert is hot and dry and the wind from the east is blowing through your tired body.

You think of the topaz temple you left behind and wish to return, but forward you must go.

With that thought there is darkness, complete blackness. You see only the light of your Guide. You feel the sand beneath your feet.

You feel the wind passing through you. But all other awareness has ceased. You feel no fear. You walk forward only guided by the lamp of you friend.

After what seems like an eternity of endless blackness, it is light again.

You have come to the edge of the river you saw in the distance, leading to the turquoise sea, but your Guide is before you and waiting.

What at this river bank are you to do? Your Guide moves forward into the sea, the water crashing in waves about him.

You can't follow him, but you can't go back. What are you to do? With an impulse of faith and courage you step forward only to find you've BECOME the Guide yourself!   You raise your staff to the east and, hearing your Guide's voice within you, you raise your hand to summon a huge and forceful east wind. The sea divides and the voice says, "And the children of God shall walk on dry land."

To both sides of the river bank are walls of water, but you walk into the center and your feet are on dry land.

You follow through knowing you have kept steadfast toward your goal, even through the torture of the elements themselves you have endured.

You now wait, looking at the other side of the sea. Still holding the light in your hand, you drop the rod onto the ground, where it becomes a serpent.

You shrink back at the power and size of the serpent, but you grab it up by the tail and in your right hand it becomes a rod again.

You are in awe of your powers.

Behind you the desert is smoking and smoldering with its heat and wind.

Raising your rod in your hand, you look toward the sky, and again you feel the Guide within. The sky is blazing a clear blue. Its color encompasses you. You feel yourself drawn upward, toward the sky, toward the blue.

Feeling the relief and joy of your journey nearing its end, you gradually start to turn, slowly, on an axis. This sensation feels familiar to you; the sensation of being lifted toward the sky is accompanied by the feeling of a hand pulling you, by your spinning.

Faster, and faster, you turn, counter-clockwise. You begin to become one with the blue sky and the air. Your body has melted away, having spun off.

There are silver shards darting through the blue sky. You are raised further upward. Silver spins around you and through you.

You feel exorcized, cleansed by the shimmering silver. You are the blue sky.

You want to stay here forever. The freedom and joy are erotic.

You feel ecstacy of a kind that you have never known before.

The blue turns to sapphire and then amethyst.

Your awareness returns. You are again surrounded by the walls of a temple. They are dark amethyst. Again, you smell the fragrance of cinnamon. The temple has no roof and you can gaze upward to the sapphire blue. The temple walls shimmer with sapphires and you see two pillars before you, leading into another room. One pillar is black and one is white.

You walk through. In the center of the room is an altar. It faces east. It is a cube of amethyst crystal. Above it is a banner.

The banner is black, with a white eight-pointed star on it. Inside the star is a yellow octagon. Standing in this temple, you have the impression of a face, a man bearded, but with his face turned to the side. You cannot actually see him, but you feel him.

You face the banner, salute the east and know that you have been touched by the hand of God.

And so ends the 20th path.

Path Journal

A. Record your emotional reactions to your path experiences here, immediately upon completion. Include any physical responses or sensations.

Date of completion: _____

Emotional responses: _____

_____

_____

Physical reactions: _____

_____

_____

What do you think these responses indicate? _____

_____

_____

B. Use this section as a diary of your experiences during the week following your completion of the path. Be sure to include how you react to things emotionally, as well as how you deal with any major issues that might arise.

Day 1: _____

_____

Day 2: _____

_____

Day 3: _____

_____

Day 4: _____

_____

Day 5: _____

_____

Day 6: _____

_____

Day 7: _____

_____

C. Review the week's experiences. How has the path affected the way you handled this week's issues? _____

_____

_____

_____

D. What special dreams has this path stimulated this week? _____

_____

_____

_____

Areas Path 20 Will Help You work On

- Gaining inner peace, joyousness, elation
- Being comfortable with your self; dealing with loneliness by accepting yourself and becoming whole
- Improving your ability to relax
- Knowing how to tap into your inner protection
- Accepting that you "can't go back"
- Developing faith and devotion, a sense of rightness
- Being able to focus on your goals
- Resisting temptation and fear
- Self-empowerment, strength and fortitude, coming from a sense of your individuality
- Strengthening your connection to your Guide
- Realizing that all Guidance comes from within
- Magic and inner transformation
- The power to remain unaffected by your surroundings

- Invisibility

- Opening the Heart Center

- Detachment and objectivity

- Teaching

- The ability to deal with emotional trauma without losing perspective

- Ability to channel higher forces

- Releasing all attachments to the physical world, and therefore no longer being controlled by physical and material circumstances

- Realizing and accepting your own power

- The ability to control the elements

- The ability to control your dreams

- Contemplation and meditation

- Learning to control the rate of your own vibration

- The will and power to make manifest your goals, and the knowledge to do what is right

- Understanding that attention is energy, and controlling the attention controls the energy

Path 19

Correspondences

— Sphere of Geburah —

We commence our journey in the Sphere of Geburah, the Radical
Intelligence.
The Hebrew Divine Name is Elohim Gebor, The God of Might.
Geburah is also known as Pachad, Terror and Fear.
The Archangel is Kamael, Prince of Strength and Courage.
The Order of Angels is the Seraphim, the Flaming Ones who are
also called the Order of Powers.
The corresponding planet is Mars.
The number is 5.
The Tarot correspondence is the four fives.
The color is scarlet.
Symbols are the pentagon, the five-petaled Tudor rose, the sword,
the spear, the scourge and the chain.
The body part is the right arm.
The chakra is the Throat Center and the corresponding gland is the
thyroid.
The incense is tobacco or dragon's blood.
Herbs are oak, nettle and aloe.
The stone is the ruby.
The metal is iron.
The living beings are the horse, the wolf and the bear.
The magical image is a mighty warrior in his chariot.
The magical phenomenon is a vision of Power.
The spiritual experience is one of energy and courage versus cruelty and destruction.
The mythological correspondences are all of the Gods and Goddesses of war.

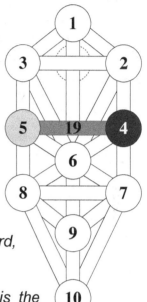

— 19th Path —

The 19th Path is called the Intelligence of all the Activities and Spiritual beings because
of the affluence diffused by it from the highest blessing and most exalted sublime
glory.
The Esoteric Title is the Daughter of the Flaming Sword.
The Hebrew Divine Name is Teth, which means serpent or tooth.
The simple letter means Taste.
The element is fire.
The color is yellow-green.

The musical note on the path is "E."

The astrological sign that corresponds is Leo.

The planet is the Sun.

The Tarot Major Arcanum card is Strength.

Stones are opal and zircon.

Herbs are catnip and sunflower.

The symbolic creatures are the phoenix, the child or the lion.

The body parts are the heart, the spine, the arms and wrists.

The path philosophy is that it is the wise man who subjugates the animal within through his thought and his humanity. It is the highest quality of man controlling the highest quality of the beast.

The magical image is a mighty warrior in his chariot.

Mythological correspondences include all sacrificed God Kings, (for example, Egyptian Osiris and Christian Jesus), infant forms of the Gods and Mighty Kings.

— Sphere of Chesed —

The Sphere of Destination is Chesed, Mercy.

It is also called Gedulah, Magnificence and Glory.

The Hebrew Divine Name is El, the Strong and Mighty God, Ruling in Glory, Magnificence and Grace.

The Archangel is Tzadqiel, Prince of Mercy and Beneficence and the Righteousness of God.

The Choir of Angels is the Chasmalim, the Brilliant Ones who are also called the Order of Dominations.

The corresponding planet is Jupiter.

The number is 4.

The Tarot correspondence is the four fours.

Symbols are the Pyramid, the Square, the Orb and Equal-armed Cross, the Crook and the Scepter.

The stones are amethyst and sapphire.

The metal is tin.

The color is blue.

The corresponding body parts are the hip, the thighs and the liver.

The corresponding chakra is the Throat Center and the gland is the thyroid.

Symbolic animals are the eagle and the peacock.

The symbolic mythical creatures are the unicorn and the dragon.

The musical note is "A."

The scent is cinnamon, clove, sandalwood and balm.

Herbs are narcissus, oak and nutmeg.

The magical image is a Strong and Benevolent King upon his Throne.

Mythological Correspondences include all of the Kings of the Gods.

The spiritual experience is an experience of the Receptical Intelligence and the formula of the tetragramatron.

Now close your eyes, and lay your mandala aside.

Invocation

"May we be encompassed by the power of the name Elohim Gebor and established in the temple of Geburah. May the portal of the 19th Path be opened to us and may we journey thereon in the power of the name Adonai Malek to the gate of the Sphere of Chesed. And in the name of El may the gate of the Sphere of Chesed by opened to us and may we be firmly established in the wonders of that Sphere."

Path

Imagine a beautiful, rich sunset.

The sky is glowing with reds, pinks and purples.

The sun shines through a light cloud cover, its golden rays streaming down from the sky.

You smell the fresh, crisp air and feel the soft breezes moving around you.

The clouds above part and the rays from the sun enfold you completely.

All around you is radiant light. You are engulfed by the light and warmth.

You gradually lose all sensation of your physical body and its weight.

You feel lighter and lighter. You experience a feeling of weightlessness.

You feel that you are being enfolded by a great being of light.

A strong, reassuring presence surrounds you.

It lifts you higher and higher.

You sense that the being lifting you up is an angel; an angel with great, massive wings.

A warm glow, a feeling of security and of love surrounds you.

You continue to float higher and higher and while you rise you're rocking gently back and forth.

It's as if you're in a hammock, swaying back and forth, back and forth.

You feel only warmth and love.

Higher and higher you float, rocking back and forth.

You hear the name, "Kamael!"; "Kamael!" It echoes again, and again. "Kamael!"; "Kamael!" Still, you rise higher and higher for an indeterminate length of time.

The name echoes again and again...."Kamael!" Kamael is the Archangel of Geburah, the "Burner of God." He is the one who burns with affection and zeal. Kamael comes from the base word Kahab, meaning to burn, to suffer, to sadden, or to make war.

All Geburah experiences are of those unable to bear this power.

Kamael provides an assistance to reach the pure divine energy.

Kamael is also called the right hand of God. He is the sword hand of Justice, justice being the restoration of lost balance and harmony.

The sword compels that which refuses the direction of love.

Kamael wages war only to end war. Kamael reigns in the world of creation and so uses Geburah powers constructively, destroying only that which needs to be destroyed.

You are lifted higher and higher still, up to the heavens.

You find yourself looking over a beautiful landscape, seeing the colors of great mother earth and all the time, Kamael is at your side.

You open your inner eyes, to find yourself standing at the base of a pentagram-shaped temple. Massive Corinthian marble columns stand at the five points of the temple. The columns are of ruby red marble, with black veins. They reach skyward.

The interior or the temple is dark and foreboding.

You stand at the base of five steps leading up to the floor of the temple and you smell sulphur and benzoin coming from it.

You freeze at this spot where you find yourself. Your heart is pounding in your chest. It becomes difficult to swallow. Your palms begin to sweat and you feel a compulsion to enter the dark temple.

There is something drawing you in, but you are afraid to take the first step.

Just as the fear reaches a point where you feel your knees are going to give way, you sense a large, muscular warrior with golden armor and a sword of fire standing at your side. Her name is Anathea.

She puts her powerful arm around you and you feel her strength enter your body.

The muscles in your legs, back, arms and neck tighten and you stand erect. You take a deep breath in and as you exhale, you exhale all fear with your breath.

With the next deep breath in, you feel joy and excitement fill your body. You feel strong and courageous again.

You take your first step up and each one thereafter comes effortlessly.

The next thing you realize is that you are standing at the top of the stairs. The temple walls are still red-veined marble inside, but through a large arch you see something gold at the center of the temple. The chamber glows brilliantly red.

You walk toward the center of the temple, with this golden-clad warrior God at your side.

You see red, orange and all flame colors flickering around the walls. It appears that the room is surrounded in massive walls of fire.

Yet, you feel only energy in this chamber, rather than the burning heat that you feared, having associated it with fire in the past.

In the center of the chamber you see a smooth ruby-red altar. It is empty except for a huge golden scale. On one side is the feather of truth, the other side is empty.

The warrior speaks to you now, "The time has come for you to look within your heart, for you to see who you truly are." The Lords of Karma await you. You look around the temple and for the first time you see figures, sitting around the five-sided temple, in red sandstone thrones.

At first these figures appear to be Egyptian, men and women, wearing kilts of black- and yellow-pleated linen. Some have the heads of birds, of wolves or of bears.

Each wears a gold necklace representing a hawk in flight. Each holds a scourge in the right hand.

As you step up to the first assessor the being leans forward and as it does so, it changes form, becoming a glowing orb that has at its center core a fiery serpent.

It feels as if a searchlight has been turned upon you.

There is no place to run, no place to hide.

You have the feeling that this being can see into your heart and mind and only the truth will be seen.

The next assessor leans forward and also changes form.

Each one in turn asks you a question: "Hast thou given due thought to the body inhabited by thee?" "Hast thou lived the fullness of time allotted thee?" "Hast thou ever loved with the body and heart as well?" "Hast thou loved with the body and not the heart?" "Hast thou kept only to the sword or the staff?" "Hast thou respected the bodies of your younger brethren?" "Hast thou stolen?" "Hast thou taken food and drink to excess?" "Hast thou spoken unjustly in anger?" "Hast thou looked upon the goods of others in envy?" "Hast thou known jealousy?" "Hast thou spoken ill of any man or woman in anger?" "Hast thou killed?" "Hast thou profaned the mysteries?" "Hast thou known pride in thyself that is false?" "Hast thou strayed from the path allotted thee?" "Hast thou been too worldly?" "Hast thou lusted after precious metals?" "Hast thou been just in the dealings of the marketplace?" "Hast thou repaid all debts promptly?" "Hast thou been generous to the needy?" "Hast thou lied to gain from others?" "Hast thou spoken like a viper to cause laughter in others?" "Hast thou been a friend?" "Hast thou hated another to the exclusion of all else?" "Hast thou been a joy to thy parents?" "Hast thou honored all faiths that are of the light?" "Hast thou given time to be at peace with the Gods?" "Hast thou turned aside from wisdom given in love?" "Hast thou listened to that which was not for thy ears?" "Hast thou lived in the light?" "Hast thou been a sword for the weak?" "Hast thou enslaved any other life?" "Hast thou faced the mirror of self?" "Hast thou taken the words of another man as thine own?" "Hast thou known all journeys end but to begin?" "Hast thou remembered the brethren of the earth, the animals and been compassionate to thy younger brethren, who have served thee as beasts in the field as well as at home?" "Hast thou ever worked man or beast beyond strength in thy greed?" "Is there one person upon the earth who is glad thou hast lived?"

No one has favorable answers to all of the questions of the assessors. But if just one person is glad you have lived, if you have given joy to just one person, the scales will balance.

The experience of the Assessors has left you feeling weak and ill.

Your soul has been exposed for all to see. For some reason, knowing that you have made just one person happy is not the soothing balm you would like it to be.

The golden-clad warrior, Anathea, is now dressed in a long, flowing white robe. She guides you off to an anteroom on the other side of the temple. The entrance is a large oak door. The sign of the tooth, Teth, is carved in the door, with a dragon below it.

The young maiden leads you in and gives you a golden goblet, of dark red wine.

You take one sip. It is bitter.

You take a second sip. It tastes better than the first.

You sit in deep concentration reviewing your life.

You see yourself as a child. You see your mother. She looks so young.

You remember the happiest times together. You remember the time she held you and told you she loved you, in the way that she knew best.

While you see yourself sitting on her lap, you remember the time that she disappointed you, or possibly hurt you.

You see into her heart and see how she felt and understand how she felt at that time. You understand why she acted the way she did.

You tell her how you feel. How you felt about the way she treated you then.

You take another sip of wine.

Thoughts of your father come to mind.

You see the best time you spent with him. You see him hugging you and telling you how proud he is of you.

You also remember the bad times, when he yelled at you and made you angry.

You can now see his motivation and you can now think as he did then and understand him.

You see your father and you tell him how you feel about the way he treated you as a child.

You take another sip and you see the face of the person you love the most... a person who may have even broken your heart.

You review an experience when you were judged unfairly.

With cold detachment, you review all these experiences and you see into the other person's heart, each time.

You forgive them all. The pain lifts from your heart.

You take a deep breath and all the sorrow lifts.

With each further breath you feel happier and lighter. You feel the energy returning and running through your veins.

You take another sip and stare out to space.

There, before your eyes, a large uncut piece of marble materializes.

You see a ray of light and a rainbow descends from above. It circles around and around on the marble. The light is absorbed by the stone. It glows with an inner radiance.

Your Guide appears and with a hammer and a chisel, one in each hand, she lands a well-aimed blow on the marble. A "perfect you" is released from the marble.

You see yourself as your perfect self; your physical appearance is perfection. You see yourself dealing with your parents, your mate and your children, as objectively and perfectly as you could possibly imagine; as you would like to! You see yourself in complete control, showing love and understanding. You are able to see into these people's hearts, to see what they really need from you; and you give it to them! You put down the golden goblet. You stand and walk across the room. You find a doorway and pull it open to find a large courtyard outside.

It is filled with lush vegetation.

You smell the damp earth and the sweet smell of juniper, laurel and flowers, including peonies, which you see growing around a fountain.

The Sun is shining; you feel the warmth of it. It beats against your body. You feel the energy of it and it feels good.

The sky is a clear, bright blue. There isn't a cloud anywhere.

You hear birds singing their sweet songs; they lighten your heart.

You walk in the garden, feeling renewed and happy to be alive.

There is a spring in your step; you feel refreshed. You have an uncontrollable urge to skip and laugh, like a child.

You are once again a child, running and skipping, carefree, all around this beautiful garden.

Suddenly, off to the side under a large group of ash trees, you see a great, red, lion! He is so large and powerful! He was asleep until he heard you.

He opens his eyes and stares at you for a while. Then he stands up, stretches and yawns. He focuses on you and slowly walks to you.

Closer and closer he comes! You freeze where you are and watch him approach. He comes to within a few feet of you and stares directly into your eyes. His pupils dilate! You stare back at him and instinctively stroke his head. He leans against your leg and you feel his weight and his strength. You continue to stroke and pet him and feel the soft hair of his mane.

You reach under his chin and scratch lovingly. He closes his eyes in contentment and licks your hand with his large, rough tongue.

You feel in complete control of this mighty beast! The two of you begin to run and play in the garden, as if he were a pup. You pick wildflowers, the most abundant being a sunflower, with its bright yellow petals and big black center.

You find a basket, made of vines. Inside are oranges, almonds and walnuts. You eat a few and feed the lion from your hand.

You grow thirsty. Almost simultaneously, Anathea brings you a ceramic jug filled with cool, refreshing liquid. It has a cinnamon taste.

You and the great lion sit under an oak tree. You continue to stroke his head and the two of you drift off to sleep.

The next thing you are aware of, you are alone in a long, narrow hallway. There is brilliant light all around.

The walls appear to be mirrors and they reflect rainbows, in a prism affect. Now you are in a blue and violet section.

You are swiftly moving along this pathway.

At the end of the tunnel you see two crystal doors. They gleam with blue light and as you push them open they ring! An azure light fills the four-sided temple that you step into.

There are stained glass walls and colored light flickers everywhere.

You smell frankincense and myrrh.

The Archangel Zadkiel is standing at the entrance. He wears a blue and pale yellow robe that flows in the breeze.

He is surrounded by the Chasmalim - the Choir of Angels known as the bright, shining ones. They are the fiery beings with the power of speech.

They line up at the violet section at the edge of the Sphere of blue light. They are warming and project the comfort of fire. They are laughter, one of the unpronounceable names of God. They bring you comfort and hope in times of trouble. Their goal is to keep you and all of us, ever mindful of advancing upward on the tree of life.

They begin to giggle. You are overwhelmed by their lightheartedness. It is difficult for you to keep a smile off of your face.

Zadkiel is the Angel that whispered in your ear as your soul descended into this incarnation. Zadkiel whispered how you should behave in this lifetime. But that memory has faded.

On your soul's journey back to God, your behavior is measured against what should have been.

Zadkiel and Kamiel are the Angels of judgment.

Zadkiel reminds you that mercy is nearer divinity than light.

Zadkiel is responsible for converting wrongs back to rights.

You look around and you see a great King, sitting on a throne of amethyst. He wears a crown of sapphire and diamonds. He stands and struts, to straighten his long violet robe trimmed in gold. His face shows exuberance and youth and the knowledge, tolerance and kindness that come with great age.

He looks at you with compassion and loving kindness.

He tells you that no matter how severe your tests and trials may be in this lifetime, mercy and benevolence ultimately awaits you.

You must strive for balance. Righteousness, prosperity and happiness are the results of right conduct, integrity and goodness.

Material wealth will be yours for the asking, but there is a price that must be paid. If you attempt to hold on to abundance it will choke you. Material wealth is scarcely fair compensation for spiritual poverty.

All these truths will come to you like a second nature, when you are ready for them. These are just a glimpse of the Sphere of Chesed.

You must now return from whence you came, and you will return back to this Sphere of Chesed at a later time when you are ready.

You walk back down the hallway leading to the blue crystal doors and the entrance of Chesed. The Sun streams through the glass walls.

You are able to look through the windows into a courtyard and there, standing under a maple tree, is a beautiful unicorn.

She looks up at you and lowers her head, as if in greeting. She sways her long white tail with joy. Around her neck is a wreath of narcissus.

You find the entrance of the courtyard and run to her side. She kneels down and allows you to jump onto her back. She strolls with you around the yard.

You feel as though you belong on her back, the two of you moving as one.

She begins to gallop around and around, faster and faster. The next thing you know you are flying, soaring on the air currents like a seagull.

The Temple of Chesed gets smaller and smaller in the distance.

You sail higher and higher upon the unicorn's back.

Suddenly, she swoops downward and you fall off her back.

Down, down, down and then, Zadkiel is at your side, slowing your descent.

You feel like a leaf, floating downward, around and around.

Until, once again, you see that beautiful sunset and you drift back to consciousness.

And so ends the 19th Path.

Path Journal

A. Record your emotional reactions to your path experiences here, immediately upon completion. Include any physical responses or sensations.

Date of completion: _____

Emotional responses: _____

_____

_____

Physical reactions: _____

_____

_____

What do you think these responses indicate? _____

_____

_____

B. Use this section as a diary of your experiences during the week following your completion of the path. Be sure to include how you react to things emotionally, as well as how you deal with any major issues that might arise.

Day 1: _____

_____

Day 2: _____

_____

Day 3: _____

_____

Day 4: _____

_____

Day 5: _____

_____

Day 6: _____

_____

Day 7: _____

_____

C. Review the week's experiences. How has the path affected the way you handled this week's issues? _____

_____

_____

_____

D. What special dreams has this path stimulated this week? _____

_____

_____

_____

Areas Path 19 Will Help You Work On

- The ability to feel and manipulate energy

- Understanding that self-acceptance leads to inner peace

- Trusting in yourself and your Guides

- Developing a sense of "gladness" at being alive, and sharing that "aliveness" with others

- Self-acceptance; you are perfect as you are

- Self-knowledge - recognizing that you have come a long way

- Cleansing - letting go of emotional blocks; being able to bring up the past and let it go

- Self-healing

- Inner-knowingness

- The ability to fulfill others' "real" needs, whether they are conscious of them or not

- Releasing your latent power and energy - empowerment

- Internal vision - being able to see inside of someone

- Precognition - the ability to foresee events

- Cognition - development of higher mental powers

- Awareness that transcends the barriers of time

- Understanding that mistakes are okay and are part of what has made you the "you" that you would not want to change; the ability to face yourself

- Knowledge that your Guides are always there to help

- Physical readjustment of your body and nervous system to accept new patterns of energy

- Opening your Throat Center

- Stimulation of your Third Eye Center

- Helping your balance and equilibrium, both physical and emotional

- Increasing psychic ability by surmounting the ego

- Learning objectivity to your humanness; acceptance of the "lower nature" in yourself and others

- The ability to forgive; mercy and understanding

- Clairaudience and clairsentience

- Accepting and dealing with Mom and Dad

- Taking everyone in your life "off the pedestal," and allowing them the freedom to be who they are

- The ability to know what you feel and communicate it, even when it's something that others do not want to hear

- Enhancement of memory

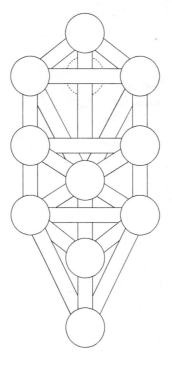

Path 18

Correspondences

— Sphere of Geburah —

We commence our journey in the Sphere of Geburah, the Radical Intelligence, called Strength.

The Divine name is Elohim Gebor, the Mighty God.

The Archangel is Kamael, Prince of Strength and Courage.

The Order of Angels is the Seraphim or the Flaming Ones who are called the Order of Powers.

The element is fire.

Symbols are the pentagram, the pentagon, the sword, the horse, the wolf and the warrior driving his chariot.

The stone is ruby.

The musical note is "G."

The mineral is iron.

Plants are absynth, rue and lambs tongue.

The incense is benzoin, sulphur or tobacco.

The planet is Mars.

The color is scarlet.

The body part is the right arm.

The chakra is the Throat Center.

The corresponding gland is the thyroid.

The magical image is a warrior in his chariot.

The mythological correspondences include all warrior Gods, among whom are Greek Athena, Roman Mars and Norse Thor.

The spiritual expression is a vision of power.

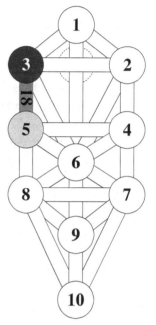

— 18th Path —

The 18th Path is called the House of Influence by the greatness of whose abundance the influx of good things upon created beings is increased; and from the midst of the investigation the hidden senses are drawn forth which dwell in its shade and which cling to it from the cause of all causes.

The Hebrew name is Cheth, which means a fence or enclosure.

The simple form of the letter means speech.

The Esoteric Title is the Child of the Powers of the Waters, the Lord of the Triumph of Light.

The color is red-orange.

The element is water.

The planet is the Moon.
The corresponding astrological sign is Cancer.
The incense is anise or camphor.
The metal is silver.
The gem is the emerald or the truquoise.
Plants or herbs are lotus, comfrey, honeysuckle and daisy.
Symbolic animals are the crab and the turtle.
The Tarot Major Arcanum card is the Chariot.

— Sphere of Binah —

The Sphere of Destination is Binah, the Sanctifying Intelligence, known as Understanding.
The Hebrew Divine Name is Jehovah Elohim, the perfection of Creation and the Life of the World to Come.
The Archangel is Tzaphqiel, the Prince of the Spiritual Strife against Evil.
The Order of Angels is the Aralim, the Strong and Mighty Ones who are also called the Order of Thrones.
The element is water.
The musical note is "B."
The stone is black opal or tourmaline.
The plants are comfrey, fern, hemlock, ivy, hemp, mulien and musk.
The color is dark brown or black.
The planet is Saturn.
The body part is the right side of the face.
The chakra is the Third Eye Center.
The corresponding gland is the pineal.
The magical image is a mature woman.
The mythological figures include the Christian Mary, the Greek Mara, Roman Mara, Egyptian Isis and all Mother-Goddesses.
The spiritual experience of Binah is a vision of Sorrow.

Invocation

"May we be encompassed by the name Elohim Gebor and be firmly established in the Sphere of Geburah. May the portal of the 18th path be opened to us and may we journey thereon by the power of the name Shaddai Al Chai through the Abyss of Daath and onward to the Gate of Binah and in the name of Jehovah Elohim may the gate of Binah be opened to us and may we be firmly established in the wonders of that Sphere."

Path

You open your inner eyes and find yourself standing in the Hall of Justice.

The Hall is called Geburah.

The twin sphinxes that guard the way into the temple stand before you.

They turn their heads toward you.

But they recognize that you have a right to be here and also that you have been here before.

They settle down once again and let you pass.

You move further into the hall.

You find a deep scarlet wall and an altar in the center of the Hall.

On the altar is a sword of flame. You stand before it and gaze deeply into the glowing color.

You have no sensation of heat, only pleasant warmth that fills you with energy; and when the flame dies down, you find that you are standing again by the pillars at the door of the Temple.

Waiting for you is the Lord of Triumph in his Chariot. He is dressed as a warrior, clad in armor, with crescent moons decorating either shoulder.

The crescent moon on his left shoulder is for mercy and the one on his right shoulder is for severity. The side of mercy smiles, whereas the side of severity frowns.

He wears a breastplate of greenish-yellow, simulating brass, the metal of Venus. It symbolizes the protection afforded by the right use of power and compassion.

There is also a square on his breastplate. It represents order and purity.

The scepter he carries is surmounted by a figure eight combined with a crescent.

He is the Charioteer and he carries his symbol of authority. It shows that dominion is the result of a blending of the powers of self-consciousness and the subconscious.

His chariot is cubic in shape, with four pillars and starry draperies and two sphinxes, one black and one white, joined at the haunches are harness to it. They pull in opposite directions, yet they look the same way.

You move onto the Chariot and stand next to the Lord of Triumph; as the sphinxes move forward you begin to travel the 18th Path.

You move out onto a vast plain.

As you travel, you see walled cities scattered over the plain.

You draw near to the first one.

You see many people lining the walls and battlements. They cheer and wave. They welcome you. You realize that they expect you to lay claim to their forgotten and long neglected city and repair it! You move into the city.

Inside, you see slums. Torn down buildings and decay surround you. The people are starving.

The royal palace itself is as bad as the rest of the city. The ruler has long been gone. No one is in power to run things here.

The people look toward you.

They want you to make their city happy and prosperous once again.

You are in shock! You are overwhelmed by the hard work ahead of you. You think of the unknown pitfalls and hurdles awaiting you.

You must think, think back and call upon your past experience! You move in your mind, back, back, to Malkuth - and you march again along the Path from Malkuth to Yesod, taking with you the intelligence of that path and those Spheres.

You move to Hod, then to Netzach, then to Tiphareth, on to Geburah and then to Chesed - and you gather about you all of the collective understandings of your past experiences as you've moved up the Tree of Life.

You feel filled with the pure physical empowerment of your experiences.

Your mind is crisp and clear.

Your drive and your understanding are complete and clear.

You find plans for the architecture simple to derive.

You have full use of your intuition. You balance and you unbalance. You understand the total necessity of rebuilding and the means of doing it.

You understand that it is your desire to better mankind, to serve mankind, even if it is at the expense of rebuilding yourself.

You understand that it is through infinite love and mercy that you exist.

Slowly now, you watch the city take on real shape and form.

Now walls are built. They enclose the city in strong arms.

They are just like a crab shell, protecting the soft inner body of the creature. Or like a turtle, protected by the hard shell within which the turtle lives.

The city is protected by its wall, the creature within its shell - just like you. You are the soul within the wall of your physical body.

All of these walls are vehicles to protect the being within and to transport that being through a world of learning, just like the chariot, which is a portable wall, or barrier, just like the warrior wearing armor.

The self is divided and the chariot is the body. It is guided by the intellect. As the charioteer, drawn by the senses, seen as the powerful sphinxes, can only move forward when those same beasts are controlled by the mind, you've driven your vehicle over the course of your experience.

In the center of the city is a place of worship.

You move to it. At this point the Lord of Triumph says goodbye to you. As he leaves, two Archangels appear.

They are Kamael and Michael. They look deadly grave. They open the door of the temple to you.

The singing winds become subdued even as their song continues, as inside you perceive silence and an acceptance of the impossible burden.

Kamael and Michael, in a deep voice begin vibrating: Aralim..... Aralim..... Aralim..... And within the dark and cool temple before you, between pillars of ebony you now see a beautiful and veiled woman.

The pillars around her bear the sign of cancer, the crab. She wears the sigil of the moon. The wind sings and becomes a vibration of sorrow.

It is too much for humankind to bear. You feel sad and cold.

Tears pour down your face. Your heart feels as if it's pierced by swords and spears.

You are enveloped by pain and darkness. You almost cannot move on. Only the vision of the Archangels can lift you up, and even they cannot remain unchanged at this level of being.

As you watch them, the form you have known them as for so long transmutes. You see them become great pillars of flame.

Then, their transmutation continues as they become great spears of pulsating light in violet, orange and scarlet and then, as you watch, they finally disappear from your sight, but you feel them as a combination of sound and mind and as a single vibration of beinglessness that contains the absolute essence of what they are.

You know that they are still with you as a protection for your frail humanity. They carry you upward as the winds die down, until about you is utter silence.

The silence around you extends in every direction.

You can't see the Temple.

You can no longer see the Angels.

You can no longer hear the wind.

There is no form, no shape, and no color.

There is nothing about you except space itself.

Utter blackness presses in upon you.

You have no body.

You feel nothing.

You are conscious of no sensation.

You are alone with the angels.

You and they, together, transmuted in this vast, formless, nothingness.

You are in the void of pure empty space.

You wait.

At first, you think, you are in a womb, waiting to be born and so you wait.

Still, nothing happens. Nothing.

What are you waiting for? Why are you waiting? You become impatient, angry. You are filled with resentment and doubt. Boredom sets in. You want to scream, but you have no voice, no lungs, no being.

What is there to do in here? You look about, but still you hear nothing, you see nothing, you feel nothing.

Maybe you should be doing something yourself? Is this a test? Your mind becomes distracted by your thoughts.

You begin a train of thoughts that you cannot stop! You become disturbed, upset and restless.

Why are you wasting time? Why are you wasting energy? After what appears an eternity a thought seeps through into your mind.

It is an answer, an answer given to you by the Archangels from the supernal world.

They have tried and tried to contact you through your mind, but you, with your busy mind, were too busy with your thoughts to hear.

The answer is "YOU are the slave of time, as are all humanity." Here you are in the Sphere of Binah, in the world of the Supernals. Time has not yet come into existence. There is no past, there is no present, and there is no future! It is your own sense of time passing that creates your anxiety.

You experience Time, Silence Understanding and Acceptance. These are the lessons and the experiences of Binah.

You exist in a pure form here.

You are held in the timeless, spaceless Sphere of Binah and you must allow yourself to just "be."

You have not been born. Nor will you be born for millions of years.

Yet you have been born and you've lived through millions of lives! You are not the chariot, but the soul that is encased in it.

You are not the shell of the turtle, but the creature within its shell.

You are not the hard shell of the crab, but the soft being that is protected by it! These vehicles, these cases are for your transport, they transport you through countless lifetimes of learning experiences.

This is the understanding of the Supernal Mother.

This is the understanding of the Sorrowful Mother.

She watches us all.

She watches our difficulty separating the Self from the Personality.

She is the sorrowful Mother, going through the birthing, the rebirthing and birthing again.

We all limit ourselves in a time capsule, in a space capsule.

But knowing the casing of the crab, the hard shell of the turtle, and the body of the soul can be separated from the gentle, pure being that it is encasing helps us to go on.

You can dismiss your earthly experience of suffering and pain and of time from your mind.

No matter how terrible is the sight, how deep is the pain, how long is the suffering, the trial will be over.

All you have to do is step out of the chariot that is your body and here you are one with the Archangels, one with the Mother.

It is by feeling and by reaching out with all of your senses that you may feel their presence and their oneness.

With this knowledge and understanding you once again grow awareness.

You feel yourself growing again within your physical mother! You find a link to your divine heritage.

A point of light grows in the darkness and, with the help of the Archangels; you have been through this genesis of the spirit.

Gently, you inch toward the opening in the womb of manifestation, knowing you may return to the root of your beingness when you need to.

You know the answer will come if you give it a chance! You feel the weight of your physical body and its five senses returning. Your awareness gradually returns to the present. You have gained the knowledge to view life with your Supernal Eyes!

And so ends the 18th Path.

Path Journal

A. Record your emotional reactions to your path experiences here, immediately upon completion. Include any physical responses or sensations.

Date of completion: _____

Emotional responses: _____
_____
_____

Physical reactions: _____
_____
_____

What do you think these responses indicate? _____
_____
_____

B. Use this section as a diary of your experiences during the week following your completion of the path. Be sure to include how you react to things emotionally, as well as how you deal with any major issues that might arise.

Day 1: _____
_____

Day 2: _____
_____

Day 3: _____
_____

Day 4: _____
_____

Day 5: _____
_____

Day 6: _____

_____

Day 7: _____

_____

C. Review the week's experiences. How has the path affected the way you handled this week's issues? _____

_____

_____

_____

D. What special dreams has this path stimulated this week? _____

_____

_____

_____

Areas Path 18 Will Help You Work On

- Learning to direct your attention inward toward self-knowledge through sensory deprivation

- Learning that the absence of the physical is restful

- Meditation; finding your inner still-point

- Acknowledgement of your extrasensory perceptions

- Acknowledgement that the real self is the "being" that lives within the "wall" of the physical self; discovery of the soul within

- Discovering a greater reality; seeing your Self as a being separate from both the body and the mind, with the power of omniscience that occurs only when the seat of consciousness rises to Binah

- Astral traveling into the higher realms

- Understanding that you already possess all that you need

- Understanding that you are part of a collective whole, and must work together to advance

- Understanding that restriction or freedom is your own choice

- Dealing with your impatience

- Dealing with the limitations of time and space; understanding that time is an illusion; ability to astral travel beyond the limits of time and space

- Releasing expectation

- The "wall" you have created around you allows you to increase your energy toward a specific objective

- Understanding that each person is made up of lifetimes of experience, unknown to others; the journey the soul is on through these lifetimes is known only to it; therefore, we have no right to judge others, nor do they have a right to judge us

- Gaining objectivity and clarity concerning your life patterns and goals

- Understanding that removing the "walls" you have constructed releases energy, and allows you to continue to grow; the ability to let go of what you have built

- Understanding that the "walls" we create maintain our energy and the structure of our lives

- Increased desire to grow beyond your own limitations

- Increased desire to serve and help others, coming from a feeling of detached nurturance, not feelings of responsibility for them

- Proficiency in dealing with physical plane matters

- The ability to deal with people and situations that encroach upon your "boundaries"

- Stimulation of the Third Eye Center

- Stimulation of the Crown Center

- Precognition increased as well as channeling ability

- Ability to conserve your energy and organize your resources

- Being able to call upon your past experience, from this and other lives, as well as previous paths

- Understanding that "everything is as it should be"

- Acceptance of responsibility

- Conquering your fears of the unknown

- Giving up your sorrow

"Man, Know Thyself"

Path 17

Correspondences

— Sphere of Tiphareth —

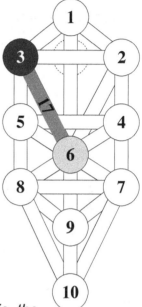

We begin our journey in Tiphareth, Beauty.

The Hebrew Divine name is Jehovah Aloah Va Daath.

It is known as the Mediating Intelligence.

The Archangel is Raphael, Prince of Brightness, Beauty and life.

The Order of Angels is the Melachim, the Angelic Kings called the Order of Virtues, Angels and Rulers.

The corresponding planet is the Sun.

The number is 6.

Symbols of Tiphareth are the Calvary Cross, the Rose Cross, the Truncated Pyramid and the Cube.

Elements are air and spirit.

Stones are topaz and diamond.

The metal is gold.

The color is yellow.

Rhe corresponding body part is the breast.

The corresponding chakra is the Heart Center and the gland is the thymus.

Living beings are the lion, the child, and the phoenix.

The symbolic creature is the sparrow-hawk.

The musical note is "F."

The scents are aloe, cinnamon and clove.

Herbs are angelica, almond, frankincense and myrrh.

The magical image is a Majestic King, a Child or a Sacrificed God.

The mythical correspondences are all of the Sacrificed Gods.

The spiritual experience is a vision of the Harmony of things and of healing and redemption; the "Christ Consciousness."

— 17th Path —

The 17th Path is known in Hebrew by the Divine name of Zain.

It is called the Disposing Intelligence, which provides faith to the righteous.

The letter Zain is the final fertilizing act, the sword or armor.

The planetary ruler of the Path is Mercury.

The corresponding astrological sign to the Path is Gemini.

The Tarot Major Arcanum Key is the Lovers.

This Path rules the sense of smell and also the hands and body extremities.

The Esoteric Title is the Children of the Voice, the Oracle of the Mighty Gods.

The Mythological Correspondences on the Path include all of the sacrificed Gods because to successfully complete the Path requires even the "death" of one's own higher self!

The color is orange.

Herbs are wormwood and cinnamon.

Stones are alexandrite and tourmaline.

The musical note is "D."

— Sphere of Binah —

We conclude our journey in the Sphere of Binah, Understanding.

The Hebrew Divine Name is Jehovah Elohim, the perfection of Creation and the Life of the World to Come.

She is known as the "Sanctifying Intelligence."

The Archangel is Tzaphqiel, the Prince of Spiritual Strife against Evil.

The Order of Angels is the Aralim, or Thrones, the strong and mighty Ones.

Binah corresponds in man to the right side of the face.

She is known as the Great Mother in all her forms, as Ama, the dark and sterile mother and as Aima, the bright and fertile mother. She is Mara, the great sea of the unconscious.

Binah is form, the container of force.

Her planet is Saturn.

Her stones are onyx and sapphire.

Her incense is civet, musk, ivy or nightshade.

Her musical note is "B."

Her sound is the deep sympathetic sound of the cello, or rainfall.

Her color is black.

Her symbols are the yoni, the triangle, the cup and heh.

Mythological Correspondences are all of the "Mother" Goddesses.

The spiritual experience is stillness.

Now, lay aside your mandala and hold its image before your closed eyes.

Invocation

"May we be encompassed by the name Jehovah Aloah Va Daath and be established in the Sphere of Tiphareth. May the portal of the 17th Path be opened to us and may we journey thereon by the power of the name Elohim Saboath through the Abyss of Daath - and onward to the Gate of Binah and in the name of Jehovah Elohim may the gate of Binah be opened to us and may we be firmly established in the wonders of that Sphere."

Path

You come to awareness in a field of sunflowers. It is a beautiful summer day.

In the field you find a dirt path of soft earth. You walk along it, noticing the faint odor of cinnamon and cloves.

As you walk further toward the south, the sun becomes brighter and brighter and you find yourself at the base of a great temple.

It is made of topaz stone, a brilliant yellow in color and it is studded with diamonds.

Above the doorway to the temple, the following words are carved: "Man, Know Thy Self!" At the front opening, on either side, is a great lion.

You walk inside.

The air within is filled with the sweet scent of cloves mixed with cinnamon and myrrh.

The temple has six walls made of polished gold.

At the farthest wall in front of you, you see a crucifix with the body of a young man on it. To your right you see a small child and to your left you see a beautiful king wearing orange robes and a golden crown.

Then, these three images disappear.

You find yourself drawn to the center of the Temple. The air around you seems to be ablaze with fire.

Around you are seven large stones. On top of each stone is a figure.

Starting at your right side, the first figure is a king. You can see his full face and he has a beard.

To his left is an old woman dressed in black and holding a cup.

Continuing on to the left, moving counterclockwise around, you see next a king cloaked in blue and seated on a high throne with an eagle on his shoulder.

Next to him is a great warrior in full armor in his chariot.

The next figure is a beautiful nude woman with a dove in one hand.

She is followed by a huntress with a bow and arrow.

Lastly, your eyes come to rest on an androgynous figure with a snake coiled around each arm.

As you watch the figures begin to circle counterclockwise around you, the fire you feel about you begins to blaze within you.

It pushes up from your feet to the top of your head.

You lose awareness of your body and become a spindle of white light.

The figures around you fade into Spheres of white light, like planets circling you, circling counterclockwise.

The Spheres are spinning faster and faster and you, as the center spindle of white light, are holding them in balance.

Experience this state of balance.

Suddenly, you find yourself standing alone.

You're aware of your body, but a veil covers your eyes as you try to see where you are.

Gradually, you see an amusement park before you.

You see lots of people and you're surrounded by noises from vendors and sideshows and people screaming and yelling as they ride the amusements.

In the distance you see a ferris wheel. You move closer, there's something that attracts you to it. It has twelve spokes and only two seats. You seem drawn toward it.

You walk to it and get on the first seat. The Ferris wheel begins to slowly carry you upward and around.

You find yourself falling asleep to the slow, even motion of the wheel's turning. When you finally return to wakefulness, it is dark.

At first there is no sense of where you are; you have no perceptions.

Then, you begin to feel the pressure of soil all around you. You try to feel your own body and you cannot. All you can sense is a small kernel of self surrounded by the enclosing soil.

Then finally, you realize that you are a tiny, little seed under the earth.

You are at first warm and protected with a feeling of being nurtured by the earth covering you, but then you feel the need to push upward toward the surface, toward where you sense there may be light.

With great force, you burst through the top of the earth.

The exhilaration of the experience is such that you keep growing now, taller and taller, toward the light.

It begins to rain.

At first you don't notice, because you're so concerned with growing up and up. You don't accept the nurturance of the rain, as you're not aware of it.

You start to wither. You become cracked and dry.

Realizing that the only way to survive is to stop growing upward and soak in the rain water, you become still. In your stillness you blossom into a flower as the refreshing water is soaked into your parts.

The image fades and forgetting what has happened, you find yourself on the Ferris wheel again. This time, though, you're in the second chair.

Around and around the Ferris wheel goes and with the gentle turning of the wheel you fall asleep again.

Awakening, you find yourself in a great forest.

You look around you to find beautiful foliage and lush greenery.

A cool breeze soothes your bark.

Bark!? You suddenly realized that you are a tree! The beautiful foliage is your own and you can feel roots extending deep into the earth.

Feel the strength and grandeur of the great tree! A wind comes from the south into the forest. All the animals are running. The leaves are rustling and tearing from your branches.

They are flying around on the wind currents about you as the full force of a storm gale hits the forest. You see other trees falling around you, and cracking in the storm.

You don't want to fall, but the harder you try to resist the wind the more of your branches rip off of you.

You struggle against it.

Finally, aware of the futility of your struggle, you accept and stop resisting the wind. In your acceptance you bend and twist and accept your fate and discover at the end of the storm that you are still standing.

Again, the image fades and you forget.

You find yourself at the carnival once again.

But this time you're not on the Ferris wheel anymore.

You are walking among the people. Booth by booth you travel through the crowd.

You see a large gathering of people in front of a man in brightly colored orange and yellow clothes who is swallowing swords. The shining silver of the sword mesmerizes you.

The man is standing in a ring of twelve flames. You are almost hypnotized by this image and as you stare, the world around you fades to darkness again.

The image of the carnival is gone! You are suspended in a black place devoid of time. In front of you lies a giant sword of silver. You are standing on its handle. As you look down, you see the handle is carved of opal and agate.

On either side of the sword is a huge pillar with no top and no base that can be seen. They seem, in fact, to stretch both up and down into infinity.

Each pillar is entwined by a giant snake.

The sweet smell of lavender hangs in the air. There is still just a faint memory of cinnamon and cloves as well.

Ahead of you, you see people walking along the flat surface of the sword. You notice that some jump off to an unknown fate, but they willingly go.

You choose to go forward, inching along the sword, one foot at a time, placing your foot carefully along the two sharp edges.

You look down. Still, all is blackness. The air is almost thick and liquid and black.

Beneath you, far below, great fissures open and close and engulf the people that have fallen down or jumped from this point.

When the fissures open, a stench rises from the bowels of the universe.

Screaming and inhuman screeches pierce the air.

As you inch your way across the sword, the howling from below evokes images of all the horrors human kind has ever known.

Images of destruction, of evil, of murder and war, rise in your mind like the stench rising from below.

You inch your way further and further across the sword.

Deep in your heart you feel the sorrow of every soul that will ever be, or has ever been. The fear of the fissures below and the weight of the sorrow you feel in your heart are so all-encompassing that just as you reach the end of the sword, your conscious mind breaks! Becoming aware again, you find yourself surrounded by a mist.

It's warm and soft, but not familiar.

Above you is the faint image of a man hanging upside down.

His legs are folded in the symbol of a cross. On his forehead appears a tiny flicker of flame.

The flame drips off of him, floats through the air toward you and enters the top of your head. It reaches into your body and travels slowly down your spine. As it goes down, you find yourself energized with the fire.

It reaches the base of your spine and you feel it pulling back up again, toward your head.

As the flame moves upward, the sorrow you felt from before is gone and a deep sense of understanding of what you have just experienced fills you.

Finally the flame, by its own power, bursts out the top of your head; you feel a total evaporation of your physical body.

It has been purged! You feel a relief and merge yourself into the mist around you! Becoming aware of a building floating in front of you, you WILL yourself, as pure energy, toward it.

The building is a temple made of onyx stone. On one side of the doorway stands a dragon and on the other side is a black crow.

You WILL yourself inside.

Once inside, you see walls made of indigo colored sapphire. There are eight sections in each of three walls. In the air is the heavy fragrance of musk.

In the center of the temple is a large chest made of lead. You move to it and look in. In it is a pool of water that grows larger and fills your vision as you look.

You lose the image of the temple and the chest and just see the ocean, broad, deep and so dark it's almost black.

In it you see the faint figure of an old woman. She seems familiar.

In one hand she holds a cup.

The expression on her face is not an inviting one, but you dive into the water anyway.

The pure consciousness you were experiencing is immersed in the rushing waters of dark sea.

After a while you cannot see a distinction between the sea and you.

And so ends the 17th Path.

Path Journal

A. Record your emotional reactions to your path experiences here, immediately upon completion. Include any physical responses or sensations.

Date of completion: _____

Emotional responses: _____
_____
_____

Physical reactions: _____
_____
_____

What do you think these responses indicate? _____
_____
_____

B. Use this section as a diary of your experiences during the week following your completion of the path. Be sure to include how you react to things emotionally, as well as how you deal with any major issues that might arise.

Day 1: _____

_____

Day 2: _____

_____

Day 3: _____

_____

Day 4: _____

_____

Day 5: _____

_____

Day 6: _____

_____

Day 7: _____

_____

C. Review the week's experiences. How has the path affected the way you handled this week's issues? _____

_____

_____

_____

D. What special dreams has this path stimulated this week? _____

_____

_____

_____

Areas Path 17 Will Help You Work On

- The ability to detach from the material world

- Being able to generate feelings of peace, harmony, joyousness, and attunement

- Being accepted

- Knowing that the more evolved you become, the narrower your path becomes; you walk the "razor's edge"

- Understanding patterns and karma

- Understanding that we lose awareness of our past lives with each incarnation until we leave our bodily attachment behind; past life recall

- Understanding that to gain control of any patterns we must first understand them

- Increasing the energy you can draw in and project out

- Grounding, stabilizing, with flexibility

- Learning to accept nurturance without obligation

- Being able to "merge" without resistance

- Freeing energy through the releasing of expectation

- Astral traveling and dream enhancement

- Merging with and accepting your feminine nature

- Enhancement of all of your physical and psychic senses

- Understanding that the clearer you are, the lighter you are, and the higher the planes that you can access

- You always have control - knowing that it is your free will to decide to repeat a pattern or to change it

- Being able to surmount the "group mind" and merge with the "universal mind"

- Feelings of "coming home;" being able to relax totally in your current situation

- Being able to "let go" and have fun

- Self-healing

- Inner stillness

- Opening the Heart, Throat, and Third Eye Centers

- Conservation

- Understanding that, "All the world is a stage, and life is a circus"

- "Waking up" - coming to an awareness of a higher awareness
- Being able to recognize yourself in all things
- Understanding opposites, and the principles underlying discrimination
- Understanding and finding the soul mate

Path 16

Correspondences

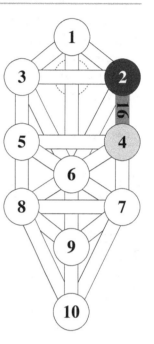

— Sphere of Chesed —

We commence our journey in the Sphere of Chesed, Glory.

It is known as the Measuring, Cohesive, or Receptacular Intelligence because it fashioneth the images of material things, bestowing peace and mercy.

The Hebrew Divine Name is El, the Strong and Mighty God, ruling in Glory, Magnificence and Grace.

The Archangel is Tzadqiel, the Prince of Mercy and Beneficence, called the Justice of God.

The Order of Angels is the Chasmalim, the Brilliant Ones, who are also called the Order of Dominations.

The planet that corresponds to this Sphere is Jupiter.

The number is 4.

The Tarot card correspondences are the four fours.

The element is fire, in water.

The color is blue.

The metal is tin.

The stone is amethyst or sapphire.

The musical note is "A."

The incense is cedar, nutmeg and clove.

The body part is the left arm.

The chakra is the Throat Center and the gland is the thyroid.

Symbols are the tetrahedron, the equal armed cross, the Orb, the wand and the scepter.

The magical image is of a mighty crowned and throned King.

The living beings are eagles and lions, dragons and bulls.

The mythical being is the unicorn.

Mythological correspondences are all of the God-Kings.

The mystical experience of the Sphere is a vision of love.

— 16th Path —

The 16th Path is known as the Triumphal or Eternal Intelligence, so called because it is the pleasure of the Glory, beyond which is no other Glory like to it and it is called also the Paradise prepared for the Righteous.

The Hebrew letter is Vau, meaning nail or hook.

The meaning of the simple letter is hearing.

The Esoteric Title is the Magus of the Eternal.

The element is fixed earth.
The astrological sign is Taurus.
The Tarot Major Arcanum card is the Heirophant.
The color is a red-orange.
The musical note is "C#."
The stones are topaz or emerald.
The symbols are the vau cross and the staff.
The incenses are storax, rose, myrtle, fennel and vervain.
The living creatures are doves.
The mystical and spiritual experiences on the Path are meeting teachers and guides,
angels and those that have gone before you.
Also, judgment and passing on all of your acquisitions to others.
The magical phenomenon is laughter and a vision of the self perfected.

— Sphere of Chokmah —

Our Sphere of destination is Chokmah, the Divine, Ideal Wisdom.
It is known as the Illuminating Intelligence.
The Hebrew Divine Names are Yah, Tetragramaton, or Jehovah.
The Archangel is Ratziel, the Prince of Princes of the knowledge of hidden and
concealed things.
The Order of Angels is the Auphanium, the Wheels or Whirling Forces, which are also
called the order of Kerubim.
The Zodiacal influence is space; the entire Sphere of the Zodiac.
The number is 2; the second Glory.
The Tarot card correspondences are the four twos and the Kings.
The element is fire in fire.
The color is grey.
The scent is musk.
The herb is amaranth.
The stones are star ruby and turquoise.
The metal is uranium.
The living being is man.
The symbols are the phallus, the tower, the wand, the line, the hexagram and the circle.
The body part is the left side of the face.
The chakra is the Third Eye Center and the gland is the pineal.
The magical and mystical experiences are those of a vision of God face to face and a
flash of mystical Light.

Invocation

"May we be encompassed by the power of the name El and established in the Temple of Chesed, Love and Mercy; may the portal of the 16th Path be opened to us and may we journey thereon in the power of the name Jehovah Tzabaoth, through the mighty

Abyss at Daath, to the Gate of the Sphere of Chokmah. And, in the name of Jehovah, may the Gate of Chokmah be opened to us and may we be firmly established in the wonders of that Sphere."

Path

You slowly open your inner eyes.

You find yourself in a garden; everything about you is lush and green.

There are pools and running streams, with beautiful foliage and flowers surrounding them.

Animals of all kinds play in the grass areas about you and you see the shadows of fish moving through the water.

A pair of doves calls to each other and the air is filled with the songs of love birds.

You set out to explore.

This is a place of great opulence. You see nature unfolding all of her bounty about you.

You leave the garden, to continue your exploration.

Outside, you see tall, large buildings, filled with all manner of comforts and treasures.

You begin to wander through a city of glistening beauty.

Everything about you is grand and glorious.

All of the people you pass are happy. You see their smiles.

They are loyal citizens of a benevolent and responsible nation.

The arts flourish here. The people are free of material needs and so you see that their minds and hearts are free to grow spiritually.

You think to yourself that the ruler of this land must indeed be benevolent! But then, you turn down a side street and you see the other side of this benevolence.

Shopkeepers raise the prices on their stands to whatever the market will bear! They are hoarding their profits, until they seem to choke on the excess! On a street corner, a group of youths sits in boredom, throwing stones. They don't seek to find employment; they know "the system" will take care of them! Their very minds are deteriorating.

You see beautiful pieces of art and literature thrown away indiscriminately, to float in the sewage of the gutters.

You see a veritable river of sewage flowing by at your feet.

You are profoundly disturbed. You realize that all are not ready to receive the opulence and the benevolence supplied by this ruler! You begin to realize that benevolence and generosity without balance can be as dangerous as tyranny and miserliness.

Look now, deep within yourself and recognize the tenuous balance of these characteristics within yourself. To balance them requires great wisdom.

Look deeply.

You realize that the more you give away, the more you give of yourself, the more will come to you.

Hoarding will choke you, as it did the shopkeepers. It will forestall you and cause you to deteriorate.

Yet, in giving, you must have wisdom, or your gifts will cause more harm than good.

This is a part of the balance of Chesed and Geburah! You become aware, again, of your surroundings.

The river of sewage is gone.

In its place is a blue Temple. It is surrounded by lush tropical gardens. Unicorns in sculptured relief adorn its sapphire walls.

The Chasmalim, the Order of Angels of the Sphere of Chesed surround the Temple and their joyous laughter fills the air.

Your spirit is uplifted, the laughter of the Chasmalim relaxes you and you begin to feel the same joy and lightheartedness in yourself.

You feel completely whole again and fully united within yourself, but also with all those about you and whose lives you have touched.

You look toward the Temple. Rising toward its door are seven steps. You recognize the steps. You see that each one represents one of the lower Sephiroh you have passed through to attain this level of being.

You mount the steps one at a time and you enter the Temple.

It is bathed in blue radiance, glorious blue radiance. Brilliant light shines through impossibly large windows of thinnest sapphire and amethyst.

This is the Temple of the Saints, the Temple of the Justified Ones.

You move forward, through beautiful hallways and the very air about you seems to glow. The halls are filled with spiritual guides and teachers. You recognize some of them! All you feel you have known for all of your life! You see people coming through that you realize you have known before. Some you recognize and some you don't.

Some are on their way into their journey through life; some are on their way out.

You see some of the most enlightened of souls; those who are completely and totally perfect and yet, have made the ultimate sacrifice for mankind - the sacrifice to retain an attachment to the physical form, that they may continue to help us all with their wisdom! From them, you feel the impulse yourself toward that perfection that they have encompassed; toward the attainment of Godhood! So, you move further into the Temple, led by your Guides and the musical laughter of the Chasmalim.

Finally, you behold a mighty and benevolent King.

He is benevolent, but wise. The Wisdom of the Sphere of Chokmah comes through to us in the form of the King in this Sphere of Chesed! Now, you feel yourself opening to the intense energy of the Temple and its King.

You open. You become filled like a vessel filled to overflowing.

Just as the surrounding kingdom is filled to overflowing with material things, you are filled with Spirit and you take your wisdom from the instruction learned outside.

You don't seek to hold onto this energy that fills you; rather, you let it pass through you and as you do, you are filled even more intensely, as a current of sheer divine will pours through you, becoming ever stronger, until your personal will and that of your Higher Self is at One with the Divine Will! Your mind absorbs your body. You feel your body, already in its astral form, becoming less and less dense, blending into all that surrounds you, until all of your awareness resides in your mind. It is as if your body and all attachment to it ceases to exist.

Next, that which is your Higher Self absorbs your mind. You feel your mind expanding, opening, encompassing a far greater reality than you ever thought to be possible. You realize that all linear thought has stopped, time has stopped, you feel infinite knowledge available to you instantly, without need for the processes of thought.

You feel that which is your Spirit, or Soul, absorb your Higher Self. You feel yourself expanding to an infinite awareness, becoming a point of stillness aware of your connectedness to all things! To be born of God, you must unite with the Divine Spark of God, the Spirit itself! Your soul is as a pane of glass as the energy passes through you and you are absorbed into Spirit, so that you may safely pass through the Abyss and the invisible Sephiroh of Daath, to pass into the Sphere of Chokmah.

As the energy pours through you, you feel your Spirit itself becoming less and less dense.

You begin to review all of your assets; those things that tie your body, mind and spirit to the physical and as each rises to awareness, you let it go.

First, you let go of your material assets, all of your things.

Next, you let go of your physical body and your attachment to it.

Becoming still lighter, you let go of all of the emotional qualities that bind you.

Finally, you let go of your mentalism itself. The intellectual body you leave behind.

Lastly, you let go of your need to control the spiritual body itself.

Everything that you have collected on your journey through life must be given away, in wisdom, before you may pass the Gate to Chokmah.

Finally, you find yourself devoid, empty, of all of your physical, intellectual, emotional and spiritual baggage.

All of your assets have been given away.

You suddenly find yourself standing before the Archangel Tzadqiel.

Tzadqiel stands with his rod of power. He upholds to you an Orb that acts as a mirror - it is the mirror of your soul.

You look deeply into the mirror and you see a vision of yourself from before you came into this life.

You see, in that vision, the purpose that was yours as you came into this life, a purpose you have since forgotten, a purpose you incarnated for and now have regained complete memory of.

You realize that all through your life, Tzadqiel has guided you through an intuitive sense of rightness and purpose to do what was good and right, to follow your pre-ordained, self-chosen Path.

But did you follow it? You automatically measure yourself against this pre-life intention. In so doing, you judge yourself; for only that which is perfect may pass the Abyss.

That which is not perfected within yourself must be confronted and left behind, to seek its own perfection or you may drop it into the Abyss itself. But nothing less than perfect may cross the Abyss.

Now, having measured and purified yourself, you move to the edge of a deep chasm.

Tzadqiel guides your Way with a staff of light.

At the edge you look down and you see no bottom. But you see vague and disquieting shapes that can't quite be seen. They move in the darkness.

For a moment you feel alone.

But then, with nothing to weigh you down, you move across.

You float, on wings of nothingness and the crossing is easy.

You float across the Abyss and ever upward, until you are absorbed into a Sphere of brilliant, silver-grey, pulsating light.

You become the light! You are overwhelmed by a feeling of Omniscience and Great Wisdom and Intense Power.

You have never felt Power, pure Power, of this magnitude before.

The energy of it flows through you.

It flows and flows, until finally you realize that what you are feeling is only a small fragment of the total Power of this Sphere.

The Power itself emanates from a Super Being who suddenly appears before you, face to face, you look at Him, seeing His face in profile! He is so brilliant that you must quickly close your eyes or be blinded.

Yet, even through closed eyelids you see His brilliance.

When you open your eyes again, you are in a Temple surrounded by twelve pillars, symbolizing the twelve signs of the Zodiac.

The Temple seems to float in silver-grey mist; but as you look more closely, you see not mist, but hundreds of thousands of stars and constellations giving off brilliance so great as to create the stardust "mist" you see! Power radiates out from the Temple in all directions and you see that there are tiny glints of light in the surrounding stardust.

These are the Auphanim, the Choir of Angels of Chokmah. It is their task to direct this pure force outward into form.

You stand entranced.

Finally, you hear the gentle voice of Tzadqiel and you see his staff of light, guiding you back across the abyss.

You are floating back, back into the Sphere of Chesed, where you began this Path.

You realize that Knowledge brought you to the Abyss and it pointed the way across. But without Wisdom you could not cross, because Knowledge had to be left behind along with everything else of your worldly life! Knowledge derives from the mind, but Wisdom derives from the Spirit.

You contemplate.

And so ends the 16th Path.

Path Journal

A. Record your emotional reactions to your path experiences here, immediately upon completion. Include any physical responses or sensations.

Date of completion: _____

Emotional responses: _____

_____

_____

Physical reactions: _____

_____

_____

What do you think these responses indicate? _____

_____

_____

B. Use this section as a diary of your experiences during the week following your completion of the path. Be sure to include how you react to things emotionally, as well as how you deal with any major issues that might arise.

Day 1: _____
_____

Day 2: _____
_____

Day 3: _____
_____

Day 4: _____
_____

Day 5: _____
_____

Day 6: _____
_____

Day 7: _____
_____

C. Review the week's experiences. How has the path affected the way you handled this week's issues? _____
_____
_____
_____

D. What special dreams has this path stimulated this week? _____
_____
_____
_____

Areas Path 16 Will Help You Work On

- Astral projection

- Expansion of consciousness; mental telepathy

- Accessing the "Universal Mind"

- Learning to be a part of everything yet detached from it at the same time

- Increasing your awareness of layers of higher consciousness, while remaining fully grounded

- Being able to use things, without being used by them

- Gaining greater body awareness and attunement to physical sensations

- Increased creativity and sex drive

- Developing values relative to the material world that work for you

- Putting attachments into their proper perspective; becoming aware of your own limits so you can rise above them

- Understanding that everyone is not ready to evolve or grow, and that this does not set them "beneath" you

- Bringing back with you a feeling of safety and protection (from Chokmah); overcoming fear

- Increasing energy and warmth, and especially your ability to control your body temperature

- Feelings of awe and humility regarding the higher aspects of creation

- Regaining past life memories that will help give purpose to this life

- Enhancement of dreaming and ability to receive messages from your Guides in the dream state

- Learning to balance giving and receiving; tempering your generosity with wisdom and discrimination

- Learning that the mind is a tool to understand the wisdom of the spirit

- Becoming conscious of your choices, and that you stay on your own particular path of growth through choice

- Inner peace

- Learning to tap into your potential power

- Learning to release your power of love

- Gaining a feeling of oneness, family, and belonging with your Guides
- "Knowingness" - gaining an inner connectedness to all things that increases the ability of "omniscience"
- Improving your sense of humor; the ability to laugh
- Contacting people who have died
- Harnessing the strong energies moving through your body
- Letting go of the mind, and the control it has over us; feelings of mental numbness; this allows higher mind to come through
- Development of the Third Eye
- "As above, so below" - understanding that the cosmic force of our universe appears in us as our neural network, through which energy flows
- Altering our perception, or "world view"
- Opening the Third Eye Center and the Throat Center
- Development of lingual skills and musical ability
- Increasing your self-value

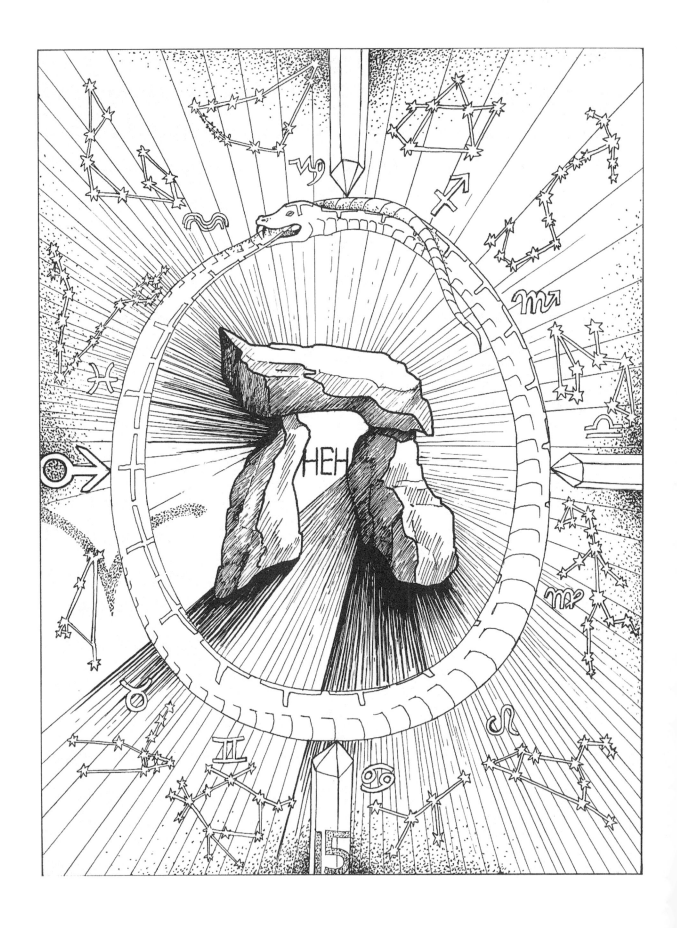

Path 15

Correspondences

— Sphere of Tiphareth —

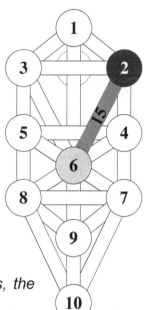

We commence our journey in the Sphere of Tiphareth, Beauty and Harmony.

The Hebrew Divine name is Jehovah Aloah Va Daath.

It is known as the Mediating Intelligence.

The Archangel is Raphael, Prince of Brightness, Beauty and Life; the Archangel of Healing.

The Order of Angels is the Melechim, the Angelic Kings called the Order of Virtues; Angels and Rulers who are responsible for creating and maintaining perpetual balance and harmony in all things.

The corresponding planet is the Sun.

The number is 6.

Tarot correspondences are the four sixes and the four Princes.

The symbols of Tiphareth are the Calvary Cross, the Rose Cross, the Truncated Pyramid and the Cube.

The stones are topaz and diamond.

The metal is gold.

The color is yellow.

The element is air.

The corresponding body part is the breast.

The corresponding chakra is the Heart Center and the gland is the thymus.

Living beings are the lion, the child and the phoenix.

The symbolic creature is the sparrow-hawk or the owl.

The musical note is an "F."

The scents are aloe, cinnamon and clove.

Herbs are angelica, almond, frankincense and myrrh.

The magical image is a Majestic King, a Child, or a Sacrificed God.

The mythical correspondences are all of the Sacrificed Gods including Egyptian Osirus, Indian Krishna and Bhudda and the Christian Jesus.

The spiritual experience is a vision of the harmony of things and of healing and redemption.

The magical phenomenon is a vision of the self made perfect and a manifestation of the "day" star.

— 15th Path —

The 15th Path is known as the Constituting Intelligence, so called because it constitutes the substance of creation in pure darkness.

The esoteric title is the Sun of the Morning, Chief among the Mighty.

It is the principle of Universal Life.

The meaning of the simple form of the letter is sight.

The corresponding astrological sign is Aries.

The planetary influence is Mars.

The element is fire.

The Tarot Major Arcanum card that corresponds is The Emperor.

Symbols on the Path are the Ankh Cross, the Orb of Dominion, the stars and constellations of the Zodiac.

The living creature is the owl.

The symbolic creature is the ram.

Stones are ruby or red jasper.

The scent is frankincense.

Plants are geranium and sage.

Herbs are cayenne pepper and dragon's blood.

The color is scarlet.

The musical note is a "C."

The corresponding body part is the head.

The metal is iron.

The spiritual experience is an insight and an understanding into the foundation and formation of genetic structure and of the solar system itself.

Mythological correspondences are the Greek Minerva, the Roman Athena and Mars and the Hindu Shiva.

— Sphere of Chokmah —

The Sphere of Destination is Chokmah, known alternatively as "The Great Stimulator" and "Wisdom."

It is called the Illuminating Intelligence.

The Hebrew Divine Names are Yah, Tetragramaton or Jehovah.

The Archangel is Ratziel, the Prince of Princes of the knowledge of hidden and concealed things; the "Herald" of God.

The Order of Angels is the Auphanium, the Wheels or Whirling Forces, which are also called the order of Kerubim.

The zodiacal influence is space; the entire Sphere of the Zodiac.

The number is 2; the second Glory.

The Tarot card correspondences are the four twos and the four Kings.

The element is fire in fire.

The color is grey.

The scent is musk.

The herb is amaranth.

The stones are star ruby, turquoise, aquamarine and lapis.

The metal is uranium or lead.

The living being is man.

Plants are fennel, buttercup and absynth.
The symbols are the phallus, the tower, the wand, the line, the hexagram and the circle.
The body part is the left side of the face.
The chakra is the Third Eye Center and the gland is the pineal.
The magical image is a bearded male figure.
The weapon is a wand, symbol of the magical Will and divine wisdom.
The magical and mystical experiences are those of a vision of God face to face and a flash of mystical Light.

Invocation

"May we be encompassed by the name Eloah Va Daath and established in the Temple of Tiphareth, beauty. May the portal of the 15th Path be opened to us and may we journey thereon in the power of the name Elohim Gebor, across the byss at Daath, to the gate of the Sphere of Chokmah. And in the name of Jehovah, which stands for the unspeakable name of God, may the gate of Chokmah be opened to us and may we be firmly established in the wonders of that Sphere."

Path

Imagine that you are in a large, crowded cathedral and a service is taking place.

You watch the service proceed for awhile; you watch as people take the holy sacrament where the body and blood of the "Christ" are symbolically offered up as sacrifice.

You begin to contemplate the concept of sacrifice.

You realize that ultimately, "sacrifice" is the death of the personality so that the higher self might live! Your mind begins to wander as the voice of the Priest drones on.

You stand at a stained glass window, watching the rays of the Sun shine through.

As they stream down, you see tiny particles of dust glinting in the sunbeams, seemingly suspended in space.

Your eyes follow the rays of light up, up, through the window.

Soon, you are rising up through the clouds following the rays of light.

Up, up, you rise, higher and higher.

The light becomes more and more intense, so as to be almost blinding.

You feel the heat.

Your skin tingles and your clothes are stripped away by pure elemental fire! You feel as if you are being pulled into the Sun itself.

You continue to rise, higher and higher.

The rays penetrate your flesh. They are burning away all that gives you weight and density.

You are being clarified and refined.

You become transparent, invisible. You are filled with a sense of freedom and joy! Eventually, out of the brilliance you begin to see a temple.

It seems to be constructed of shafts of multicolored sunlight.

You look more closely. The floor, the walls, and the ceiling are golden topaz.

In the center of the temple floor is an equal armed red cross.

It is enclosed in a hexagon of yellow and surrounded by a six-pointed white star.

The temple itself is hexagonal in form as well; the roof is a three-sided pyramid.

You smell the fragrance of frankincense and myrrh, which permeate the air all about you.

Soon, you sense a presence at your side and when you turn to look, you see the glowing form of the Archangel Raphael. His radiance is bright enough to equal the Sun! He holds a spear pointing downward, as a symbol of peace. He is the Prince of Light, a vanquisher of darkness, bringing in the light from the east point in any magic ceremony.

Associate him with protection, with perfection and with power. He is a great intercessor, continually praying for mankind. He nods in recognition of your presence and just by his glance you are filled with love and a feeling of belonging.

He is your Guide along the first part of this Path.

He steps aside so that you can see the Choir of Angels, the Melachim. These beings are Rulers, Kings, and are responsible for supplying points of balance. They keep the entire solar system and galaxy in balance and prevent them from running into each other.

On a smaller scale, they keep your body in balance. When you or they fail, your body becomes diseased, your mind becomes insane, and your emotions become unbalanced. Death ultimately occurs due to these imbalances.

Surrounded by all this brilliance, you have difficulty differentiating these light beings from the temple itself. As you continue to look around, the temple and the beings surrounding you fade into greater and greater brilliance.

You feel weightless in a void of brilliant white light.

You begin to have the sensation of turning, slowly, on a vertical axis.

You try veering to one side, but like a toy top, you automatically "right" yourself.

You realize that you have the innate ability to keep yourself spinning in an upright and perfectly balanced condition. As long as you stay centered, you can maintain your balance easily. When you veer off to one side you feel the pull of centripetal force pulling you further off balance.

At one point, you almost fall, in you experimentation! But at that moment, the Melachim exert their influence to keep you upright and in perfect balance and all through this you feel that twisting and turning and spinning around a central axis. And you maintain your balance and stay upright.

As time goes on, your balance becomes more and more finely tuned, until you barely have need of the balancing aid of the Melachim at all! At the moment of your greatest centering and balance, you become aware of a shaft of light streaming down from overhead.

You feel its white brilliance enter your body through the top of your head. It fills your Crown Center at the top of your head.

Then it moves down to fill the Third Eye Center at your brow.

The white light continues to move down through your body. You feel it fill your Throat Center and then you feel it move downward to open your Heart Center with white light. You feel the light and the radiance! You feel the light beaming outward from you now in all directions, from your Heart Center! The light in you moves downward again to fill your Solar Plexus Center with brilliance and down still further to illuminate your Sacral Center, the lower balance point of your being.

Finally, it moves down to lighten and energize your Root Center at the base of your spine! You feel the light and energy expand in all directions around you.

Your very consciousness is expanding.

You feel more perceptive. You feel more vibrant. You are filled with a wonderful feeling of love and of understanding and you are now able to see the Melachim clearly! They take form before your eyes! You look at the Archangel Raphael as well, and his face now has features that you can see clearly. He extends his hand to you. You firmly take hold of it. He walks you out of the glowing Temple of Tiphareth.

With him you look out over the celestial hilltop that the Temple is seated upon. You look out over a golden and glowing valley toward a setting sun and you see the first star of night appear, low on the horizon. You feel a faint warm breeze and a deep feeling of peace and security fills you.

You stand quietly looking out over the land as the day turns slowly into night. There is no need to speak. As the light disappears, Raphael disappears, too, although you still sense his presence at your side. His thoughts come to you automatically.

He says, "Now, there is someplace else for you to go. You are ready." A star rises to your right, its rays streaming down to envelope you. Before you know what is happening, you are following the starlight, moving upward once again.

You are moving through space now, surrounded by the dark night, stars shining all around you.

You feel the softness of feathers beneath you and look down; you realize that you are being carried upward upon the wings of a great and silent owl. He glides upward following the air currents that follow the luminescent path projected by the star! You look at the night as you fly upward, especially at the constellations. Many you recognize easily, others you cannot, for they are as yet unknown to man! As you continue to fly, the owl's flight moves into a downward swoop; you briefly loose your balance and fear you will fall! You stiffen and begin to lose your center, but then you realize you are still supported, not truly alone and recalling the lesson of centering, you quickly regain your balance! The owl continues his upward journey.

Now, as you move upward you settle down with enjoyment, looking at the star groups around you. You identify the Little Dipper, Polaris, the Milky Way, Aries and Pisces! Constellation after constellation becomes familiar. Never before were you able to identify them so easily! The owl now changes his angle of flight. He pulls up his head and flaps his massive wings as he slowly descends to what appears to be a grassy plain.

You land in the center of a ring of massive stones. They make primitive arches and resemble Stonehenge on Earth.

You climb from the owl's back, and he disappears.

The night sky is now becoming lighter, turning faintly blue. In a shadow among the monoliths you see a being seated on a large stone throne. You move closer to see it is a warrior in armor cloaked in a long red robe. On his head is a crown of ruby; each stone is set in iron. In one hand he holds a golden cross whose top end is a circle, an ankh. In the other hand he holds a glowing orb.

You slowly walk toward him, not knowing what to expect. He looks powerful and frightening. He motions for you to come closer. In a deep, gentle voice he says, "So you have come to find wisdom! You are on the Path of rediscovery!" He steps down from his throne and walks to your side. He motions you to follow him toward the ring of stones.

The Sun is now rising and shines first on the rock formation in the sign of Aries. You stand looking at the formation. The Sun shines through the arch onto your face and momentarily you experience what it is like to be an Aries. To feel the energy and urge to move forward constantly, no matter what the odds. You remember experiences you've had with Aries people and then you remember a past life you experienced as an Aries.

As the Sun moves forward, it begins to shine upon you from each of the twelve signs of the zodiac in succession.

It shines upon you from Taurus and you experience the implacable solidity and strength of Taurus, you recall the people you know who are Taurians and you remember a past life as a Taurus.

It shines upon you from Gemini and you experience the flexibility and capriciousness of Gemini. You recall Gemini people in your life and you remember a life time as a Gemini.

It shines upon you from Cancer and you experience the deep emotional sensitivity and nurturing need of Cancer and you recall the Cancer people you have known and you experience a past life as a Cancer.

It shines upon you from Leo and you experience the pride and idealism of Leo. You recall the Leo people you have known and re-experience a past life you have had as a Leo.

It shines upon you from Virgo, and you experience the sharp and discriminating mind, the love of service of Virgo. You recall Virgo people you have known and you relive a past life you have experienced as a Virgo.

It shines upon you from Libra and you experience the balance, artistic harmony and mediating ability of Libra. You recall people you have known who are Librans and you recall a past life you have lived as a Libran.

It shines upon you from Scorpio and you experience the depth of emotion and ability to transform through suffering that is Scorpio. You recall Scorpio people you have known and relive a past life as a Scorpio.

It shines upon you from Sagittarius and you experience the searching mind and need to experience that is Sagittarius. You recall Sagittarians you have known and relive a past life as a Sagittarian.

It shines upon you from Capricorn and you experience the responsibility and guidance, the building nature that is Capricorn. You recall Capricorns you have known and relive a past life you lived as a Capricorn.

It shines upon you from Aquarius and you experience the uniqueness, the humanitarian and objective understanding that is Aquarius and you recall the Aquarians you have known. You relive a past life as an Aquarian.

It shines upon you from the last of the Astrological signs, Pisces. You experience the totally empathic and receptive nature of Pisces and recall Piscean people you have known. You relive a past life as a Pisces.

After having experienced the experience of all the signs of the zodiac through the Sun's light, you become aware of the Auphanim - the Order of Angels of the Sphere of Chokmah. They are the wheels that are the origins of karma and cycles. They are the wheels of the universe where beginnings and endings meet, so that everything evolves out of itself.

As you watch them, you know that only through the understanding, letting go and forgiveness of your own transgressions can you evolve and return to the wisdom of Chokmah! Suddenly, a brilliant light flashes all about you as Ratziel, Archangel of the Sphere of Chokmah, appears. He radiates a warmth and love that is far greater than seems your own ability to receive at this time.

Ratziel is the holder of the Book of Wisdom and you know that through him any question you have may be answered. Questions fill your mind and he answers without words. In your heart, you hear.

Your answers will all come to you consciously in time. You will be born around the zodiac many times. You will learn with each incarnation. In time, you will obtain the Wisdom of the Book of Ratziel that was first given to Adam. You must listen for the secrets he whispers about the stars! Ratziel now enfolds you in his arms and you slowly drift back into the stars that you know so well by now.

You drift back to beautiful mother Earth, to the time and place that you know as now.

And so ends the 15th Path.

Path Journal

A. Record your emotional reactions to your path experiences here, immediately upon completion. Include any physical responses or sensations.

Date of completion: _____

Emotional responses: _____
_____
_____

Physical reactions: _____
_____
_____

What do you think these responses indicate? _____
_____
_____

B. Use this section as a diary of your experiences during the week following your completion of the path. Be sure to include how you react to things emotionally, as well as how you deal with any major issues that might arise.

Day 1: _____
_____

Day 2: _____
_____

Day 3: _____
_____

Day 4: _____
_____

Day 5: _____

_____

Day 6: _____

_____

Day 7: _____

_____

C. Review the week's experiences. How has the path affected the way you handled this week's issues? _____

_____

_____

_____

D. What special dreams has this path stimulated this week? _____

_____

_____

_____

Areas Path 15 Will Help You Work On

- Increasing cognitive ability; increased awareness, clarity and alertness
- Mental telepathy and clairaudience; improved physical vision
- Astral projection
- Insight into the infinite
- Freeing consciousness and perception; gaining the "vision" to know where you're going
- Learning to listen to your inner voice to find answers
- Learning to raise your consciousness through controlling the rate and direction of the spinning flow of your energy
- Maintaining your balance and harmony in all ways
- Aiding past life recall

- Increasing ability to embrace peace and happiness

- Clearing and opening all of your chakras, especially the Third Eye

- Freedom resulting from self-forgiveness, and the forgiving of others

- Empathy; knowing how it feels to "walk in someone else's shoes"

- Insight into others, and ability to accept others

- Knowing that there is a purpose to everything, that everything is part of a perfectly meshing universal mechanism that you can now begin to see

- Increasing wisdom

- Oneness with God

- Wholeness; recognizing that the whole is always greater than the sum of its parts

- Gaining solidity and rootedness; establishing order; improved organizational skills

- Reassessment of your life, with a reassertion of goals, and the knowledge that you are on the right path

- Developing assertiveness and a "take charge" attitude

- Burning, sizzling, sparking away blockages

- Rebirth

- Increasing heat production, and healing ability

- Healing illnesses from past lives

- Studying sciences, such as astrology

Path 14

Correspondences

— Sphere of Binah —

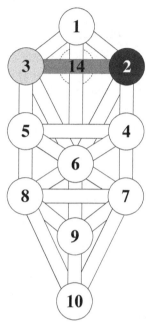

We commence our journey in the Sphere of Binah, "The Lord God" or "God the Mother."
The Hebrew divine name is Jehovah Elohim.
The corresponding planet is Saturn.
The element is earth.
The mineral is lead.
Gems are onyx, sapphire and pearl.
The colors are indigo and black.
Plants are ash, cypress and the opium poppy.
The perfumes are musk, allum and civit.
The Tarot correspondences are the four threes and the four Queens.
The magical image is a mature woman or matron.
The symbols are the brooding dove and the Holy Spirit.
The "weapon" is the cup, symbol of the intuition.
The Archangel is Tzaphqiel, the beholder of God.
The angelic order is the Aralim, meaning the Strong, Mighty Ones, the Supporters or Upholders, or Thrones.
The Gods which correspond are the Roman Saturn, the Greek Cronos, God of Time, Maya, Greek God of the Power of Illusion, Kwan Yin, Goddess from Chinese Buddism, Yin, from the Taoist tradition, the Hindu Kali and the Egyptian Isis.
The musical note is "B."

— 14th Path —

The 14th path is The Illuminating Intelligence, so called because it is the scintillating flame which is the founder of the concealed and fundamental ideas of holiness and of their stages of preparation.
The Hebrew Name is Daleth, the door, or "Gate of Heaven."
The Esoteric Title is The Daughter of the Mighty Ones.
The Tarot Major Arcanum which corresponds is the Empress.
The planet is Venus.
The color is emerald green.
The musical note is "F#."
Animals are the sparrow, the dove and the swan.
Plants are myrtle, clover and rose.

Stones are emerald and turquoise.
Scents are sandalwood and myrtle.
The "weapon" or "tool" is the girdle.
Goddesses who correspond are Aphrodite, Greek Goddess of Love and Freya, the Norse Goddess of Love.

— Sphere of Chokmah —

Our Sphere of destination is Chokmah, The Supernal Father, called the "Great Stimulator."
Hebrew Divine Name is Jehovah, meaning the unpronounceable name of God.
The corresponding planetary influence is the Zodiac, acting through Uranus and Neptune.
The Archangel is Ratziel, the Herald of God.
The Order of Angels are the Auphanim, or Wheels.
The symbol is man.
The colors are violet and grey.
Stones are aquamarine, lapis and star ruby.
The metal is lead.
Plants are fennel, buttercup and absynthe.
The perfume is musk.
The magical image is a bearded male figure.
The "weapon" is the wand.
Gods are Matt, the Egyptian God of Truth, Thor, the Norse God of Learning and Writing, Palace, the Greek God of Wisdom and Zeus.
The corresponding Tarot cards are the four twos and the four Kings.
The musical note is "C."

Invocation

"May we be encompassed by the name Jehovah Elohim and established in the temple of Binah, Understanding. May the portral of the 14th path be opened to us, and may we journey thereon in the power of the name Jehovah Tzabaoth, across the abyss of Daath, to the gates of the Sphere of Chokmah. And in the name of Jehovah, may the gate of Chokmah be opened to us and may we be firmly established in the wonders of that Sphere."

Path

Imagine that you are very, very small... so small, that you can fit inside of a lily flower. You are sliding around and around the smooth, silky petals, slipping down into the very center of the flower.

You slip down and down, into the stem of the flower. It's like a long and narrow slide. Further and further you slip down, surrounded by total darkness.

You lose all sense of your surroundings. You are weightless and you are without form. You are only aware of spinning, down and around, down and around.

All physical sensations are gone. You have no awareness of a physical body and you have no awareness of your surroundings. You float effortlessly down the dark tunnel-slide.

The slide drops you into a sea that warms and soothes your soul.

You are totally relaxed. You float, totally alone. There are no thoughts of the past and there are no thoughts of the future. You simply are.

You explore yourself and find that you are pure energy, no longer physical. You are of the essence of God. You are the seed of the Spirit.

You are going back, back to the magma matta - the "Great Mother of All." You are going back to the great giver of life, Aima, the Fertile Mother. Aima, giving, yet limiting and confining, like the womb.

Going back to Mara, the "Mother of Sorrow," who deprives each of us, for a purpose, so that we migh learn and grow from that learning. She takes away from us, but replaces that loss with something better. For every sorrow, there is an equal and opposite joy, through a connecting time axis.

We, with our limited view of the entire picture, are unable to see the Great Mother and her influence completely. The time in her womb is our time of rest. It is our time between lives. It is our time to assess and evaluate our state and to plan for our future experiences.

The Great Mother, Aima, receives all input and eliminates all that is not fitting and sends out each soul in its proper direction.

Some she sends across the abyss into the light, some she sends back to Chokmah, into the God-Source, if that soul is ready and seeks no more earthly lessons.

On this path, she will send you across the abyss to the Sphere of Chokmah! Tzaphqiel, Archangel of the Sphere of Binah, appears to you now! He is the beholder of God, the One who contemplates divinity. It is through Tzaphqiel that you are able to see yourself in relation to the great reality. He is the spirit of light. He is the eye between the worlds and the patron of meditation and contemplation.

Feel his presence, while floating in the dark, deep sea of Binah! It is through Tzaphqiel that you glimpse the nature of Kether.

You now sense the Great Mother of all as a beautiful, patient and understanding woman. She emerges from the sea, a cup in her hand.

The cup is the Aralim, the Choir of Angels in this realm. They are the containers and holders of divine energy. They act like condensers, or reservoirs, providing regulation and stabilization for the divine being of Chokmah.

The Aralim are the womb that holds your seed and supports you now. They are the matrices, which give form to pure energy. They are the dark holders of light, the silent holders of sound. They are the dry containers of liquid, the cold containers of heat. They are the matrices of your body now.

You feel your soul, the energy that is you, being poured from the cup held in Binah's hand into your body, at the start of its physical life. You remember and you know that at the completion of your cycle your soul will be poured back into the Sphere of Chokmah.

This is the mystical birth symbolized in the act of baptism.

The Aralim bring the water of eternal life to you now.

You feel Aima, the Great Mother, holding you in her arms. She pours holy water over your body. It flows and flows, clear and pure, until you become wholly immersed in Her waters, becoming a part of Mara, the Great Sea of the universal unconscious.

You are without form, without emotion, without mind, without desire, totally without any separate sense of self. Your soul begins to expand outward, finding itself in all things as it begins its journey across the abyss at Daath, toward its source, toward Chokmah, the Sphere of pure power, the universal wellspring of energy.

As your awareness expands outward through the abyss, it grows and grows, far greater than you could have ever imagined. You sense a part of yourself in all things and a part of them in you. You are moving toward wholeness.

You absorb the opposite polarity to yourself, the ultimate gift of the Sphere of Chokmah.

The Auphanim, who are the Order of Angels of the Sphere of Chokmah, create the full circle and direct your energy so that it is complete. They make beginnings and endings meet, so that everything evolves out of itself. Like the serpent winding around the Tree of Life, you are once again complete when your soul reaches the Sphere of Chokmah.

Experience your wholeness, now, as you can only here in this Sphere! With your completeness, your awareness and vision expand exponentially. You are able to see the blazing glory of the temple of Chokmah, contained in a single pulsating column of light dazzling in every color of the rainbow and other colors you have never dreamed before! In the column of light you momentarily see the bearded face of a Great King shining forth. The sheer power of his will washes over you like a mighty wave. You look away and when you look back, you again see only the blazing temple, against a backdrop of millions of stars.

Ratziel, Archangel of the Sphere of Chokmah, appears before you.

You see a star shining over his shoulder, one star brighter than all the rest. It is your star, and he is whispering something to you, but you are unable to hear him.

You sense he has great wisdom to impart to you, but you are unable to hear him no matter how closely you listen! You struggle to hear, but realize that Ratziel does not speak in words you can yet understand. As you perceive this, you are filled with a feeling of known and understood destiny and purpose, though you are unable to put words to it! The star grows brighter. You know that it is your star and your path to follow now! As you watch your star grow brighter and brighter, Ratziel disappears in a flash as the light continues to grow while totally enveloping you. You feel a building of energy that seems to come both from yourself and from the brilliant temple of light. The tension builds and builds, until you are spewed forth in a massive explosion, back across the Abyss, into the ocean of the Sphere of Binah.

You float, as the turbulent waters that received you slowly return to calm. You begin to explore the new wholeness that you feel, the new sense of purpose, of "rightness" in your life.

Slowly now, you begin to feel sensation return to your body, as your soul re-enters following its journey to the supernals. You are filled with a sensation of new found wholeness, a sense of purpose and destiny and the energy to pursue it.

And so ends the 14th path.

Path Journal

A. Record your emotional reactions to your path experiences here, immediately upon completion. Include any physical responses or sensations.

Date of completion: _____

Emotional responses: _____
_____
_____

Physical reactions: _____
_____
_____

What do you think these responses indicate? _____
_____
_____

B. Use this section as a diary of your experiences during the week following your completion of the path. Be sure to include how you react to things emotionally, as well as how you deal with any major issues that might arise.

Day 1: _____
_____

Day 2: _____
_____

Day 3: _____
_____

Day 4: _____
_____

Day 5: _____
_____

Day 6: _____
_____

Day 7: _____
_____

C. Review the week's experiences. How has the path affected the way you handled this week's issues? _____
_____

D. What special dreams has this path stimulated this week? _____
_____
_____
_____

Areas Path 14 Will Help You Work On

- Increasing energy and the healing warmth you emit

- Increased energy especially flowing through the hands, aiding "laying on of hands" types of healing work

- Increasing sensory perception and sensation, and your ability to interpret what you receive

- Ability to diagnose illness psychically

- Meditation

- Cleansing and clearing blockages in yourself and others

- Increasing your future directedness and sense of anticipation

- Union of the male and female within you

- Feeling the parts of yourself as fragmented sections of a whole that you are learning to bring together

- Ability to experience total freedom with self-responsibility

- Ability to grow beyond your self-imposed limitations; recognizing that the limitations you have set define you, and that you can redefine yourself by changing those limitations

- Being able to take a chance, to go beyond what you think your limitations are, and grow

- Enhancement of creativity and wisdom

- Pregnancy - the ability to create life, or give life to your dreams

- Acceptance of responsibility, especially for the power of your own mind and will

- Becoming a clear channel for your higher self; gaining insight into what wholeness is, and opening your higher perceptions
- Receiving clear messages concerning what you are to do and become; gaining a sense of rightness, purpose, and clarity regarding your own path in life
- The ability to see and feel the "white light" and other things beyond the visible spectrum
- Opening of all of the psychic energy centers, especially the Third Eye and the Crown Centers
- Cosmic orgasm
- Sensing yourself as an energy being
- Ability to re-center and establish your own rules and boundaries, thereby creating balance within yourself
- Being able to control your own energy, and keep it smooth, balanced, and fully integrated
- Gaining the ability to understand others who don't speak your language, by paying more attention to feeling than to words
- Understanding the principle of polarity
- Becoming secure in what you know
- Learning to relax and "go with the flow;" accepting the lack of permanence in all things
- Increased sex drive and sensuality
- The ability to return to the "space" you experienced in Binah at will
- Rebirth - the Third initiation on the Tree of Life

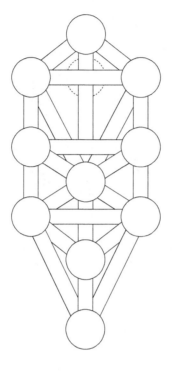

Path 13

Correspondences

— Sphere of Tiphareth —

We commence our journey in the Sphere of Tiphareth, Beauty.
The Hebrew Divine Name is Jehovah Aloah Va Daath.
The Archangel of the Sphere is Raphael.
The Choir of Angels is the Malachim or Angelic Kings.
It is called the Mediating Intelligence.
The Planetary correspondence is the Sun.
It is symbolized by a vision of Universal Harmony.
The color is a bright, golden yellow.
The number is 6.
The magical images are a Majestic King, a Child and the Sacrificed God.
The stones are topaz and diamond.
The metal is gold.
Plants are almond, angelica, ash, chamomile, cinnamon, frankincense and, of course, sunflower.
The musical note is "F."
Symbols are the truncated pyramid and the cube.
Mythological and relgous correspondences to Tipareth include Jesus, the Christ, The Buddha, the Egyptian God Osirus and the Greek God Apollo.

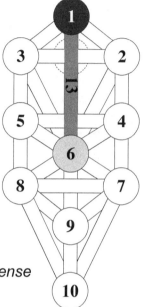

— 13th Path —

The 13th Path is known as the Uniting Intelligence because it is itself the Essence of Glory and the consummation of Truth.
The Hebrew letter for the path is Gimel, meaning Camel.
The planetary influence on the path is the Moon.
The corresponding Tarot Major Arcanum card is the High Priestess.
The elements on the path are water and spirit.
The symbol is the virgin, she who is the repository of unblemished cosmic memory.
The stone is moonstone, pearl or crystal.
The scent is jasmine.
Plants are star anise, coriander, ginger, orris root and lily.
The color is blue.
The musical note is the "G#."
The mystical experience is a vision of light.

— Sphere of Kether —

The Sphere of Destination is Kether, the Crown.
The Hebrew Divine name is Eheieh, God the Creator.
The Archangel is Metatron.
The Order of Angels are the Chayoth Ha Qadesh, or, the Order of Seraphim.
There is no corresponding planet.
The number is 1.
Tarot correspondences are the four Aces.
The color is brilliance, pure white with specs of gold and silver.
Symbols are the crown, the point and the swastika.
The Magical Image is an ancient bearded king who can only be seen in profile.
The spiritual vision is Union with God.
It is called by the titles, "Existence of the Existence," "Concealed of the Concealed," "Ancient of the Ancients" and "The Primordial Point."
A mythological and religious correspondent is the Hindu God Brahma, always shown with two faces, one looking forward and one away, that we may only see one at a time.

Invocation

"May we be encompassed by the name Jehovah Aloah Va Daath and established in the temple of Tiphareth, Beauty. May the portal of the 13th path be opened to us and may we journey thereon in the power of the name Shaddai Al Chai, across the mighty abyss to the gate of the Sphere of Kether. And in the name of Eheieh, may the gate of Kether be opened to us and may we be firmly established in the wonders of that Sphere."

Path

Take a deep breath... and now take another.

In your mind's eye you see yourself back in the Sphere of Malkuth, moving through the winding tunnels, the deep caves and hidden spaces deep within the earth as you repeat the first of your lower initiations on the Tree of Life, the initiation of the earth element.

It's easier this time, to let go of your attachments to the things of the physical plane, to find your way deep into the recesses of yourself, to experience the rebirth that frees you from the flesh.

As your spirit is freed from its fleshly container, you feel an expansion of the energy of your Root Center, moving upward from the base of your spine.

You now find yourself floating in the Sphere of Yesod, Sphere of the Moon herself, as you again experience the second of your lower initiations. It's easy this time to reach out beyond yourself to let the feeling nature flow freely within you; you look into the mirror of your unconscious, of your inner self without fear, comfortable with what you see. You see the haze and formlessness of this lowest of the astral Spheres surrounding you, but you find your way through this hazardous realm easily and instinctively, never being drawn from your path, because your knowledge of self is so complete. You have already passed the initiation of air and are at home in this Sphere.

Your Sacral Center now becomes energized as you free the energy of your etheric body, attached to the lower astral plane and the Sphere of Yesod. A warm flush moves upward from your Sacral Center, just below your navel.

You move on, upward to the Sphere of Hod, where you again review the lower initiation of water. You feel yourself floating, lost in an endless sea, floundering in your own and others' emotions, identity threatened. You look back over the ages of human civilization and conquer each fear attached to your humanity. By the power of your mind you again complete the initiation of water, with ease. You have been here before! In the Sphere of Netzach, you face again the lower initiation of fire. You feel your whole being consumed by fire. It surrounds you and burns from you all that you were. You are left with a feeling of purpose, creativity and direction.

Now, you feel your Solar Plexus Center opening and a massive burst of energy moves upward from the area of your diaphragm, as you again complete the four lower initiations! It lifts you upward! You move upward into the center of the Tree of Life, into Tiphareth, the temple of the Sun.

It is so beautiful. A sense of hope, harmony, beauty and balance surrounds you.

You look around. You stand in an eight-sided cathedral. The walls seem to be made of light in every shade and every color.

Rainbows are reflected in every dimension.

The Archangels Raphael, Michael, Gabriel and Auriel each occupy a corner of the temple. Raphael is in the East, Michael in the South, Gabriel in the West and Auriel in the North. They each radiate light, love, wisdom and compassion.

The Choir of Angels chants their devotion to the invisible unmanifest.

You sit down in the middle of the temple and effortlessly join the Choir in its devotions.

Emerging right in front of you suddenly is a beautiful, mystical woman. She is sitting in a throne on top of a lotus flower cushion.

Her throne is supported by six lions. A moon floats above her head.

She radiates an intense aura and in her many hands are innumerable symbols of purity, wisdom, compassion, dedication, concentration, generosity and spirituality.

In this very majestic form she smiles at you. From her Crown chakra, a very bright beam of light emerges to focus on your own Crown chakra. Another beam of light, red, focuses from her Throat chakra to yours. Then another yet emerges from her heart and an emerald light focuses on your Heart Center. She fills you from head to toe with infinite love and compassion, purifying your body, your mind and your speech, like the ocean constantly washing the pebbles on a beach.

You realize that you are not your physical self anymore. You started a long time ago, in the astral triangle, from the Sphere of Malkuth, the physical and you have grown.

In order to arrive here in the Sphere of Tiphareth you have shed layers and layers of your outer garments. You have conquered your desires and attachment for and to the material world. Attachments to people, to circumstances and to places, no longer control your action.

Feelings of anger, impatience, jealousy, greed and egotism have all disappeared.

Here, in the Ethical Triangle that begins with Tiphareth, there is no room for them.

You also realize that Tiphareth and the Ethical Triad, is not your true destiny. Your home is in the Supernals, in the World of Atziluth.

This beautiful, kind, warm Priestess knows that you have worked hard during your journey thus far. She signals to you that she is pleased with your progress.

You look around again now and realize that you are still in the middle of the temple, but the wall of the temple no longer exists.

Surrounding you now is a circle of light. It radiates from the Archangels.

A pure vibration generated by the chanting of the Choir of Angels surrounds you as well.

At this point you are the pure and natural being, the soul and center of the universe, the King in your own Kingdom and you are also the dot in the middle of the circle.

Outside circumstances cannot affect you anymore. The pain, the agony that accompanies birth, aging, sickness, suffering and death, are only illusions in the astral world. In the world you are in now, here in Tiphareth, only peace, love and joy and harmony exist.

And yet you want to share this peace and harmony with all the beings that are still struggling in the planes below.

You look to the Priestess for tools and hints of how to share this joy; she smiles again, admiring you for your willingness to share and for your tremendous courage to forsake your newfound treasure, the peace and the joy of Nirvana, for the sake of others.

Radiating from her Crown chakra, her throat and her heart, again, an immense ball of light forms and is absorbed into your own Crown chakra, Throat chakra and Heart chakra again! By the power of your own will, by an act of compassion, you wanted to sacrifice your physical body into the pure natural energy being that you are, so that you can receive the light, the love and the power.

By your Will, spurred on by your compassion, you want to sacrifice this new found balance that you have, by reaching out to other beings.

With the light that you have received from this Priestess-Goddess, you radiate light now yourself.

A strong beam of light, like a shower pouring out from your Crown chakra, bathes people that you know, as well as those that you don't.

You continue to shower down light, love and pure energy onto humans, animals and even the plants of the earth.

This is, for you, a point of transmutation. You have become the Christ that died on the cross. You have become the Buddha that became enlightened, but still came back to share the doctrines.

You exist for the sake of sacrificing yourself to help others.

You rest. You think that your journey has finally come to an end, and yet, somehow, the yearning from the soul is still not satisfied, the yearning for your continued upward movement, the very evolution of your own soul.

The Sphere of Tiphareth is only a place of incarnation, only a place for the form to transform into matter.

You ask the Angels and the Priestess-Goddess to help you to move upward on your journey once again, to find your true destiny.

Touched by your sincerity, the Archangels take their places with Raphael in front of you, Gabriel behind you, and Michael to your right and Auriel to your left. The Priestess-Goddess allows her form to merge with yours. You feel lightness and tremendous energy filling you. You have formed the hexagram, with the power and elements of air, water, fire, earth and spirit.

You begin to spin. Faster... and faster... and soon you are rising upward, not knowing where you are going, but feeling as if you are being drawn upward by suction, a force more powerful than you have ever imagined.

You have a sensation of diffusing and elongating. There is no perception of height, length or depth; only a vast energy field.

You are in the Abyss of the cosmos.

Floating in it are specs of gold and silver shimmering, like writing. It's as if other souls are on the same journey, also seeking their final destiny.

"What are you looking for?" you ask yourself.

You have heard that no man has lived after he has seen God. Where can you get a description? How can you define the indefinable? None of your six physical or even psychic senses can help you anymore.

You have heard that God is the beginning and the end. He is the primordial point, the point of everything that is. He is the "I am that I am". He is the eternal OM.

In the abyss the moment of waiting, of not knowing what you are waiting for, reminds you of your first entrance into the Sphere of Binah; the concept of timelessness, except in Binah, you know you are waiting to be born, in the Abyss you are waiting to be one with the eternal... to be without beginning and without end.

Suddenly, you realize that you are expanding. There is no above and no below. There is no left and no right. There is no darkness and no light. Duality does not exist.

It is the vibration of motion that is going on. Still, and slowly, the vibration builds up.

The breath of God surrounds you. At first you barely hear it, but slowly it gets louder and more encompassing.

You begin to hear barely perceptible vibrations that form words to you - words that are not spoken, but formed of the very breath of God.

You cannot see Him; you can only perceive the infinite breath of the Divine. You did not notice it in the beginning because you were so involved with your own breath, but as His breath enfolded you, you could no longer tell one from the other. It was as if you and He breathed the same breath. You are truly made of the image of God.

You continue to breathe as one and from this pure, concentrated, uninterrupted movement, two nebulas gather. The momentum builds up.

The Divine Spark ignites. Light emanates from light and manifestation takes place.

Every time you breathe you utter the Holy name of Life. Every time you breathe you are one with God. Every time you breathe you manifest as the divine One.

Out of love and compassion, God desired to be transmuted in Tiphareth as the sacrificed God. He also is the child that is redeemed in Malkuth. The child in Malkuth has learned to abandon the self, sacrificing it to the good of a higher purpose. It rises to Tiphareth. From the desire for the love and the learning and the joy of union with his creator, finally, he finds his way back to be one with the eternal.

You are the Creator; you are the Sacrificed God; you are the point of transmutation and you are also the Created - one with light, love and pure essence.

Having fulfilled your mission you thank each of the Archangels and the Choir of Angels, too. You thank the Priestess-Goddess, who now appears even more the Goddess. You make a promise to continue to help the others on the Path, just as they have helped you.

As you complete your thanks, you find yourself back in Tiphareth, the temple of the Sun. You are more secure, peaceful and balanced than ever before. You feel a beam of energy constantly entering the top of your head now, passing through you and radiating outward to all upon your level and below.

You feel like the Sun yourself, having the newfound capacity to channel the energy from its highest source out into the world around you, energizing, uplifting, healing and bringing wholeness to all those you come in contact with! Feel this energy, now, pouring through you as the energy of transmutation and joy.

Now, bring your attention back to Malkuth, slowly, back to an awareness of your physical being and this time and this place, which you now realize is equally all a part of the God Source!

And so ends the 13th Path.

Path Journal

A. Record your emotional reactions to your path experiences here, immediately upon completion. Include any physical responses or sensations.

Date of completion: _____

Emotional responses: _____
_____
_____

Physical reactions: _____
_____
_____

What do you think these responses indicate? _____
_____
_____

B. Use this section as a diary of your experiences during the week following your completion of the path. Be sure to include how you react to things emotionally, as well as how you deal with any major issues that might arise.

Day 1: _____
_____

Day 2: _____
_____

Day 3: _____
_____

Day 4: _____
_____

Day 5: _____
_____

Day 6: _____
_____

Day 7: _____
_____

C. Review the week's experiences. How has the path affected the way you handled this week's issues? _____

D. What special dreams has this path stimulated this week? _____

_____

_____

_____

Areas Path 13 Will Help You Work On

- Aligning, cleansing, clearing, balancing yourself
- Grounding, yet elevating your consciousness at the same time
- Clairaudience - hearing voices giving higher guidance
- Enhancement of your feeling nature
- Becoming more objective to yourself and others
- Being able to remain open without pain
- Increasing your energy flow and your ability to produce and channel energy
- Increasing the healing energy in your hands
- Radiating feelings of joy, love, and oneness
- Being able to access the universal mind as opposed to your individual mind
- Meditation
- Flushing negativity
- Accepting yourself as part of God, and therefore good and worthy
- Increasing your ability to feel and perceive energy
- Being able to release yourself, altering your consciousness as you might do through drugs, but achieving this state without them
- The ability to manifest your thoughts more quickly
- Releasing blocked emotions
- Recalling past issues so that you can lay them to rest; understanding the past

- Improving your ability to project your thoughts; empowerment leading to fulfillment
- Acquiring a desire to help, heal, and serve others, even at the risk of losing your hard earned balance; gaining the ability for self-sacrifice, to others or to a higher cause
- Teaching ability; being able to share your "peace" with others
- Being protected and being able to protect others
- Omniscience; recognizing your link to all things
- Learning to achieve oneness through breath control
- Creativity
- Self-responsibility
- Opening and balancing all of your chakras
- Gaining greater clarity and increased sensitivity in using your psychic and physical senses
- Releasing the flow of the kundalini force within you

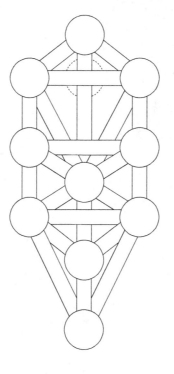

Path 12

Correspondences

— Sphere of Binah —

We commence our journey in the Sphere of Binah, called the Sanctifying Intelligence and known as Understanding.

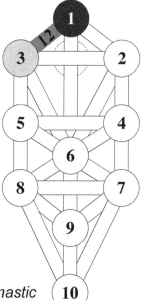

The Hebrew Divine Name is Jehovah Elohim, the Perfection of Creation and the Life of the World to Come.

The Archangel is Tzaphqiel, the Prince of the Spiritual Strife against Evil.

The Order of Angels is the Aralim, the Strong and Mighty Ones who are also called the Order of Thrones.

The planet is Saturn, the Lord of Karma.

The element is primal water.

The color is dark brown or black.

The metal is lead.

The stones are pearl, star sapphire or onyx.

The musical note is "B."

Plants, herbs and scents are myrrh, musk, civet, ash, cypress, mastic and cinnamon.

The body part is the right side of the face.

The chakra is the Third Eye or Brow Center and the corresponding gland is the pineal.

Symbols are the cup, the womb and the tomb.

The mystical experience is an intuitive and all-seeing understanding.

The magical image is a mature woman.

The mythological figures include all of the mother goddesses.

— 12th Path —

The 12th Path is called the Sanctifying Intelligence, the Foundation of Primordial Wisdom, known as the Intelligence of Transparency because it is that species of Magnificence called Chazchazit, which is named the place whence issues the vision of those seeing in apparitions.

It is the Creator of Faith.

The Esoteric Title is The Magus of Power.

The Divine Name is Aloeth Elohim, Goddess of Goddesses, or the Great Mother.

The Hebrew letter is Beth, which means house.

The meaning of the Double Letter is Life-Death.

The color is yellow.

The musical note is "E."

The Guide on the Path is the Archangel Tzaphqiel.

The planetary influence is Mercury.

The Tarot Arcanum Card is the Magician.

The element is water in fire.

Symbols are the house, the wand and the caduceus.

Plants, herbs and scents are mastic, sandalwood, mace, storax and clove.

The metal is quicksilver.

The stones are opal and agate.

Living beings are apes, swallows and the ibis.

The mystical experience of the Path is freedom from Karma through choice and will, coming from understanding.

The Path philosophy is that we begin our magical mystical transformation to pure beingness through the exercise of our will with understanding and thereby speed our vibration.

Ultimately we work the highest of magics, the transformation of the self.

— Sphere of Kether —

The Sphere of Destination is Kether, the Crown, called Rashith ha- Gilgalim, the beginning of whirling, the Primum Mobile or First Mover, which bestoweth the gift of life in all things and filleth the whole Universe.

The Hebrew Divine Name is Eheieh, the Divine Essence.

The Archangel is Metatron, Prince of Countenances, he who bringeth forth others before the face of God, who is born of man.

The Order of Angels is the Chayoth Ha Qadesh, the Holy Lifing Creatures, which are also called the Order of Seraphim.

The elements are all elements.

Symbols are the point, primordial stillness, the swastika and the wheel of life.

The sound is a whisper, the breath itself.

The musical note is "D."

The scents are ambergris and almond.

The stone is diamond.

The color is white brilliance.

The body part is the crown of the head.

The chakra is the Crown Center and the gland is the pituitary.

The magical image is a vision of God, face to face.

The mythical figures include, Brahma and all Gods who are the ultimate root of all things.

The spiritual experience is a vision of that from which you have come and to which you shall ultimately return.

Invocation

"May we be encompassed by the power of the name Jehovah Elohim and established in the Sphere of Binah, Understanding. May the portal of the 12th Path be opened to us and may we journey thereon in the power of the name Yod Heh Vau Heh to the gate of the Sphere of Kether, the Crown. And in the name of Ehieh, may the gate of Kether be opened to us and may we be firmly established in the wonders of that Sphere."

Path

You open your inner eyes.

As you do so, you find yourself in a cavern. Rock is all around you.

You recognize this place as the Sphere of Malkuth. You look about you with familiarity.

Ahead of you, you see an opening. Above you is a wide crack through which pale light shines.

You walk forward, and stand beneath the light. It encircles you. It is as if your whole being becomes filled with the light that shines from above.

You feel yourself becoming lighter and the light lifts you up... up... up... up.

As you rise, you recognize levels of being you've passed on earlier journeys.

You are carried past Yesod, the airy Sphere of the lower astral.

Past Hod and Netzach, the water and fire Spheres of the upper astral planes.

You pass into Tiphareth, seat of your Higher Selfhood, where the light grows so bright and golden, you almost want to linger.

But still, you are drawn upward.

So, you let go of the wonders of Tiphareth and you are drawn up past the Spheres of Geburah and Chesed.

Finally, you have reached the edge of the Abyss itself, the invisible Sphere of Daath. Here, the light about you falters and dims.

But never the less, it carries you across.

It deposits you, finally, in the Temple of Binah.

As you come to rest in the Sphere of Binah, the light continues to dim.

It gets fainter and fainter, until at last you rest in total darkness.

The air about you is totally still.

You feel so exalted, so high, yet so alone and isolated and yet around you, you perceive warmth in this darkness... a sense of security... a feeling of protectedness that generates a feeling of well-being.

The feeling of well-being fills you.

It is as if vast arms surround you in love and warmth.

You realized that this Sphere is the womb of the Goddess, the womb that gives you life and the calm and the serenity of the tomb to which you return at the end of life.

It is the place of your beginning and your ending.

You recognize that you are with the Goddess now! As soon as you realize this the light returns! You look about you. You find yourself in a rough hewn pyramid.

In the center of the pyramid your eyes become fixed by a three-sided chest or ark, upon which lies the staff of Mercury.

You move forward and gaze at the chest and the staff.

After a few moments, you become aware that the triangular walls of the pyramid are all covered with eyes.

Eyes that do not blink! At first you think that they are looking at you! Then, you feel that they are actually looking through you! Finally, you realize that these eyes see all that is, all that was and all that ever shall be on earth and in all of the worlds! You quake at the thought of their omniscience, their all knowingness.

Suddenly, the eyes all seem to become more alert to your presence! Tzadqiel, Archangel of the Sphere, and the owner of these far-seeing eyes, appears before you.

His brilliance is almost more than you can bear to look at, yet he is to be your Guide on this Path. His purpose is to help you to truly see, in every way.

Tzadqiel points toward one wall. As if you are watching a motion picture, scenes begin to unfold in front of your eyes.

You see yourself watching a young, very gifted child. You see the child drawing happily, painting. He completes his work, and he shows his drawing to a pleased and excited mother! Soon, you see the same child, older now, painting beautiful pictures and you rejoice at his achievement, his talent. You feel the deep pleasure of the Great Mother flow through your whole being as she to watches his progress, his own ability to create.

The scene changes again. You see the same child, but still older, grown, in fact, into a youth. You see him rejected in love.

The scene shifts yet again and you see him, in rage, rending his paintings.

Your whole being is filled with sorrow as you feel the incredible grief of the Great Mother. Her sorrow is unending, immeasurable.

But beyond her sorrow, you feel her infinite understanding and her patience.

You marvel that she can have these positive feelings in the midst of her sorrow and know that it is these that you are here to learn! The scene on the wall is still moving forward and you continue to watch. You see the young man, now fully grown, sitting behind a desk.

You wonder where his paintings are. He doesn't look happy.

You see that he has cut himself off from his own need to be creative when love was withheld from him.

You join your own sorrow to that of the Great Goddess.

Now, the scene on the wall shifts again and you see this man again, now an old man, bitter and unhappy. He pushes those who would love him away, he is filled with feelings of inadequacy and stifled self-expression.

You taste the salt-tears of the Goddess and your own sorrows deepen.

You marvel at her infinite patience. Yet you cannot yet share it.

The scene on the wall blanks out momentarily and the air drifts into silence.

You try to understand what you have seen and then, suddenly, the wall becomes animated as another scene appears upon it.

You see a new child before you. Somehow, you know that this is the same child as before, reborn.

You see the child frustrated and angry. He is looking for something that he doesn't know he's lost! You feel the Goddess all about you and you hear her Sigh.

Ahhhhhhhh.............

The scenes continue to pass on the wall. Faster now, and you see that this child, too, matures to an embittered man, following the same patterns as the previous life, unknown to himself, and yet you still feel a sensation of infinite patience emanating from the Goddess! You marvel! Tzadqiel shows you more and more lifetimes for this youth. The scenes flash by with an incredible rate of speed. Most are the same. Most show him embittered and lost.

But finally, at last, we see this child in a new incarnation where he at last picks up the brush and paints again. This time his mother turns away. She gives no praise. But still, he paints and you hear the Goddess sigh again.

Mmmmmmmmmmmm..........

You see that he is not gifted in this life. His paintings are rough and crude. But yet he takes joy in them.

Again, you hear the Goddess sigh.

Her sigh is of reassurance.

Shhhhhhhhhhhhh..........

You see him struggle to achieve. It is his will and his choice to succeed, where before he failed.

In his struggle, you see his life blossom, in love and happiness and you feel the deep and great joy of the Goddess.

It flows through you and fills your whole being.

Now, you begin, finally, to glimpse her understanding, which goes so deep because it is all encompassing.

She shared in all of his joys and sorrows. But her instant understanding had seen the totality of his soul's journey from start to finish.

But while you dally in your thoughts on this, Tzadqiel is busily showing more scenes.

The wall is not still.

Your attention is drawn now to these new scenes and you are shocked! These scenes are intensely familiar to you. They are of your own life! You gaze at each of the scenes that he shows to you and you begin now to see patterns in your own life.

You see patterns of self-doubt, of insecurity, of fear, of inhibition, of blocking yourself, of depriving yourself, of anger, of guilt and on and on.

You trace these patterns back to your childhood and as the scenes shift before your eyes, you see another being that you recognize as yourself from a previous life! You see the origins of the patterns! You see the hand of the Goddess in the restrictions on your life and soul that created these patterns! You see again the action that eventually forced you, or will force you, to break free of the pattern and so, you see yourself now in this life, knowing the need to break free, feeling the fear of failure and of loss and uncertainty, and yet, as you move forward into the unknown, you feel the Aralim, the Angelic Host, the Thrones of the Sphere of Binah, holding and supporting you! They act as a lens that will help you to focus yourself and grow more and more refined, while essentially remaining yourself.

You feel yourself becoming lighter and lighter.

You break free of your own self-forged bonds! You realize now that all Karmic patterns are your own creation, established by yourself in order to achieve the ability to grow beyond them! This is a part of the Understanding of the Sphere of Binah.

You float free now, no longer within the Sphere of Binah, having understood the nature of cause and effect, you have become self-responsible.

You no longer need the womb of Binah! All around you, you see light.

It moves and flows around you.

You see worlds born out of fire, growing into planets! You see teeming metropolises on those evolving planets! You see them growing, building, aging and then dying! You see them turning to cinders in space, consumed by the explosions of their own Suns. You see whole civilizations and worlds that are born, grow and die, only to be born again! As you see more and more of these things, your understanding of the Sphere of Binah grows! With this newfound understanding, you become more and more aware of your own actions.

You begin to see, in every action you take, its eventual result.

So, you begin to plan your actions with care and in so doing get only positive and foreseen results! At first your progress is slow. But soon you gain confidence and speed! Before long, you no longer need to act to achieve your aim! Your thought is enough to achieve the results you seek! Now, indeed, you are truly a magician! As you realize this, you realize that in this exercise of your Will, you have transformed yourself and in transforming yourself, you have transformed your world! You become aware that this power of thought resulting in action is now happening very quickly - so quickly that you feel a shaking of your very spirit! Your innermost being is vibrating so quickly; the vibration within you moves quicker and quicker, until finally, you burst forth into pure brilliance! The brilliance echoes and contains a soft whisper.

EEEEHHHHH..........

HHIIIIIII..........

AHHHHHHHH..........

EEEHHHHHH..........

HHIIIIIII..........

AHHHHHHHHH.........

The air is still about you. All about you is white brilliance. You feel only the motion of your own spirit, moving to the breath.

Ahhhhhhh...........

Hiiiiiieeeee.......

Ahhhhhhhhh.........

The light is so bright; you can look about yourself only with closely squinted eyes.

But soon, you see before you the Archangel Metatron. You are looking at his back, as he himself is face to face with God, the only being in the cosmos who may look upon God and live! The light that he sees is so brilliant that his body cannot fully block it and it is this brilliance shining through him that fills the place that you are in! Metatron, youngest Archangel. He was born, like you, a mortal. He was raised up by God. It was he that gave the Kabbala to Adam. He is the scribe of God.

It is from here, the Sphere of Kether that perfected souls choose to go into the vast darkness where only God has looked or to return back to the wheel of life once more.

You remain here, in the eternal now, hearing the rhythm of the breath of God, the breath of Ehieh.

Until, finally, the normal breath of waking consciousness returns to you.

You wake, as from a deep sleep.

And so ends the 12th Path.

Path Journal

A. Record your emotional reactions to your path experiences here, immediately upon completion. Include any physical responses or sensations.

Date of completion: _____

Emotional responses: _____

_____

_____

Physical reactions: _____

_____

_____

What do you think these responses indicate? _____

_____

_____

B. Use this section as a diary of your experiences during the week following your completion of the path. Be sure to include how you react to things emotionally, as well as how you deal with any major issues that might arise.

Day 1: _____

_____

Day 2: _____

_____

Day 3: _____

_____

Day 4: _____

_____

Day 5: _____

_____

Day 6: _____

_____

Day 7: _____

_____

C. Review the week's experiences. How has the path affected the way you handled this week's issues? _____

_____

_____

_____

D. What special dreams has this path stimulated this week? _____

_____

_____

_____

Areas Path 12 Will Help You Work On

- Dissolving creative blocks
- Getting in touch with your true creative ability
- Becoming aware of what your own blockages are, and what is needed to overcome them
- Learning to identify your emotional "buttons;" getting in touch with your own karmic problems
- Getting more in touch with yourself; knowing that you must lose who you are in order to value who you are
- Learning to let go of your identification with your resistance and blocks
- Learning to be responsible for everything that you project and create
- Learning that understanding frees you from limitation; let go of your fears through understanding
- Relaxation and balance

- Knowing that there is a purpose for everything you pass through; understanding your own purpose now
- Judge yourself - do not base your self-image on other people's opinion of you
- Understanding cycles, and recognizing them in your life and in your world
- Recognizing that all of your thoughts are things and will manifest; you are a magician already
- Recognizing that emotion powers thought
- Being able to be totally receptive
- Developing foreknowledge through the activation of the Third Eye
- Forgiving yourself, accepting your humanity
- Being able to expand your consciousness upward, through the Crown Center
- Astral projection
- Energizing the right side of the body, and the upper half of the body; general intensification of energy
- Purging; dealing with your anger, and redeeming the energy through healing
- Dream enhancement and understanding
- The ability to see "through" things
- Increasing communication with your Guides
- Increasing your ability to use your Throat Center, the creative will; through assertion you learn to release your bonds and "go with the flow"
- Allowing your higher self to manifest its creativity through your lower personality
- Being able to clearly recognize cause and effect, by seeing the whole picture
- Being able to see truth, and understand that there are no rights or wrongs

Path 11

Correspondences

— Sphere of Chokmah —

We commence our journey in the Sphere of Chokmah, Wisdom.

The Hebrew Divine Name is Jehovah.

The Esoteric title is the Illuminating Intelligence.

The Archangel is Ratziel, Herald of God.

The Choir of Angels is the Auphanim, or Wheels, or Whirling Forces, often called the order of the Kerubim.

The Planetary correspondence is the Sphere of the Zodiac acting through Uranus, or according to some modern Kabbalists, through Neptune.

The element is fire in fire.

The color is grey.

The stone is aquamarine, lapis or star ruby.

The metal is lead.

Symbols are the phallus, the line and the yod.

Plants are fennel, buttercup and absinthe.

The corresponding body part is the left side of the face.

The chakra that corresponds is the Third Eye Center.

The number is 2.

The Tarot correspondences are the four twos and the four Kings.

The mythological figure is the Greek God Uranus, the ultimate "father" of the Greek pantheon of Gods, whose children castrated him and also Neptune, "father" of the ocean of existence.

The weapon is the wand, symbol of the magical will and divine wisdom.

The magical image is a bearded male figure.

The spiritual experience is a vision of God face to face.

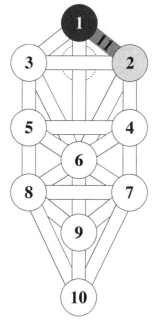

— 11th Path —

The 11th Path is known as the Scintillating Intelligence because it is the essence of that curtain, which is placed close to the order of the disposition, and this is a special dignity given to it that it may be able to stand before the face of the cause of causes.

The Hebrew letter for the Path is Aleph, meaning ox.

The esoteric title is "The Spirit of Aether."

The element is air.

There is no corresponding Planet or Sign, although some modern Kabbalists equate it to Uranus.

The stones are topaz and chalcedony.

The scent is galbanum.

The color is bright pale-yellow.

The musical note is "E."

The mythological correspondences include the Crocodile, Egyptian symbol for creative energy, The Green Man, who personifies spring and the Greek Dionysus Zagreus, whose death symbolizes initiation.

— Sphere of Kether —

The Sphere of Destination is Kether, the Crown.

The esoteric title is the "Admirable or Hidden Intelligence" because it is the Light giving the power of comprehension of the First Principle, which hath no beginning.

The Hebrew Divine name is Eheieh, God the Creator.

The Archangel is Metatron.

The Order of Angels is the Chaioth Ha Qadesh, the Order of Seraphim.

The number is 1.

The Tarot correspondence is the four Aces.

There is no planet that corresponds to Kether, although some modern Kabbalists place Pluto here.

The color is brilliance, pure white with specs of gold and silver.

Symbols are the Crown, the Point, the Swastica and the thousand-petaled lotus.

The corresponding body part is the cranium.

The chakra is the Crown Center.

The magical image is an ancient, bearded king who can only be seen in profile.

The spiritual vision is Union with God.

The mythological or religious figure is the God Brahma, whose two faces look away from one another, one into Creation, one into the Ain Soph Aur of the unmanifest.

Invocation

"May we be encompassed by the name Jehovah and established in the temple of Chokmah, Wisdom. May the portal of the 11th path be opened to us and may we journey thereon in the power of the name of Metatron to the gate of the Sphere of Kether. And in the name of Ehieh, may the gate of Kether be opened to us and may we be firmly established in the wonders of that Sphere."

Path

Find yourself in silent darkness.

Go within.

Put all your thoughts aside.

Put aside the day you've spent.

Put aside your plans for tomorrow.

Forget.

Forget the facts that clutter your mind.

Yes, there are many things you want to know, much knowledge you desire.

But, for now, put all of that aside.

Let go of your intellect.

The time we have chosen to spend together - NOW - is special.

Silently, in the darkness, we have been traveling on a journey.

Together, like small children, waiting; waiting together, in the cosmic darkness. We have been waiting in safety; waiting in anticipation, on the precipice of discovery.

You become aware of your breath.

Breathe in slowly... breathe out.

Again, breathe in... then slowly breathe out.

Be aware as you become energized by your breath.

Become aware that the universe around you is breathing in and breathing out, with you.

You are in a very high place, far from the earthly plane.

You feel infinitely subtle.

All is very still.

The air is cool and crisp.

Beneath your bare feet, you feel cool white marble.

Beneath the marble platform you are standing on are twelve white pillars. You know these are the zodiacal signs, dividing up all that is.

You are standing very close to the edge of the platform, but you know that you will not fall over the edge.

All around you, you see the starry heavens and you feel the ever-revolving "machinery" of the universe moving around you.

Now, you fix your sights on an even higher place, if you can imagine that.

All is clear and a blue-white glow surrounds you.

Slowly, again, you breathe in and out.

Floating, in the distance before you, is a mountain.

You cannot see its base because you are so high up on your marble platform.

All is cool and calm and you feel as beautiful and cool as the marble you are standing on.

The mountain in the distance has soft white fog surrounding it, blurring its image.

You can hardly keep yourself from going toward it.

You become aware again of your breath, and as you breathe in and out you feel your Heart Center become warm and energized. You begin to feel the energy of it radiating out from you.

In your Heart Center, in your mind's eye, you can see the letters YHWH and you hear the sound reverberate within you.

You feel yourself floating up higher still.

In the air around you, you hear the sound of wheels turning.

It sounds almost like small wooden wheels turning. As if, in fact, a million small softwood mills were turning and grinding the grains of life, back into the very component energies that comprise them.

The sound is not obtrusive, but rather is soft and lovely.

It's as if you held a few grains of wheat between your fingertips and softly crushed them.

You feel like one of those grains, slowly releasing your innermost being, allowing the life energy to flow, uninhibited by form.

The radiation pouring from you is growing more intense and you feel in tune with the vibration of the sounds around you.

Again, you look toward the mountain and you realize that you have grown closer to it and have left your marble platform behind.

On top of the mountain, you see the Archangel Ratziel.

You hear his voice loudly proclaiming something and cannot understand his words.

You let the words enter your ears without the need or desire to comprehend and for one very brief moment you have a crystal clear vision of all of creation. You see children being born, growing and dying, you see whole species coming into existence, completing their cycle and fading from existence. You see stars being born and dying.

You perceive, for just an instant, the ebb and flow and structure and organization behind all physical manifestation. You recognize infinite Power, tempered with Wisdom.

You feel your Throat Center begin to vibrate and, almost in the moment of your comprehension, your insight is stolen away, remaining only as a memory.

Ratziel is holding in one of his outstretched arms a book made of clear, blue sapphire.

You can see that the book has writing etched on it.

This book has been passed down through the ages, to Adam, to Abraham, to Jacob, to Moses and finally to Solomon the Wise.

You want this book! But in despair, you see the writings make no sense to you. You cannot rely on your intellect now. With all the words you have read and all the knowledge you have acquired, you have not yet gained the wisdom of this book, or the wisdom adequate to comprehend it.

In this small instant, the letters YHWH, YAWAY, vibrate within you and outward from you.

You reach out to touch the book.

Suddenly, stars appear all around and above you.

Energy generates through you and from you. It forms a straight line, a rod, and vibrates through you.

Finally, circling back and completing itself around you, the circle expands and expands toward the infinite.

There is no time, for all time is within you. Within the circle you have become.

You, the initiate, have encompassed every grain of existence at once and you realize, that this is where true Wisdom begins.

You have attained Wisdom with Knowledge, not Wisdom by Knowledge.

You are now rising upward, even further.

The stars have a new meaning to you.

Inwardly you understand the order and working of the cosmos, without having to process this knowledge through your intellect.

The beauty and the wonder of the cool, blue mountain are surpassed by the blazing white stars around you.

The planets that you know pass you by and you pass others still that you have no names for. The universe moves through a dance of life that you intuitively understand and encompass.

The brilliance that began at your Heart Center has blossomed out from you in all directions.

You realize, in the blazing beauty of what's all around you, that you are one of the stars also.

You have become whole and you feel yourself moving back even to the origins of the star, as you release more and more energy, becoming more and more subtle, until you feel yourself as the nebula, that vortex of energy that gives birth to the stars! Suddenly, but still softly, you break through the darkness of this universe, to brilliant whiteness again. But this time, you are much, much more subtle and higher up the planes.

You feel as if you are standing on top of a cone-shaped field of energy.

When you look about, all you see is blazing whiteness - a very alive, very electric whiteness, like cosmic dust.

You have entered the Sphere of Kether and you notice that this brilliance is mostly coming forth from the Angelic host of this Sphere, the Qioch Ha Kadesh. They are with you here, on your journey to become whole again.

They are all around you and they appear to vibrate as burning coals of fire. They are not like the other angels you have encountered along your way. They seem almost the building blocks of the four elements, without being of the elements themselves.

You see them as spinning four-spoked wheels of energy, like the swastika, each with an all-seeing eye at its center.

This is a beautiful place and it is a place that, as the purified being that you have become, you can connect with.

The connection is the white brilliance about you. It is the same energy you have felt in the center of your being and you feel excited at finding what you have been searching for all these timeless eons.

You glow.

You radiate.

You are one with the brilliance.

You oscillate between being vaporously cool and blue-white, to blazing hot-white.

All the while, you are feeling the glory and the splendor of the oneness with the source of your being.

You see a thousand-petaled lotus unfolding from your Crown Center and are consumed by its light.

You feel a presence in front of you. It is very large. It is the Archangel Metatron.

You sense that he is young and you feel anticipation.

You know that he is the only one that has seen the face of God.

He instructs you to again become aware of your breath. You slowly breathe in and then slowly breathe out.

Silently, inwardly, as you breathe, breathe in and hear the sound O...............

As you breathe out, hear the sound Mmm..........

Until you vibrate inside to the sound of OM.

OM.

OM.

Again, and again, vibrating inside.

You feel yourself merge with the Archangel Metatron, feel yourself becoming this infinitely large, youthful being, born of man, who alone can see God.

Before you, in the blazing white light, appears a King, bearded and crowned. But he only shows you one side of his face. He looms, vast and limitless. You are filled with awe and wonder.

There is a quickening of the radiation within you and without you.

You cannot tell if the bearded King is slowly turning the hidden portion of his face toward you, or if you are being drawn to that hidden side.

But all at once and with a blazing flash, you and that hidden place are one! You are together in a huge, cosmic explosion.

You are and then you are not.

Slowly, you feel awareness return, as the Archangel Metatron releases you from his being.

You feel your consciousness begin to drop back into that state that now is your natural state of awareness, but you bring with you the understanding of all that you have experienced.

And so ends the 11th Path.

Path Journal

A. Record your emotional reactions to your path experiences here, immediately upon completion. Include any physical responses or sensations.

Date of completion: _____

Emotional responses: _____

_____

_____

Physical reactions: _____

_____

_____

What do you think these responses indicate? _____

_____

_____

B. Use this section as a diary of your experiences during the week following your completion of the path. Be sure to include how you react to things emotionally, as well as how you deal with any major issues that might arise.

Day 1: _____

_____

Day 2: _____

_____

Day 3: _____

_____

Day 4: _____

_____

Day 5: _____

_____

Day 6: _____

_____

Day 7: _____

_____

C. Review the week's experiences. How has the path affected the way you handled this week's issues? _____

_____

_____

_____

D. What special dreams has this path stimulated this week? _____

_____

_____

_____

Areas Path 11 Will Help You Work On

- Energizing, especially the Crown Center and head
- Learning the feeling of emptiness, stillness - pure existence; a vessel waiting to be filled
- Being able to recognize symbols, especially of infinity, active in your life
- Being able to join earth and spirit within yourself
- Relaxation, calmness, peacefulness
- Astral projection
- Invincibility; the ability to be unaffected by that which is external to you
- Taking with you a feeling of womb-like protection
- Finding the ultimate seed of creation within yourself
- Recognizing that you are just as responsible for your inner creations as for your outer ones
- Understanding that breath is life
- Releasing all blocks to your energy flow
- Gaining insight into that which is unmanifest
- Nurturing a need to be of service to all
- Understanding that you can best be of service by letting the creative force work through you unhindered by your personality
- Increased sexuality, sensuality; orgasmic
- Increasing your ability to "merge" with another
- Feeling the rhythm of the universe
- Feeling part of all
- Sensing the natural order and adjusting your timing to it
- "Explosive stillness"
- Being able to expand your own energy and consciousness to affect others
- Being able to comprehend the elements of creativity
- Enhancement of mental and theoretical creativity
- Understanding the interaction of good and evil, and their "balance"
- Increased perceptual sensitivity

- Release of kundalini energy, raising your vibration

- Recognition that you are part of something infinitely greater than you, or your ability to comprehend

- A feeling of knowledge within, without knowing consciously what you know; wisdom

- Understanding that wisdom comes from the heart, knowledge from the head

- To know something, you must recognize that it is a part of yourself

- Activation of the top four chakras, and synchronizing their action

The Lightning Flash

Invocation

"I proclaim a working of the final Path in our journey to higher consciousness, the Path of the Lightning Flash, whereby we may bring our higher understandings learned from our journey upward on the Tree of Life into manifestation."

Path

We commence our journey in the Sphere of Kether, the Crown.

The Hebrew Divine Name is Ehieh.

The planetary correspondence is the first swirlings of life and of being.

The element is all elements.

The color is white brilliance.

The herbs are ambergris and almond.

The stone is the diamond.

The symbol is the crown.

The mystical experience is one of enlightenment.

The body part is the cranium.

The chakra is the Crown Center and the corresponding gland is the pituitary.

The Path of the Lightning Flash takes you down the Tree of Life from Kether to Chokmah, then on to Binah and across the Abyss at Daath to Chesed. From Chesed you proceed across the Tree again to Geburah and then onward to the balance point on the Tree of Life, Tiphareth.

From Tiphareth you move downward, still on your return journey, to the Sphere of Netzach and across the tree to Hod, then down to the middle of the Tree again, in Yesod. Finally, you return once again to the Sphere of Malkuth, where your journey began and where you may begin to manifest the results of all you have learned, in the ultimate achievement — the spiritualization of matter.

The planetary correspondence of this Path is, again, the entire Zodiac.

The element is all elements, on all levels of experience.

The color is white, which contains all colors.

The herb or incense is lotus, to unlock the higher mysteries.

The stone is clear crystal or diamond, which hardened within the earth achieves its perfection; also, the prism, which breaks white light down into all colors.

Symbols of the Path are the staff of power, the thousand petaled lotus, the lightning flash and the serpent or snake.

The mystical experience is one of being filled as a cup would be filled: with energy and inspiration.

The Tarot Arcanum is the World or the Universe.

The Sphere of Destination is Malkuth, the Kingdom.

The Hebrew Divine Name is Adonai Malek.

The planet is Earth.

The element is earth.

The symbol is a gateway or a cavern.

Colors are all shaded natural hues.

Stones are the fossil and the herkimer or rough diamond encased in rock.

The herbs are ivy or willow.

The body part is the feet.

The chakra is the Root Center and the corresponding gland is the gonads.

"May we be encompassed by the power of the name Ehieh and established in the palace of Kether, the Crown. May the portal of the Path of the Lightning Flash be opened to us and may we journey thereon in the power of the name Jehovah, to the gate of the Sphere of Malkuth, the Kingdom. And in the name of Adonai Malek, may the gate of Malkuth be opened to us and may we be firmly established in the wonders of that Sphere, filled with all of the experiences of our journey."

You open your inner eyes.

About you, all you can see is white brilliance.

Your eyes are dazzled. You see nothing but light.

You hear the whispering sounds of many voices and yet all of the voices are One and the One Voice is God.

You allow yourself to drift, devoid of consciousness, in the vast sea of blinding and dazzling light.

The brilliance consumes you, until you are totally immersed and one with it.

You cannot tell if you are the brilliance or if it is you!

There is no separateness. All is one.

You are filled with a consuming joy. It uplifts you, fills you with pure radiance and you feel yourself rising higher and higher, toward the very center of the brilliance.

At its center, you feel a burning. It could be hot or cold, yet it washes away any last remnants of resistance.

The Crown of your head opens.

You are becoming One with Metatron, Archangel of this Sphere!

With him, you look upon and you experience the blazing Glory of God!

You sink deep into the light, where all is stillness. Here, you may remain for an eternity, to return ultimately to the great darkness of the Night of God, or you may do as others have before you and return now to the world of man; to aid and to help your fellow seekers!

Your thoughts drift to your journey.

You feel a great vibration building about you.

It's as if the universe itself is shaking.

The motion is so great, it seems that you can withstand it no more!

You see and feel about you a glorious explosion of brilliance and with it you are propelled outward.

You travel with tremendous speed and you move through a silvery gray light.

At last, you come to rest, in the Temple of Chokmah.

You are floating freely among the stars.

You see the course of planets moving through their orbits about you, in familiar and comfortable patterns.

You see patterns within patterns.

As you look, all of these patterns become the pages of an enormous book!

You hear the voice of the Archangel Ratziel reciting endlessly the wordless patterns of eternity.

The left side of your head and face begins to tingle as you become filled with this knowledge! Your forehead begins to feel as if it's expanding outward as your Third Eye becomes activated.

Ratziel hands you your copy of the Book! Then, he wordlessly disappears!

You feel your body begin to rise and you float outward over an incredibly deep chasm. There is no bottom to be seen, only flickers of half-formed images and snatches of inhuman sound.

You recognize the Abyss and that you pass over its edge.

But although there is darkness beneath you, with your book of knowledge, you have no fear.

You float over the edge of the Abyss and finally come to rest in the warm dark "womb" of the Sphere of Binah.

You feel the warmth now, of the Eternal Mother all about you. All is darkness and warmth.

You are surrounded by an ocean of cosmic amniotic fluid!

All about you is still. Yet you feel the nurturing exchange of life force with the Universal Mother, as if you are a child still in the womb.

A tear drops upon the right side of your face.

Instantly the right side of your head and face become alive and energized.

Tzaphkiel, with his all seeing eye appears before you, a glowing figure in the darkness of the Mother's womb. He touches his own single eye and then he reaches out and touches your Brow Center, activating your Third Eye and you feel as if his hand actually moves inside of your head, opening a long unused channel and light enters!

This unused organ opens further and you see with your own Third Eye the vivid colors and glories of the Mother; the darkness that was is banished!

You couldn't otherwise see in the darkness, for to see her you must see with your inner vision, the vision that She gives you — vision of your past, your present and your future, vision allowing you to see readily the relationship of cause and effect.

The brilliance around you increases. You remember again, your journey and with your free will, you will yourself back across the Abyss at Daath.

Again, you see the darkness below, the flickering of half seen horrible forms and the inhuman sounds that you have come to associate with Daath.

But with an assertion of will, you shut out the unwanted sounds and sights and see only the Shining Sword Path that leads you cleanly and easily across the Abyss and into the blue light surrounding the Temple of Chesed. A unicorn awaits you. You mount him, in an astral body that is new and awkward to you.

Tzadkiel, Archangel of the Sphere of Chesed meets you at the Temple, smiling. He sees that you have elected to join the souls working from the Sphere of Chesed in guiding and helping humanity.

He takes your left arm and places in your left hand a royal blue sapphire! You feel the blue light of the sapphire flow up your arm and into your Throat Center, opening it. You feel so much energy that you feel the need to sing and laugh! The Chasmalim, the brilliant ones, join in with their laughter and song!

You are lost to their joyous song and see only the mighty and benevolent King of the Sphere of Chesed smiling down at you.

Finally, you remember your journey again and are swept onward.

You move now to the Sphere of Geburah.

Haniel, Archangel here, meets you at the Palace entrance. He is dressed in his suit of armor, glowing in all his might!

He touches your right arm and instantly you, too, are clothed in invincible armor!

He places in your right hand an iron sword; you know it is not meant for hurting, this sword, but for protection, for justice and for balance and for eliminating that which is unnecessary and not beneficial to your well being or to that of the others in your care.

A red glow comes from the sword. It travels up your right arm and into your Throat Center again. Again, your feel your throat open and a sound emerges — this time you raise your voice in a powerful chant, as the sword fills you with its power.

You may wield it only by your will united with that of the Divine!

You turn, with Chamael and you salute the Master of this Sphere, Elohim Gebor!

Now, you may resume your journey.

You again direct your vibration downward, down into the golden Sphere of Tiphareth.

Golden light shines now directly into your heart, and you feel a still denser astral form collecting around you.

You are consumed by the golden light that emanates from your own Heart Center.

Raphael, Archangel of the Sphere, places his hand on your breast and instantly, you are cleared of all hurts, washed clean of all transgression from this or in any other life. You feel the healing energies of love move through you!

A phoenix, mythical bird of this Sphere, flies high above you. You feel yourself one with him, having followed the same path of transformation.

Raphael, Lord of Music, hands you his lyre and you feel it become a part of you. You will now have the ability to hear his music in your heart, the music of your own Higher Self. You will have the ability to play it for others, as well!

You are ready, now, to continue your journey onward, into the Sphere of Netzach, Sphere of elemental fire!

You feel yourself falling, falling, through tongues of brilliant green fire, until finally you fall into a green sea and you are again dowsed by the waters of the Mother!

You feel a denser body around you now. You feel the coolness of the water splashing about you. You play beneath a waterfall, looking upward at the golden sphere of the Sun.

Roses grow all about the pool where you bathe and all manner of green and growing things abound all around. The very air has a green caste to it! You smell the fragrance of the roses and hear the sounds of living things all about, from insect to animal life. You become filled with abandon, filled with a love of all life!

You play, like a child, freely in the water, with the Elohim, Choir of Angels of this Sphere. You see a myriad of others who have also taken this journey and some who are only beginning it and you see no differences among you! You are all one, all moving in the direction of the forces that move all life!

A whirlpool forms about your feet, pulling you down. You let yourself be pulled in, offering no resistance. It pulls you in all the way up to your chest and you feel an opening happening in your Solar Plexus Center. It's as if a door is opening and an inrush of the watery fire of Netzach fills you!

Haniel, Archangel here, appears before you, lighting your way with his fire as you sink beneath the waters to swim, carrying with you, eternally, the waters of life and the joy that fills you now!

You swim forward, through a wall of green elemental fire, across the Tree of Life once more and into the Sphere of Hod, Sphere of elemental water! Soon, placid water surrounds you, cool, soothing and deep.

Haniel leaves you now and the Archangel Michael, from the Sphere of Hod appears to you, meeting you as you walk up and out of the waters surrounding his temple. You recognize, once again, the palace of Hod, with its black and white checked floor and its roof of orange stone.

You enter the temple, feeling totally at home here now. You see the scepter of Mercury, messenger of the Gods, lying on the altar. You breathe deeply, feeling your solar plexus open and expand. Michael takes up the scepter and holds it to your solar plexus. A burst of white light is drawn down through the top of your head and through each chakra in turn, until the Solar Plexus Center becomes the focus of that light. You know now that with your breath and your mind you, too, are to be a messenger!

You feel your legs grow lighter and fleeter and you look down, to see the Wings of Mercury upon your own heels! You feel the burning fires of the mind all about you, the spiritual flame that kindles your thirst for knowledge, for ritual and for the sharing of this with your fellow man.

You are carried outward upon that flame, through the upper astral plane, bright with its spiritual flame and downward again into the denser flame of the lower astral plane and into the airy, violet colored Sphere of Yesod.

As you approach the Garden of Yesod you actually see images and thought patterns floating in the surrounding violet cloud-like atmosphere.

Some of these are your own and some are those of others. You see that many of these thought patterns are old and outworn and you readily see the ways in which they might be altered.

They float all around you. You see thought-images of past and present, just as you see souls entering and leaving the physical plane by way of the Gate at Yesod.

You cannot now be trapped by any of these thoughtforms, no matter how frightening, or disturbing, because you know and recognize them as your own creations.

You continue to float downward and you come to rest in the Garden of Yesod; its surrounding wall now appears very insubstantial, as if you no longer need its protection, having created your own and learned to travel the highways of the lower astral plane in safety.

The Moon rises and its glowing white orb fills the horizon.

You lay back on a slab of crystal, smelling the sweet odor of night-blooming jasmine, gazing at the ever changing landscape around you, forming and constantly changing into and out of one another, in a dance that once brought fear and confusion, but now feels comfortable.

This Sphere of Yesod, that once was so treacherous, with its many pitfalls and emotional pulls, is now seen as simply one more aspect of self and of reality with your newfound knowledge and understanding. You know easily what is real and what is not and how to see the truth hidden in riddles.

Gabriel, Archangel of the Sphere of Yesod, appears floating toward you from the glowing orb of the Moon. As he moves, you feel a tug at your Sacral Center, just below your navel.

You look down to see the silver cord that you know connects you to your physical body far below in the Sphere of Malkuth.

You look toward Gabriel, but in his place, you see a mighty stag.

The pull of the silver cord gradually becomes a tugging in your loins. You feel an intense light energy coming through it to you from the stag! You realize that your Sacral Center is being fully opened!

The stag moves toward you, appearing to float through the violet currents of the astral light.

As he comes closer, he again changes into a tall youth, naked and beautiful. He comes closer still, and the youth seems to change into a beautiful maiden, with crescent moon upon her brow.

Then, the maiden changes back into the youth, until gradually you see them both, first one and then the other, then both in the same body, male and female.

Your own body becomes mightily energized as you feel the union of your own spirit, readying itself for the plunge into matter!

The youth touches you and you are transported down again into the Sphere of Malkuth.

You open your inner eyes. You are in a cave. You feel the pulse beat of the Great Goddess about you.

Sandalphon, Archangel here, helps you to your feet. Long unused muscles stretch.

You feel the energy of this Sphere flowing through your body, awakening it.

The energy finally comes to rest in your Root Center, at the base of your spine.

Here it can flow freely to all parts of your being as needed.

Sandalphon leads you now, slowly, up a narrow passageway.

Up, up, into the sunlight!

You turn, and look back at the Sphinx, representative of the Goddess on Earth, having given birth to you once again.

Sunlight pours through you!

You feel union of Sun and Moon, male and female in your innermost being.

"And so ends the Path of the Lightning Flash."

Path Journal

A. Record your emotional reactions to your path experiences here, immediately upon completion. Include any physical responses or sensations.

Date of completion: _____

Emotional responses: _____

_____

_____

Physical reactions: _____

_____

_____

What do you think these responses indicate? _____

_____

_____

B. Use this section as a diary of your experiences during the week following your completion of the path. Be sure to include how you react to things emotionally, as well as how you deal with any major issues that might arise.

Day 1: _____

_____

Day 2: _____

_____

Day 3: _____

_____

Day 4: _____

_____

Day 5: _____

_____

Day 6: _____

_____

Day 7: _____

_____

C. Review the week's experiences. How has the path affected the way you handled this week's issues? _____

_____

_____

_____

D. What special dreams has this path stimulated this week? _____

_____

_____

_____

Conclusion

The Lightning Flash Path is not a traditional Path on the Tree of Life at all. After guiding Pathworkers up the Tree, I found that time and again they came back to repeat the Path 32, saying that after completing the final Path (11) they felt ungrounded. So, with the help of my Guides, I created the Lightning Flash Path.

The Lightning Flash follows the pathway down the Kabbalistic Tree of Life that energy takes as it enters into matter. It helps you to ground and center once again after the other Paths are completed. It also has a deep affect on your psyche as you follow the 'Flash' all the way down through each type of consciousness and reconnects you with the parts of yourself inherent to each Sephiroh. It imparts an unconscious appreciation for how to manipulate energy to create form. By bringing the focus back down to Malkuth, the Sphere of the Earth Plane, you make all of the tools and insights you have gained on your journey fully available to you in your daily life.

Now, you have returned from your journey. Take time to assess what you have learned, how you have grown, during the six months or however long it has been since you first began your Pathworking. Look at the world around you. What are you bringing into your world now? What are you creating? Where do you want to go from here? It is your life, and it is your journey to continue.

Many Pathworkers repeat the entire journey several times over before they feel they have fully assimilated what they need to know now. Some go back and repeat just specific Paths if they are having new challenges in their lives that they feel a specific Path may help with. For example, if you are having difficulties with finances, repeating Path 32 is helpful. If you have health challenges in your life any of the Paths touching upon Tipareth or Path 29 will be helpful. Or even a combination of these. Once you have gone through the Paths in order, you may repeat them in any order you want in the future. I do suggest that periodically you repeat the entire journey in order as a way to re-order and re-balance yourself. The section at the end of each Path where I have recorded what many other Pathworkers have experienced and learned from it will help you to know which one to use to help yourself to rebalance and work through life's many tangles. Most importantly though, will be your own record of how the Path specifically affected you, and what you saw being affected in your own life when you were on each Path's journey.

Each time you repeat a Path or even the entire Tree, your experience is different because you are different. Each time you will grow in new ways, and you will experience new things. Sometimes you will experience things you missed the first time around. Sometimes your experience will include things not on the Paths as I have written and read them.

Know that if your mind wanders from a Path, it is still part of YOUR journey. Make note of that. If you fall asleep while walking a Path, that is often your own higher consciousness putting your waking mind out of the way so that the imagery and information can be better assimilated. Never fear. You will get the information, whether you were reading it or listening to it.

I am very excited that in today's world with new technology available I am able to offer all of the Paths to seekers everywhere on my website, www.sandyanastasi.com. Please go there, if you haven't already, and listen to the Paths. If you don't have a computer, the Paths are available for purchase on my site or by mail on CD. If you have no CD player, I suggest you either have someone read each Path to you when you do it, or read each Path individually into a recorder and play it back so you can close your eyes and allow yourself to move through each guided visualization as instructed. You may enjoy reading them as well, but the experience will be far more effective if it is audio.

When I walk a Path myself, I first listen to it, then go back and read it. I make sure that I hold a stone or crystal significant to the Path, that I wear the color of the Path, that I sleep with the Tarot card for the Path beneath my pillow during the week I am working on its Path, and that prior to lying down to listen to the Path I burn incense or anoint myself with an oil significant to the Path. Always, as I enter the Path, I gaze at my colored mandala and allow my consciousness to move into and through it and onto the Path I have chosen to do that day. By doing all these things, I attune my vibration to the Path immediately, and achieve the deepest experience I can.

I welcome you, fellow traveler, to a journey of the soul that may last a lifetime and beyond.

About the Author

Like many who realize their psychic gifts later in life, Sandy Anastasi awakened to her abilities in her late 20's. She understood that many people develop deep psychological problems because their psychic abilities are misunderstood and often blocked. These insights and an inner need to pass on her knowledge and abilities led her to begin teaching others to develop their own psychic gifts. She believes that if you are psychic, you MUST use your gifts, or at least learn to control them, or they will use you!

Sandy has many psychic gifts, but she believes her greatest to be the ability to identify and emulate the gifts of others. Because of that she is uniquely suited to teach people to open and develop those very gifts in themselves.

Sandy has been a professional psychic and astrologer since 1979. She holds a B.S. degree from Adelphi University and has teaching certifications in several fields. In addition to teaching, Sandy has worked as a Safety Engineer, and owned her own small book store for many years before retiring to become a full time psychic counselor, writer and teacher. Sandy's writings include books on Astrology, Kabbala, and Tarot, as well as psychic development.

Sandy has also appeared on many radio and television shows over the years, most notably *Crossing Over* and *Cross Country* – both television shows hosted by her good friend and former student, John Edward. She currently lives in Florida with her husband and four dogs.

Additional Products and Services

If you enjoyed this book, you may be interested in the many other products and services offered at www.SandyAnastasi.com.

Personal Readings With Sandy Anastasi

Are you interested in communicating with your guides and Higher Self in order to obtain key messages that can help you overcome the challenges you will be facing in the future? Or would you like to revisit and learn important lessons from past lives you may have lived? Are you interested in finding out just how astrologically compatible you are with your friends, family, and significant others?

The benefits of having these insights are HUGE. Many people can live for decades without having access to such information, which can provide a critical insight in how to move on and move up in life. And there are many options to fit your specific needs, such as:

- Channeled Readings
- Past Life Reading Using Tarot and/or Astrology
- Death and Afterlife Charts
- Astrology
- Astrology Comparisons

For a limited time only, I am still willing, able, and excited to take on new clients. However, I can only handle so many one-on-one sessions in a given week and I'll always give scheduling preference to my loyal client base. So if you're interested, please book as soon as possible in order to get your spot! Rates and additional information can be found at www.SandyAnastasi.com.

Workshops and Classes

Many of my clients find that the workshop environment is an ideal way to make large gains in their skills and understanding of these topics. And I agree, because workshops provide many benefits and opportunities that cannot be wholly replicated in book format. These advantages include:

- In class demonstrations for hands-on experience.

- Immediate feedback from myself and other skilled instructors.

- The ability to meet with other highly motivated people that are interested in this area of learning and development.

- Question and answer sessions for those burning questions on your mind.

- An environment full of high energy from the instructors and other students.

- An affordable cost compared to one-on-one training.

For a current listing of available workshops, please visit www.SandyAnastasi.com.

Appearances, Interviews, and Lectures

I also am available for appearances, interviews, and lectures outside of the classes and workshops already listed. Please inquire for availability, topics, and (if applicable for the particular format) pricing.

Books and Audio CDs

If you're like a majority of my friends, colleagues, and clients, then I know that an interest in one genre will turn into an eager desire to explore them all... and that's a good thing! Often some your biggest insights and 'ah ha' moments will come in areas you least expect it. So while your primary interest may be in spiritual channeling, experience in tarot reading may be the key to unlocking your ability (or at least guiding you into the right direction).

In terms of topics, my 30+ years of experience and training has allowed me to create over 100+ books and CD sets covering the following:

- Crystal and Stones
- Divination
- Dowsing
- Energy Healing
- Healing
- Kabbala
- Meditation
- Numerology

- Philosophy

- Psychic Development

- Psychic Protection

- Channeling and Spirit Communication

- Radionics

- Tarot

So regardless of which genre you're on now, there is something for everybody and something to expand into to diversify your skills and talents.

Most Popular Products

- The Psychic Development Series (books and CDs). This six-part series will systematically teach you drills and techniques that will greatly improve your current psychic abilities, regardless of your current skill level. Topics covered include: energy balancing, how to send and receive information, remote viewing, radionics, channeling/mediumship, soul retrieval, and much more!

- Basic Tarot (books and CDs). Using the Rider Waite deck – The meanings of all the cards are discussed as well as their history and many uses. Students may use any deck utilizing 78 cards. The basic Celtic cross layout is used while finishing with students doing simple but accurate readings

- The Astrology Series (books and CDs). This series will teach you the many components of reading, creating, and interpreting astrological charts. Part 1 begins with learning the basic meanings of the symbols, planets, and houses while the advanced levels cover the nuances of lunar nodes, interceptions, decans, and other important topics that are often ignored or misunderstood.

- The Psychic Development Workshops (transcripts and CDs). These expand upon the book series listed above, particularly in the following topics: psychic self-defense, seeing and feeling the aura, using the pendulum, astral travel, crystal gazing, and psychometry.

- Kabbala Pathworking (books and CDs). A unique experience in exploring the 22 paths of the Kabbala; an ancient system that becomes a roadmap to delineating the soul path to enlightenment. A series of guided visualizations on each Path are designed to open the doors of your unconscious to the energies of the Higher Self and the God consciousness within.

Free Support Materials

In order to help you get the most out of the content of the books and tapes, many of the exercise sheets and other support materials are freely available for download online at www.SandyAnastasi.com (For example the crown chakra mandala and the psychic development aptitude test). There you will also find free gifts and bonuses, such as a downloadable chakra meditation audio that you can use to balance your body's energy system. You are allowed (and highly encouraged) to give and distribute these materials in whatever ethical manner you deem appropriate to others that have an interest in this type of journey.

CPSIA information can be obtained
at www.ICGtesting.com
Printed in the USA
BVHW011723310719
554778BV00002B/5/P